"The contrasts you develop betwee[n] startling. You remind us that the c[...] men are not the whole of American culture, however central and universal these writers may like to think they are. I appreciated the fact that you follow writers who include indigenous people in their construction of 'wilderness.' And I liked that you mention African American writers."

— JULIE ALLEN
Professor Emerita, Sonoma St[ate]

"Jonah Raskin's *A Terrible Beauty* is a [...] work of cultural criticism. The author [tak]es as his central subject the 'wilderness of words' at the heart of American literature, and offers a compelling new take on the forms of capture, captivity and the captivating that define our relationship to the wild."

— TILAR J. MAZZEO
Clara C. Piper Associate Professor of English, Colby College

"Wilderness set the new American nation apart from its European sources and defined the American Dream, though American culture has treated it as something to fear and control, seeing it, in Yeats' phrase and Jonah Raskin's title, as *A Terrible Beauty*. Raskin explores that tension across an enormous span of American literature, from the earliest explorers to F. Scott Fitzgerald. It's an illuminating, painfully revealing, and ultimately inspiring journey."

— DENNIS MCNALLY
Author, On Highway 61: Race, Culture, and the Evolution of Cultural Freedom

"Into the wild we go in *A Terrible Beauty* as Jonah Raskin explores American writers from Henry David Thoreau to F. Scott Fitzgerald, demonstrating the formative omnipresence of wilderness in American literature and thought. We need a cultural dimension to the environmentalist proposition of 'rewilding,' a rewilding of our minds and hearts, and here Raskin points the way, learnedly but unpretentiously. Take a walk on the wild side!"

— CHRISTOPHER PHELPS
Associate Professor of American Studies, University of Nottingham

A
Terrible
Beauty

BY JONAH RASKIN

The Mythology of Imperialism

Out of the Whale

The Weather Eye
(EDITOR)

Puerto Rico: The Flame of Resistance
(CO-AUTHOR)

Underground

My Search for B. Traven

James Houston

For the Hell of It

Homegrown
(CO-AUTHOR)

American Scream

Natives, Newcomers, Exiles, Fugitives

The Radical Jack London
(EDITOR)

Field Days

Marijuanaland

James McGrath: In a Class By Himself

Rock 'n' Roll Women

Burning Down the House

A Terrible Beauty

The Wilderness of American Literature

JONAH RASKIN

REGENT PRESS
Berkeley, California

[Paperback]
ISBN 13: 978-1-58790-278-9
ISBN 10: 1-58790-278-8

[Ebook]
ISBN 13: 978-1-58790-279-6
ISBN 10: 1-58790-279-6

Library of Congress Control Number: 2014942514

Cover design by Paul Veres

Book design by Mark Weiman

Publisher's Cataloging-in-Publication

Raskin, Jonah, 1942-
    A terrible beauty : the wilderness of American
literature / Jonah Raskin.
    pages cm
    Includes bibliographical references and index.
    LCCN 2014942514
    ISBN 978-1-58790-278-9 (paperback)
    ISBN 978-1-58790-279-6 (ebook)

    1. American literature--History and criticism.
2. Environmentalism in literature. 3. Wilderness areas in
literature. 4. Wilderness areas--United States.
I. Title.

PS88.R37 2014   810.9
                          QBI14-600162

MANUFACTURED IN THE U.S.A.
Regent Press
Berkeley, California
www.regentpress.net

For Eleanor,
who helped give birth to my
first book four decades ago,
and who helped give birth to this one, too.

CONTENTS

ACKNOWLEDGEMENTS

The wild is a territory not a part of the agency of humanity.
It could be a strip of earth in your own backyard or it could be
Yosemite. Wherever it is it takes care of itself.
— GARY SNYDER

You can't keep the wild out of your fields. You can't build a
fence to prevent the forest from entering your farm.
— WENDELL BERRY

American literature was my first love in college; in writing this book I've gone back to a subject that ignited my intellectual passions at Columbia College more than fifty years ago. To be true to myself I've had to write this book. It could be that I will write another, but it seems unlikely that I will write one that has taken as much time, energy and discipline as this one. Since the wilderness is inextricably connected to nearly everything else about American literature, writing about the wilderness has meant that I've had to write about form, voice, style, and the lives of the writers, along with history, culture, economics and ecology.

I've talked about this book for years. I have had encouragement every step of the way, except from publishers and agents. Professor Bryant Brantley took me through the pages of medieval literature and invited me to his class to talk about wilderness. That was an early boost. The English Department at Sonoma State University (SSU) allowed me to teach a class about the wilderness in American literature that helped focus my ideas. Discussions with students further sharpened my thinking. Steve Norwick from the SSU Environmental Studies Department lent me dozens of books and took me on my first venture into an official wilderness area. Chip McAuley listened to me talk about the writers and the books I have featured in these pages. Robert Friedman read early drafts and encouraged me to stay the course. The library at SSU obtained hard-to-find books from other California libraries through LINK+. At the front desk, Jack Ritchie helped immensely. I also found rare books at the New York Public Library when I was away from home.

Some of the ideas in *A Terrible Beauty* found expression in essays and articles published in *Rain Taxi, The Sierra Club Newsletter,* the *Redwood Coast Review* and *The Point Reyes Light.* I hope that Eric Lorberer, Vicky Hoover, Stephen Kessler and Tess Elliott know how important it was to be able to publish in their pages. At KQED, Mark Trautwein provided ample time for me to air my views on environmental issues. Talking to members of the Sierra Club in Lake County enabled me to test my ideas and to listen to theirs. My editor and publisher, Mark Weiman at Regent Press in Berkeley, rallied around this book and brought it into print. James McGrath gave me a subscription to *High County News* that kept me abreast of environmental issues in the West. (The June 9, 2014 issue contains a stunning article about the destruction of the Arizona wilderness along the border with Mexico. Author Ray Ring describes the "renegade roads" created by the U.S. Border Patrol in the name of national security. "It's probably the worst violation ever of the spirit of the 50-year-old Wilderness Act," he writes.)

Two writers profoundly influenced my own thinking about American literature and the American continent: F. O. Matthiessen and Peter Matthiessen (no relationship). Roderick Nash's *Wilderness*

& The American Mind showed me the richness and the complexity of the subject. I hope the reader might think of this volume as a companion to Nash's: where he has explored ideas and organizations I have mapped narratives and tropes. He's an historian; I'm a cultural critic. Our approaches, I think, yield similar and yet very different insights into art and politics in America.

I want to thank the following people for guidance and inspiration along the way: Paul Wirtz, Candi Edmondson, Anne Teller, David Loeb, Diane and David Albracht, Sterling Bennett, Dianne Romain, Nicolette and Bill Niman, Dee and Peter Swanhuyser, David Bolling, Mark Dowie, Bill Pinkus, Thora Lares, Thaine Stearns, Eric Foner, Daria Foner, Jeff Jones, Elizabeth Herron, Sherril Jaffe, J.J. Wilson, Gael Delmar, Patrick McMurtry, Ralph Benson, Eleanor Stein, Bernardine Dohrn, Rue Mapp, John Hart, Mark Trautwein, James Morton Turner, Gary Snyder, David Kupfer, Teresa Baker, J. Baird Callicott, Curt Meine, Steve Costa, Doug Brinkley, Ken Brower, Steve and Ann Dunsky, Tess Elliott, Nancy and Kevin Lunny, Amy Trainer, Sarah Baker, Timothy Williams, Anne and Steve Halliwell, Stacey Tuel, my two brothers, Daniel and Adam, and all my hiking and backpacking companions.

Ellen Komp proved to be an excellent proof reader and a cogent critic who nudged me gently along the road. Last but not least I want to express my gratitude to Christopher Phelps, Tilar Mazzeo, William Ayres, Dennis McNally, LMDV, and Michael and Eleanore Kennedy.

I began work on *A Terrible Beauty* in 2007 and continued to work on it for seven years while I pursued other projects that resulted in books and articles about farms, farming, foraging, marijuana, Jack London, oysters, national parks and more. Most of those projects took me outdoors: from mountains to valleys and to deserts and seashore. What I mean to say is that while this book was nurtured in libraries it was invigorated in the open air. Near the end of my research the fiftieth anniversary of the

Wilderness Act approached. I followed the public discussions, attended meetings and talked to wilderness advocates.

Some of their intensity rubbed off on me. Contemporary debates and conflicts about the wilderness shaped my thinking about American literature. I suppose that I enjoy a kind of Double Consciousness on the subject; it seems to go with the territory. The phrase "Double Consciousness" was first used by W. E. B. Du Bois (1868-1963) in a magazine article and later in *The Souls of Black Folk* to describe the strange experience of African Americans. "One ever feels his two-ness," he wrote. Du Bois also noted that Double Consciousness meant "always looking at one's self through the eyes of others." I have borrowed the term and the definition and applied it to writers who weren't African American but who also felt a sense of duality and division. They too had a sense of "two-ness," though it didn't derive from the experience of slavery, segregation, and geographical and psychological separation from Africa. Writers in the United States have articulated the alien sense that Americans have felt on a continent where they were not native and that was home to civilizations and culture other than those of their ancestors. Americans and un-Americans, they were outcasts, Ishmaels and strangers in a strange land.

This book is obviously about the past. I think it's also about the present and the future, though readers may well come away from *A Terrible Beauty* with a whole range of ideas and feelings, perhaps contradictory. Over the past few years, longtime wilderness advocates have told me that the wilderness has lost much of its mojo in the last fifty years. I think that's about right. Today, many other environments — open space districts, parks, wetlands, watersheds, wildlife refuges, working landscapes, land trusts and more — claim the imagination and human energies. The Sonoma Land Trust is one of the local organizations that make a big environmental difference in my part of the world.

It may be that the wilderness will not loom large in the world of the future. But there will continue to be interest in wilderness, if only because it played a significant part in the history and culture of North America for hundreds of years. Ironically, the wilderness as a place that came to be synonymous with America and the United States began as a transplanted European trope. The wilderness trope went wild in America. Perhaps the unfolding contemporary environmental crisis will lead to new critical thinking and new narratives about the wild and the wilderness. I expect it will. Indeed, it's changing all the time. Writers, artists and ecologists talk today about "urban wild," "rewilding" and the meaning of wilderness in an era of global climate change.

The title for this book, *A Terrible Beauty*, comes from William Butler Yeats's poem, "Easter 1916." The full line reads, "A terrible beauty is born." I like to think that Yeats would feel that the phrase "a terrible beauty" applies to the continent of North America. Settlers, colonists, explorers and pioneers have certainly been so terrified by its awesome beauty that they have wanted to destroy it. Herman Melville grasped the concept. "Warmest climes but nurse the cruelest fangs," he wrote in *Moby-Dick*. "The tiger of Bengal crouches in spiced groves of ceaseless verdure. Skies the most effulgent but basket the deadliest thunders." The "mysterious, divine Pacific" is also home to the white whale. Attack the wild and the wild will seek revenge, Melville seems to say. Aim to destroy it and it will destroy you. "A terrible beauty is born." Native Americans in Sonoma County, California, where I live and work, tell me that their ancestors didn't understand how and why white men were able to cut down sacred forests and not be struck down dead. Global warming, they tell me, is nature's revenge. It's not modern science, but it's a compelling narrative that Herman Melville and Emily Dickinson would appreciate.

— *Santa Rosa, California*
October 2014

AH, WILDERNESS!

The word "wilderness" appears in the title and just once in the body of Eugene O'Neill's 1932 romantic comedy *Ah, Wilderness!*, which takes place in Connecticut on July 4, 1906. The main character, the son of a prosperous newspaper owner, recites the famous lines from *The Rubaiyat of Omar Khayyam*:

> *A Book of Verses underneath the Bough,*
> *A Jug of Wine, a Loaf of Bread – and Thou*
> *Beside me singing in the Wilderness.*

O'Neill's point seems to be that the wilderness has vanished, that we long for it and turn invariably to poets and writers who have written about it and to artists who have depicted it to recapture that which has been irrevocably lost. Ah, Wilderness! So far away and yet oh so close.

From the beginning, the continent of North America has been a place of great beauty and a space of terrible destruction.

The word "wilderness," which could mean a wasteland as well as a wonderland, summed up almost all of the contradictions. Fierce and fickle, savage and strange, it was the twin and the double of itself, elusive and mysterious, an immense womb and a vast grave-yard that brought life and death, endless creation and unending destruction. For the literal minded the wilderness was nothing more than an aggregate of trees and forests. For imaginative writ-ers from Nathaniel Hawthorne and Emily Dickinson to Nelson Algren and Arthur Miller, it had little to do with a place on a map but rather signified a state of mind and an inner emotional land-scape of isolation, alienation and existential dread.

Dickinson described her own "Wild Nights." Hawthorne explored the "wilderness of sleep." Algren mapped the "neon wil-derness" of the city, and, when Miller decided to craft a play about the Salem witchcraft trials that would serve as an allegory for the anti-communist "witch-hunts" of the Cold War era, he noted, "I would not only be writing myself into the wilderness politi-cally but personally as well." Even the naturalist John Muir wrote whimsically and metaphorically about the untamed California landscape and about the "manners of the wilderness."

The wilderness gestalt changed radically in 1964 when President Lyndon Johnson signed into law the Wilderness Act, which created the National Wilderness Preservation System and gave birth to specific Wilderness areas that might be desert, forest, mountain, or valley. From then on there was lower case wilderness and upper case Wilderness, and sometimes the lower case wilder-ness was less tamed than federally protected Wilderness areas that often became playgrounds for the wealthy who could afford to take long vacations, make long journeys and spend heaps of money.

The idea that a wilderness might be part of a government system would have shocked the Puritans who thought of the wilderness as the world outside and beyond: the quintessential

"Other" that threatened Christianity and civilization. From the beginning, civilization and the wilderness, the tame and wild were two sides of the same coin, though early settlers usually didn't and couldn't see the similarties.

It wasn't until Thoreau came along in the 1850s that anyone articulated a kind of Double Consciousness about the continent itself that aimed to fuse opposites rather than push them apart. "What we call wildness is a civilization other than our own," Thoreau argued, playfully. By the time of the American Renaissance, it became clear to writers such as Herman Melville that the barbarians turned out to be civilized and the civilized, it seemed, were as barbaric as any barbarian.

For hundreds of years, Americans have not been able to live without the precious wild that they turned into a kind of fetish. But they have not been able to live with it, either. They have fenced it off and hired rangers to protect it and they have trashed it and polluted it. The wilderness is dead! Long live the wilderness!

I would like to see more wilderness protection, though I know that more wilderness areas all by themselves will not automatically ensure that the earth will survive global climate change, pollution, and environmental destruction. Still, the wilderness is one essential part of a program to preserve, conserve and restore. We need a new wilderness consciousness. We need renewed protections for clean air, clean water, uncontaminated soil and endangered species. American literature reflects the history of environmentalism and the threats to it. By showing us the past it can provide guideposts to the future.

American writers tracked — perhaps more poetically and empathetically than writers in any other Western culture — the interface between specific local, and immense continental environments on the one hand, and human beings on the other, whether the environment was represented by forest, wilderness, desert or wasteland.

In America, art sprang from the earth itself, and from the labors of the men and women who wrestled with it, tamed it and were beaten down by it, too. In "Song of Myself," Whitman boasted, "I loafe and invite my soul," but his poetry pulsates with lumberjacks, miners, sailors, blacksmiths, stevedores, and more who engage with forests and mines, on lakes and rivers, and in villages and towns all the way from New York to California. Much the same could be said for the work of Melville (think of his sailors), Twain (his Mississippi River pilots), Cather (her Nebraska farmers), Hurston (her Florida field workers) and Faulkner (his Mississippi plantation owners and slaves). North America itself haunts our literature. She's also a character in her own right.

In this book I have followed wilderness narratives, wilderness tropes, and "wild form" — that unique American mode of expression — from the age of the explorers in the seventeenth century to the age of the gangsters in the twentieth. Novelists and poets in the U.S. adopted and explored "wild form" long before Kerouac arrived on the scene with *On The Road*. But he was the first, as far as I know, to consciously use the term "wild form" to describe the kind of experimental fiction that he wanted to write. A keen student of American literature, of Melville, Jack London, Thomas Wolfe and Saroyan, he understood that his predecessors had eschewed tame English forms and experimented with wild American forms.

I have written about Roger Williams, James Fenimore Cooper, Mark Twain and Willa Cather, but at the heart of this book, I think, are the poets, essayists and novelists of the American Renaissance: Emerson, Thoreau, Hawthorne, Melville, Whitman and Dickinson. They are among the wildest writers that our nation has ever seen. My purpose throughout has been to look at American literature with a renewed sense of awe and wonder as though for the first time and to enable readers to look at the terrible beauty — the sacredness of the North American

continent and the destruction of it — through the eyes of our
poets, essayists and novelists. Literally and figuratively American
writers are nearly all wilderness writers. They write about the wilderness and they have written themselves into the wilderness, too.

I have not explored every major wilderness book in the vast
literature of the United States. A case in point: John Steinbeck's
The Grapes of Wrath (1939), perhaps the last great novel about
the wasteland and the wilderness, those two indelible polarities
in American writing about the environment. As singer and songwriter Bruce Springsteen noted, the wilderness in *The Grapes of
Wrath* is "that isolation that seems to be part of the American
character." The wilderness and isolation go back to the days of
the early Puritans. Near the end of the novel, Tom Joad, the Okie
ex-con turned California visionary, describes the spiritual journey
of preacher Casy — and simultaneously offers one of Steinbeck's
explicit moral lessons. "He went out into the wilderness to find
his own soul," Joad tells his salt-of-the-earth mother. There, Joad
explains, Casy learns that "a wilderness ain't no good, 'cause his
little piece of a soul wasn't no good, 'less it was with the rest, an'
was whole." Springsteen added that the power of the novel derives
from its ability "to reach in and pull you out of that wilderness,
into the world." In these pages I have not aimed to be all-inclusive
and encyclopedic, but rather to suggest approaches, readings and
ways of interpreting with help from cultural critics, writers and
artists like Springsteen.

Editors and teachers have told me that literary criticism is
dead, unless it is based in theory, and that readers no longer read
books about books unless they're theoretical. If that is the case,
then this is also a book meant to persuade the nation to return to
its classics. Why? Because our literature is a mirror in which we
have recorded ourselves and our landscapes. In the pages of *The
Scarlet Letter, Moby-Dick, Leaves of Grass, Walden*, and elsewhere

we see ourselves and recognize ourselves as killers and as lovers, lovers who kill and killers who love. We are Captain Ahab and Moby-Dick. We are Hester Prynne and the scarlet letter, leaves of grass and Walden Pond. We peer into the classics and look at great beauty and terrible carnage. American literature is a wilderness of words, no more artificial than the wilderness of trees and forests, deserts and wastelands that human beings have created.

Critics in America, though not around the world, often aim to keep art pure and to separate it from social concerns, causes and movements, environmental as well as overtly political campaigns. There is no way to keep art pure; the whole concept is false and misleading. Art is connected to life and life to art and the wilderness is at the heart of both art and life in the Americas. I have tried here to look at the wholeness of American culture and at the same time I have aimed to respect individual voices and styles. The wilderness makes us whole and divides us from one another. I mean this book to serve as an introduction to American literature. It's for those who have never read James Fenimore Cooper and Emily Dickinson and it is also for specialists: environmentalists, ecologists and scholars of the American novel.

Will we survive as a species? Will the earth itself survive, or will it be destroyed? Those are the questions that our writers have always asked. Their answers have usually been ambiguous, complex and contradictory. Return now to those exhilarating days of yesteryear when Europeans met Indians in the wilderness and the slaughter began.

CHAPTER 1

EXPLORERS & COLONISTS

Sebastian Cabot, Henry Hudson, Robert Juet & William Bradford

THE CLASH OF CIVILIZATIONS

Europeans framed their encounters with Indians as the clash between the civilized and the savage and rarely recognized that the Indians enjoyed civilizations of their own or that Europeans themselves behaved as the worst sort of barbarians. In fact, the Indians of North America belonged to oral cultures and, alas, kept no written documents. If only they had history would have been very different. The sailors aboard European ships belonged to the Old World and at the same time to the brand new culture that sprang from Gutenberg's invention of movable type that made possible the rapid dissemination of information about the New World. The printing press, that wonderful yet diabolical machine, aided and abetted the invasion and the occupation of North America. *Extra! Extra! Read all about the savages and their wild lands.* In a letter written at sea on February 15, 1493, Columbus claimed that he saw "trees of

a thousand kinds and tall, and they all seemed to touch the sky."
The island of Hispaniola, he insisted, was "a marvel" and its veg-
etation a "wonder to behold."

From the beginning, that unholy trinity — the printing
press, the map and the musket — gave the voyagers an advan-
tage in their barbarous encounters with the hospitable Indians.
All over the world, the culture of the book, the newspaper and
the legal document battered down print-less cultures in forests,
jungles and mountains. As the communications guru, Marshall
McLuhan, noted in *Understanding Media*, "Tribal cultures...may
be greatly superior to the Western cultures in the range and delicacy of their perceptions," but they were often at a disadvantage
when confronted by the culture of the written word that gener-
ated "separateness of the individual, continuity of space and of
time, and uniformity of codes." Against the onslaught of Bible
and musket, tribal societies used every weapon, every tool and
every means at hand to repel, contain and outwit the invaders.

For hundreds of years, the writers who chronicled the age
of exploration created white gods and dark-skinned devils. They
were guilty of thinking in terms of binary oppositions — good
and evil — and rarely saw the evil in themseles and the good
in the Indians. From the start, however, a vocal minority punctured big holes in the official stories. In his wake-up call to all of
Europe that he entitled *The Very Brief Relation of the Devastation
of the Indies* (1552), the Spanish cleric Bartolome de las Casas
(1484-1566) documented Spanish "acts of force and violence and
oppression." He recorded a whole world "destroyed and depop-
ulated by the Christians." Prophetic las Casas saw New World
wonders turned to New World wastes.

Near the start of his gruesome narrative of torture, slavery
and genocide, he emphasized his own terrible and terrifying experiences. "I saw all these things I have described," he wrote. While

he empathized with the Indians, he didn't try to see the world through their eyes, perhaps because he recognized that Europeans often inserted their own ideas into the minds of the Indians and then ascribed them to the Indians. In the language of today, they "projected" their thoughts onto the Indians they enslaved, exploited and murdered.

Sebastian Cabot — the sixteenth-century, Venetian-born explorer and cartographer — knew more about the world than just ocean winds and sea currents. A philosopher and a cultural ambassador, he noted that, "Our people and ships may appear unto them strange and wondrous and theirs to ours." Cabot had the good sense to understand that the wonderful went both ways. It would be a stretch to call him the father of American writing, but he shared with the writers of the American Renaissance a knack for looking both ways that might be called Double Consciousness.

When Cabot died in 1557, the English novel had not yet been invented. It didn't arrive until about 1719 when Daniel Defoe published *Robinson Crusoe* and a year later *The Adventures of Captain Singleton*. Cabot and his fellow explorers kept logs and recorded facts, or what they took to be facts. They were literate in that they could read and write, and literary in the sense that they told vivid stories. The first American writers were often sailors, soldiers and missionaries.

The early tales about North America might be divided into two groups: those that presented the continent as a hostile place, and those that described it as hospitable. The hostile writers called it a "wilderness." The hospitable writers dubbed it a "garden." Sebastian Cabot, with his sense of dualities, might have recognized that the garden and the wilderness were opposites and twins. He might have looked at the wilderness and seen it as a rambunctious garden and the garden as a tamer version of the wilderness. Neither the gardeners or the wilders, however, suggested that Europeans turn their ships around and leave the New World "untrammeled," to borrow the key word that's used in the 1964 Wilderness Act. Preservation and conservation didn't occur to the "gardeners" or to the "wilders." They were all colonizers, albeit with competing notions of what a colony ought to look like, and whether to colonize with the whip and the chain or the cross and the sacred text, or perhaps all of the above.

Not surprisingly, tales about gardens and about wilderness weren't born with the arrival of Europeans in North America. In fact, they are older than the Old Testament. Tales about the wild are as ancient as the Assyrian epic, *Gilgamesh*, which was originally inscribed on clay tablets that date from as far back as 2100 BCE. Thousands of years went by and no one knew about the amazing Assyrian tablets until they were unearthed at the ruins of Nineveh in 1850, a year before Melville published *Moby-Dick*, a coincidence that's almost too good to be true.

WILD & TAME

A mythmaker and an Orientalist, Melville would have regarded *Gilgamesh* as a curious and wonderful artifact. His contemporaries, Thoreau, Emerson and Hawthorne would have agreed. The story of the clay tablets and their discovery in 1850, reads like a tale out of the pages of Hawthorne's *The Scarlet Letter*, in which musty manuscripts come to life. In 1857, seven years after they were unearthed, scholars officially decoded the cuneiform characters, though the tablets would collect dust in the British Museum for years. In 1872, George Smith, a curator, realized their importance for Biblical studies, but it wasn't until 1916 that the first modern reader — the great German poet Rainer Maria Rilke — recognized the literary significance. "These truly gigantic fragments," he wrote, "belong with the supreme works that the conjuring World has ever produced." Melville might have reached much the same conclusion.

Like *Moby-Dick*, *Gilgamesh* describes the journey of a hero across a mythic landscape that links monsters and men. Like *Moby-Dick*, it describes the amity and enmity between men from opposing worlds, though, unlike *Moby-Dick*, it also offers portraits of powerful women. The authors of *Gilgamesh* were closer to matriarchal cultures than Melville. The ancient epic boasts far more female characters than the testosterone-fueled pages of *Moby-Dick:* Aruru, a goddess of creation who makes the wild man Enkidu; Ishtar, the goddess of love and war; and Shamhat, who embodies pleasure. Like the ancients, Melville recognized the paradoxes inherent in the human condition, and, like them, he brought down terrible death and destruction in *Moby-Dick*, perhaps the wildest American book ever written.

Gilgamesh suggests that the wild and the tame are two sides of the same coin. Melville reached the same conclusion. "We may have civilized bodies and yet barbarous souls," his narrator and main character observes in *Redburn* (1849), a mini-epic in which he makes fun of "snivilization" and praises sailors as "ocean barbarians." Melville's American sailors hunger for wild places, wild men and encounters with wild beasts. In *Moby-Dick*, Ishmael must have his "pagan friend," Queequeg. So, too, Gilgamesh, the king, can't exist without Enkidu.

In his essay, "The Oldest Story in the World," the poet and translator Stephen Mitchell observes that Enkidu, the "wild man," is Gilgamesh's "double," as well as his "opposite and mirror image" and that the Assyrian gods send Enkidu to confront Gilgamesh in order to "civilize him." Wild, naked Enkidu is himself humanized by the erotic arts of Shamhat, a temple priestess. Sex takes the animal out of him even as it draws out his animal self.

The wild and the tame, the primitive and the civilized are ominously and beautifully entangled in American literature. As Stephen Mitchell suggests, the world of Gilgamesh, "like ours, is not black and white." He adds, "there is ultimately nowhere to stand, no side we can ultimately take and not cut ourselves off from the truth." The walled city, Uruk, is both paradise and tyranny; its walls necessary and yet arbitrary.

Humans are forbidden to enter the "Cedar Forest" that's guarded by the monster, Humbaba, who is a force of nature like Moby-Dick, the white whale. Environmental awareness existed in Assyria in 2100 BCE. When Gilgamesh kills the monster, Humbaba, in part because he wants to be a famous warrior, "a gentle rain falls into the mountains as if the heavens themselves are weeping for the consequences of that act."

Fast-forward to *Sir Gawain and the Green Knight*, the fourteenth-century English epic that revives the tropes of the wild and the tame. Sir Gawain, an emissary from King Arthur's court, ventures into the wilderness and enters into deadly combat with the Green Knight, a gigantic warrior who towers above everyone else. Not only immense and monstrous, he also has a dual identity. The Green Knight is the lord and master of the castle and he's also the wild man of the wilderness who lives to kill. The virtuous Sir Gawain proves himself, not only in battle with the Green Knight, but also by deftly avoiding the snares set by his seductive wife, the mistress of the castle.

Unlike Gilgamesh, unlike Enkidu and unlike pagan Ahab, Sir Gawain is a devout Christian and not supposed to have sex with married women. Moreover, he's the great-grandfather of the knights of the forests in Cooper's novels. The seductive lady of the castle is also the great great-grandmother of the rambunctious women who appear in the lyrics to rock 'n' roll songs, such as Lou Reed's "Walk on the Wild Side" and "Wild Thing," a pop culture anthem sung by Jimi Hendrix, Jeff Beck and Warren Zevon among others. For rock 'n' rollers, the wild signified sex, drugs, raucous music, and defiance of conventionality, not woods or forests.

Nineteenth-century American poets, novelists and essayists didn't study ancient Assyrian epics and *Sir Gawain and the Green Knight*. They didn't intentionally transfer Gilgamesh, Enkidu, Gawain, the Green Knight and the gracious lady to the forests and frontiers of the New World. But they created archetypal characters in epic narratives as though they knew subconsciously that the wild and the tame, the beastly and the human, the world inside and outside the walls of the city, were inextricably connected. The New World brought writers into the world of myth even as the Old World set itself apart from the world of myth.

PARADOX OF THE PIONEER

In *Studies in Classic American Literature*, D. H. Lawrence suggests that to understand American literature from Benjamin Franklin to Walt Whitman, it helps to recognize that "Somewhere deep in every American heart lies a rebellion against the old parenthood of Europe." Lawrence added that, "most people have come to America...to get away from everything they are and have been." As he well knew, hordes of Europeans fled from kings, popes, lords, ladies and servitude of all kinds. They came to America to escape from the past and to enjoy freedom. Still, more than a few brought the past with them, along with their parents and the notion of parenthood itself. For every child who rebelled against the ancestry of Europe, dutiful daughters and sons accompanied mothers and fathers and imported patriarchal values. Lawrence himself recognized that "no American feels he has completely escaped" the mastery of Europe. Indeed, many didn't want to escape; others tried and failed. Europe and the European held on.

Lawrence's notion that Americans are in perpetual flight shows up in modified form in *Love and Death in the American Novel* (1966). The author, Leslie Fiedler, writes about disobedient boys and rebellious men who rebel against women, the institution of marriage and civilization itself. "The typical male protagonist of our fiction has been a man on the run, harried into the forest and out to sea, down the river or into combat — anywhere to avoid 'civilization,' which is to say, the confrontation of a man and woman which leads to the fall, to sex, marriage and responsibility," Fiedler wrote. The typical American male protagonist, if such a character exists, might be more complex than Fiedler allows. Maxim Gorky (1868-1936), the modern Russian novelist, certainly thought so. He looked at James Fenimore Cooper's Natty Bumppo — as archetypical a protagonist as any in American fiction — and saw a more nuanced character than Fiedler allowed.

"As an explorer of the forests and prairies of the New World he blazes trails in them for people who later condemn him as a criminal because he has infringed their mercenary and, to his sense of freedom, unintelligible laws," Gorky wrote. He added, "All his life he has unconsciously served the great cause of geographical expansion of material culture in a country of uncivilized people and — found himself incapable of living in conditions of this culture for which he had struck the first paths." The Russians had their own literature of the frontier. Their Wild West was in the East, at the opposite end of the continent from Moscow and St. Petersburg.

Gorky read American literature through the lens of Russian society. Fiedler read it through the culture of post World War II U.S.A. when mad men fled to Madison Avenue to become advertising executives or took to the road to become wanderers and adventurers. Both the Beats and the organization men longed to

be wild men, the roles played to perfection by the leading young
male actors of the day, James Dean and Marlon Brando.

D. H. Lawrence's notion that "most people" came to America to
get away from "everything" doesn't include European explorers such
as Sir Francis Drake, Henry Hudson, Robert Juet and John Smith,
who brought *everything* they could from the Old World to the New
World. Moreover, they didn't have the benefit of hindsight that one
finds in *The Great Gatsby*, Fitzgerald's Jazz Age riff on the wild and
the tame that mythologizes the origins of America. At the end of the
novel, the narrator Nick Carraway imagines European sailors as they
spy "the green breast of the new world" and fall under its magical spell.

Real sailors, like their fictional counterparts, were also enchanted
by North America. Thomas Pownall, an eighteenth-century English
colonial administrator, wrote that, "Everything made a vivid impression" and that his "imagination was all suspense" — if one can
imagine that intriguing idea. The continent would give rise to "genuine wildness of imagination," to borrow a potent phrase that F. O.
Matthiessen uses in *American Renaissance* (1941), not to describe literature in the U.S., but Emily Bronte's *Wuthering Heights* (1847), an
atypical nineteenth-century English novel in which the wild and the
tame clash and collude until one doesn't know what side to choose.

The poets, essayists and novelists who belonged to the
American Renaissance pushed the imagination into wild territories
within and without, but they had no monopoly on "genuine wildness of imagination." Dickens pursued it and so did Emile Zola,
Fyodor Dostoevsky, Emily and Charlotte Bronte. An outgrowth
of the Romantic Movement, imaginative liberty as one might call
it expressed global discomfort and disenchantment with imperial
order and the rapaciousness of class society that led, Heathcliff
explains in *Wuthering Heights*, to a conundrum in which "the
tyrant grinds down his slaves and they don't turn against him: they
crush those beneath him." Melville explores the phenomenon in

Moby-Dick; Thoreau reflects on it in *Walden* and in his essays.

Two hundred years before Bronte and her American contemporaries launched their literary expeditions into unexplored territories, Henry Hudson was excited by the strange and wonderful New World that he saw before him. An Englishman and a Londoner, he sailed under the Dutch flag with a crew that was part Dutch on the eighty-five-foot *Half Moon*. Only Hudson and Juet, his English first mate, kept logs. Self-confident and self-willed, Hudson set out on his voyages with a son. He took nearly everything he wanted and needed: compasses, clocks, muskets, food, drink, swords, ideas about the nature of human nature and preconceived images of humanity that influenced the course of action he followed when he arrived on the shores of what's now New York.

Born and bred in an era of war and conquest, Hudson and the early seventeenth-century explorers exported war and greed to North America. Opportunistic, they advanced their own personal interests as well as those of mercantile enterprises such as the Dutch West India Company. Historian Douglas Hunter describes Hudson as a double agent who was officially employed by the Dutch and secretly working for the English. That may be, though he behaved like a loyal company man. He turned back from his 1609 voyage — which he hoped would bring him to the Northwest Passage and to the wealth of India — because, as he explained in his journal, he wanted to "save victuals, wages and tackle." Not a reckless spender, he kept New World secrets until the day he died. On his way home, he stopped in Ireland. The Mayor of Dartmouth, Thomas Holland, reported that, "one Henry Hudson an Englishman late of London…has discovered some special matters of great consequence which he would not impart."

Hudson never shared his New World secrets, though he and Juet wrote accounts of their voyages that were published in England in 1625 — nearly a century before the appearance of Defoe's *Robinson Crusoe*. Hudson called the world on the other side of the Atlantic, "the Land." Juet called it "the Land" and "the Country." Juet named the inhabitants the "people of the Country" and "the people of the mountain." Neither he nor Hudson used the word "wilderness." They saw and experienced a continent that we might call pre-wilderness America, though the word wilderness was already available to them.

In fact, it appears in Shakespeare's *The Merchant of Venice*, which was written and performed in the 1590s, as reports of the New World circulated across England. Shylock speaks of "a wilderness of monkeys" an image that suggests an infinite number of monkeys, a kind of chaos of monkeys. Hudson and Juet saw no monkeys and no wilderness, though they saw all make and manner of creatures: a superabundance of life itself. As the *Half Moon* left the known world, Hudson entered a magical territory where he saw fog and ice as he had never seen them before. Nearly everything was bigger than anything in Europe; there were great bear, deer, whales, foxes, fowl and a "great river."

Hudson magnified the greatness of the New World. He gazed in wonderment at the "pleasant land" and at the "green things that did there grow" and sent sailors on a scouting expedition to "see what the Land would yield that might be profitable." The men took stock of everything they saw, noted the birds and fish they captured and killed: 40 lobster and 118 codfish, all on one scouting expedition, and an "incredible number of seals." Hudson also recorded an encounter with a whale that swam under the ship and "Yet by God's mercy we had no harm." From the start, whales surfaced in the literature about North America.

Nearly everything that happened, Hudson ascribed to the hand of God, not to man or men. He didn't fully believe in human agency, though he was a powerful agent himself. With one eye on God and the other on gold, he noted that timber was abundant and suitable for building ships that could sail across the

Atlantic and carry rich cargos to Europe. The Indians stored so much corn that it was "enough to load three ships," he wrote after a brief sojourn on shore that took him inside the well-constructed round houses of the inhabitants. Juet was as eager as Hudson to loot and pillage. He also wrote that, "the Land" offered "a very pleasant place to build a town on."

In Juet's eyes, "the Land" was a paradise of "goodly trees," "great and tall oaks," "rare minerals" and "very sweet smells." He saw what he called "woods," but nothing that prompted him to use the word "wilderness." The inhabitants of the land — "the People of the Country" — were quiet, civil, merry, and "very loving," he insisted. They were, he added in his journal, "very glad of our coming." The natives near the island of "Manna-hatta" served the sailors platters of venison, made speeches and expressed reverence for the wanderers who gave as little back as they could. Juet traded "trifles" for oysters, grains, grapes and pumpkins.

Despite the gifts and the friendship, he suspected that the Indians meant to "betray" him and the sailors on the *Half Moon*. "We durst not trust them," he wrote. He could not believe that strangers would freely offer them "love, tobacco and Indian wheat." The Europeans shared wine and brandy with their hosts, hoping that the intoxicated natives would disclose their plans. They only learned that alcohol "was strange to them" and that they didn't know "how to take it." Sailors kidnapped two Indians, held them captive and beat them bloody. Before long, Juet began to use the word "savages" to describe the "People of the Country."

A native climbed aboard the *Half Moon*, purloined a pillow, two shirts, and a bandolier used to store shot and powder. He was promptly killed, whereupon the Indians fled "into the woods." Before long, they regrouped on the shore, aimed arrows at the sailors but did not inflict injuries. One native tried to overturn a small boat with sailors aboard. The *Half Moon's* cook cut off one of his

hands with a sword and the native drowned. Juet loaded and fired
a small cannon known as a "falcon" and took credit for killing several "savages" on shore. His narrative would be repeated hundreds
if not thousands of times over the next three-hundred-years with
variations on the theme of murder, robbery and betrayal.

On his 1609 journey to North America Hudson discovered
something more valuable than a passageway to India, though
he was disappointed that he had failed to accomplish the task
assigned him by the Dutch East India Company. On August 20,
1609, he decided to abort his mission and use "all diligence to
arrive at London." In his journal, he noted that he was "void of
hope of a Northwest passage" — a feeling far removed from the
human "capacity for wonder" and the "aesthetic contemplation"
that Fitzgerald attaches to the Dutch sailors at the end of *The
Great Gatsby*. Hudson was downright disappointed.

He and Juet sailed briefly up the river that would be named
the Hudson, turned around and went home with a sense of defeat.
In 1610, on yet another voyage, Juet led a mutiny against Hudson
and set him adrift in a small boat, never to be seen or heard from
again. Europeans could be treacherous to their own kind. The
European powers were no more loyal to their foot soldiers, sailors and sea captains than the foot soldiers, sailors and captains
were loyal to them. Sebastian Cabot's failed expedition in South
America led to his banishment from Spain. Even Columbus
(1451-1506) was arrested and jailed by the authorities. Gorky
was right. The explorers "served the great cause of geographical
expansion" and then they were condemned as criminals.

When Thomas Holland, the Irish mayor, debriefed Hudson
at the end of his 1609 voyage, he explained that Hudson described
"the coast of America." The sailors on *The Half Moon* didn't know
that "the Land" stretched all the way to the mythical land called
"California" where Sir Francis Drake arrived in 1579, repaired

the *Golden Hinde* and met the peaceful Miwok who brought him food to eat. Colonization of America proceeded from the East, the West, the North and the South. In 1609, the year of Hudson's next-to-last voyage, the English established Jamestown, the first real European settlement in North America, though the Spanish had an outpost in what is now Florida. The French founded Quebec the previous year. Before long, Europeans plunged into the woods, scaled mountains, followed rivers upstream and collided with Indians.

Africans arrived in Virginia in 1619, a year before the Pilgrims, and while they weren't slaves at first, they were quickly enslaved. The slave trade would go on for centuries, cost millions of lives and make great fortunes for Europeans and Americans. Africans cleared forests, plowed and planted fields and labored on plantations. With "sweat and brawn," the historian, W. E. B. Du Bois observed, they helped to "beat back the wilderness, conquer the soil, and lay the foundations" for what would become "a vast economic empire." African Americans soon learned to love the wilderness that they tamed. "If you want to find Jesus, go in de wilderness," one slave song goes. Another offers the line, "I found free grace in de wilderness."

Two Strange Dutchmen

Two strange agents of the Dutch empire, Harmen Meyndertsz Van den Bogaert and Adriane Van der Donck, were among the earliest Europeans to live in the woods, speak Indian languages and report what they saw and heard. Van den Bogaert was the stranger of the two men. Born in 1612, he was a barber and a surgeon. When he arrived in New Netherlands he was 18. At 23, he led an expedition into Iroquois territory to mend fences with the

Indians and negotiate beneficial terms for the lucrative fur trade. A man of many roles — diplomat, negotiator, anthropologist and detective — Van den Bogaert adapted to his environment and was accepted by the Indians. Whatever fears he might have had about the Iroquois and the forest they soon vanished. The Indians assured him that he "must not be afraid" and that they presented "no danger" to him. He went calmly where no Dutchmen had gone before: into Indian villages that were "so neatly made that it was a wonder" and to feasts with salmon, bear, beans, pumpkin and strawberries, and where he saw paintings of dogs, deer and snakes. At night, Van den Bogaert slept peacefully under the stars. He felt comfortable enough with the Indians and with his own anxieties to confess "I do not know" when he didn't have answers or understand the strange world he saw. Few European travelers in the woods of America would echo those four words.

Near the end of his life, Van den Bogaert was indicted on charges of sodomy with a black servant. He fled into the Mohawk valley, but he was captured and imprisoned in what is now Albany, New York. He escaped from his cell but drowned crossing a river he hoped would bring him to freedom.

Adriaen Van der Donck went into the woods shortly after Van den Bogaert, and, while he didn't use the word "wilderness" he noted that, "The whole country is covered with wood." He added, "There is all too much of it." The myth of the superabundance of the New World, expressed by Juet and Hudson, was echoed by Van der Donck. A utopian, he depicted the Indians as dreamers, egalitarians and sun worshipers who told him that a goddess had created the universe. Why the Dutch worked so hard, the Indians didn't understand, nor did they grasp why in Holland, "one man should be so much higher than another." To European settlers who worried that too many trees had already been cut down, Donck replied, "there can be no scarcity of wood." To those who worried that the animals of the country "will be destroyed," he had a ready answer, too: "There will not be an end to the wild animals." If environmentalism, as it came to called, arrived early in North America in the work of Roger Williams for example, so did the counter argument that insisted on infinite plenty.

VIRGIN LAND, HIDEOUS LAND

The quintessential English soldier of fortune, John Smith (c.1580-c.1631), saw "good woods," "spacious tracts of land," and "incredible abundance" in the New World. In almost all of his books, he emphasized the steps that were necessary for the creation of a prosperous colony. Smith erased Indian names and substituted English names. *Accominticus* became Boston and *Anmoughcawgen* Cambridge. He also described Virginia as Massachusetts's "Virgin Sister." The myth of the "Virgin" land would be nearly as popular as the myth of the wilderness.

Smith insisted that his tales were true, though he embellished, exaggerated and fictionalized. The New World practically required fictionalization. "I have been tossed and tortured into so many extremities," he wrote as though he was a character in a Defoe novel. His volumes are almost all how-to books. He had all the right answers for skeptics wary of the advertisements for the New World.

Smith warned husbands not to run away from wives, instructed children not to abandon parents and advised servants not to escape from their masters. Probably everything that he hoped and prayed would not happen, had already happened. Even as he created a new order in the New World, he meant to preserve and protect the old order in Europe. In the wilds of Virginia, he assured readers, an English boy might find happiness with the daughter of an Indian chief. Indeed, when Indians took him hostage and held him prisoner, he explained that, "God made Pocahontas, the King's daughter, the means to deliver him from his captivity."

A poster boy for the colonization of the New World, the ubiquitous Smith created myths about himself as a superhero who was "a slave to the Turks and a prisoner among the most barbarous savages." He escaped captivity and worked his way to the top of the social ladder. "Wars in Europe, Asia, and Africa," he noted, had taught him "to subdue wild savages in Virginia and New-England." He added that, "strange accidents" had befallen him all his life. "How often up, how often down, sometimes near despair," he wrote. His books helped to lay the groundwork for English novels by breaking down barriers between truth and the make believe.

In *Nova Britannica*, an unabashed advertisement for the settlement of Virginia published in 1609, the author Robert Johnson described the landscape as both a garden and as a wilderness and called for men and women to emigrate or to invest their money — to "adventure." Johnson never set foot in Virginia though his absence didn't prevent him from describing the "earthly paradise" he was certain existed. The notion that America "should remain wilderness" with "wild beasts" and "savage people" he found totally unacceptable. The wilderness had to be conquered.

Johnson emphasized the seemingly endless forests of the New World and reminded potential investors that Europe's forests had been "spent and wasted." Indeed, by 1600, European timberland had already been depleted. America could supply all of Europe's growing need for wood; there would be ample employment for carpenters, sawyers and coopers. Not surprisingly, the tree was, in Johnson's view, the most apt emblem for the colonial enterprise. Like its heartiest trees, the plantation at Virginia was "firmly rooted" in the ground with "limbs strong and branches fair."

Unlike the Cavaliers who settled Virginia, many of the New Englanders were Calvinists who thought of the world as wicked, a notion expressed at the very start of John Bunyan's Puritan classic, *The Pilgrim's Progress.* "As I walk'd through the wilderness of this world," Bunyan wrote. Published in 1678 to great acclaim, his book captured the Puritan vision of the world as a place of "cheats, games, plays, fools, apes, knaves, and rogues...thefts, murders, adulteries, false-swearers."

The wilderness of New England had all those elements and more, including wild Indians and dark forests. To the early English settlers, it was a Godless land in which their religious faith was sorely tested. To reach the Promised Land, the Pilgrims had to pass through the perilous wild and resist the kinds of temptations that Bunyan warned against. A century earlier, Sebastian Cabot had set down rules for behavior: no blasphemy, ribaldry, dicing, carding, "nor other devilish games." The Pilgrims reaffirmed his edicts.

William Bradford, the author of *Of Plymouth Plantation* (1630-1651), presented himself as a pious Pilgrim and as a righteous colonist who condemned the Indians as "savage and brutish men." He described the landscape as "a hideous & desolate wilderness." Eager to see what lay beyond the forest, he climbed a tree and looked for a "more goodly country." He saw none. Trees spread everywhere but he vowed that for the sake of God he was "ready to perish in this wilderness."

When Englishmen took up with Indians, Bradford found them "base." The point was to band together and to prevent "drunkenness & uncleanliness" and put a stop to "sodomy & buggery." Still, the wild called to the tame English. It was impossible to prevent settlers from drifting beyond the "Hedge." Thomas Morton — the "lord of misrule" as Bradford called him — created a freewheeling, boisterous colony, "New English Canaan," which he described in his book of the same name. For Morton, the New World was "very beautiful and commodious" and "like our parks." As though Adam himself in the Garden of Eden, he wandered in the forest, identifying the trees he saw. "There are such infinite flocks of fowl and multitudes of fish," he wrote.

The Indians he met were "full of humanity" and not "a dangerous" people. They reminded him of "the wild Irish" and he condemned the Puritans who slaughtered them. At New Canaan, Morton and his fellow utopians, with help from Indians, set up a Maypole and enjoyed "revels and merriment after the old English custom." They drank beer, sang songs and had sex with the Indians in what was probably the first countercultural community on American soil.

Hawthorne revisits New Canaan in his short story "The Maypole of Merry Mount" in which he rewrites colonial history and describes the triumph of the Puritan ethic and the Puritan ethos over the party of mirth and gayety. In Hawthorne's fictional account, Endicott, the governor of the Massachusetts Bay Colony, destroys the maypole and the whole community that surrounds it. Endicott insists that his soldiers cut the long, luxurious head of hair of the Lord of the May. Hawthorne observes that the Puritans were burdened with superstition and that they "peopled the black wilderness" with devils and "ruined souls." Moreover, he suggests that this early chapter in the annals of colonial society was emblematic of American history. "The moral gloom of the world overpowers all systematic gayety," he wrote.

Woodstock hippies and their descendants would surely have disagreed with him, though historians of the 1960s have described the 1969 rock concert at Altamont in California — just months after Woodstock — as the death knell of the counterculture. Hawthorne's own Double Consciousness enabled him to see New Canaan through the eyes of both the party of gayety and the party of gloom, and to imbue Endicott with a sense of compassion and even wisdom. While Hawthorne was attracted to "wild mirth" he felt that maturity required that it be left behind along with exuberant youth, and that responsible adult citizens ought to turn to work, reverence and parenting.

*

Tales of the "earthly paradise" and the "New World" — a phrase as potent as any in the history of advertizing — lured men, women and children to the shores of North America and then into the vast hinterlands that Hudson and Juet only glimpsed. Pioneers plunged into forests on foot, horseback and canoe and later by steamboat, railroad, in covered wagons and on rafts. Hunters, outlaws, soldiers, missionaries and naturalists followed them. In the wilderness they found themselves, discovered riches, battled Indians, chopped down trees and whole forests, made clearings, built cabins, hunted, fished, farmed, escaped from the dead weight of the past and projected onto the land, as though it was a tabula rasa or huge blank canvas, their dreams, nightmares, hopes and fears.

CHAPTER 2

PURITANS

Roger Williams, Mary Rowlandson, Cotton Mather & William Faulkner

HOWLING WILDERNESS

The modernist fiction writer, William Faulkner (1897-1962), called his collection of Mississippi hunting stories, *Big Woods,* as though to register disapproval with the word "wilderness." The four related tales — "The Bear," "The Old People," "A Bear Hunt" and "Race at Morning" along with Faulkner's commentary — recount the initiation into manhood of a young Southern white boy. They also describe the transformation of the "big woods" into a "howling waste." Faulkner meant the phrase "howling waste" as an ironical commentary on the Puritan motif of the "howling wilderness." All through the seventeenth and for much of the eighteenth century Puritans rarely used the word "wilderness" without also using the word "howling," though what they actually heard they didn't say. "Howling" derived its power to terrify precisely because it came from everywhere all at once.

If Faulkner could have encountered just one seventeenth century wilderness writer, that man would have to be Roger Williams (1603-1683), the wildest Puritan in seventeenth-century America. A Calvinist theologian and the founder of Rhode Island, Williams was a maverick minister, poet, ambassador, spy, adjunct to English military officers, trader, translator and backwoodsman, too. One might call him an incipient CIA agent. Williams spent most of his life in a place that he called a "pagan wilderness" by which he meant that it wasn't inhabited by Christians but rather by Indians who didn't believe in his God.

Of all the many biographers, scholars and students of William's life and work, Perry Miller — the paramount twentieth-century authority on all matters Puritan — probably appreciated him more deeply than anyone else. Still, Miller also noted that Williams was "the worst kind of virtuous man, a perfectionist" who "demanded that the rest of the world conform to him, rather than he to them." Miller described Williams as the first literate Englishman who lived "intimately with the Indians." He also noted that he had a "violent imagination" and an "aptitude" for "allegories." Indeed, violence and allegory run all through his work, which sometimes seems to presage the stories of Franz Kafka and the poems of T. S. Eliot.

Born in 1603 in England, Williams died in 1683 in New England. A truly transatlantic figure, he moved back and forth across the Atlantic. Caught up in the revolutions and the civil wars of the seventeenth century, both in London and on the edge of the emerging British Empire, he helped turn the world upside down and to make history in England and New England. Faulkner would have recognized his big, bold achievements.

At the very start of *Big Woods*, he describes the dualities inherent in the archetypal Puritan pioneer who holds "Bible and jug in one hand and (like as not) a native tomahawk in the other."

Moreover, Faulkner describes his mythic Puritan as "a married invincible bachelor, dragging his…family behind him into the trackless infested forest…scattering his ebullient seed in a hundred dusky bellies through a thousand miles of wilderness." Williams was as complex a historical figure as Faulkner's archetypal Anglo Saxon pioneer, though by all accounts he was less sexually active. He went into the wilderness alone in a canoe on a cold winter day, in flight from the colonial authorities in Boston, though his wife and children soon joined him. Williams preferred the Bible to jug whiskey, and while he adopted Indian ways, he never carried a tomahawk or shot a bow and arrow. If he went native it was largely to survive. During a period of intense conflict between whites and Indians in New England, he had to remind Governor Winthrop that he had not "turned Indian" and had not joined forces with the "wild Americans."

Williams was the first Englishman in the New World to recognize the wilderness as a trope. In a real sense he invented the American wilderness. He was also the first literary figure to write a series of poems about it. As Perry Miller noted, "No other New England writer makes quite so much of an incantation out of the very word 'wilderness.'"

The English invasion and occupation of North America gave new meanings to the words wilderness and wild though curiously neither appears in *A Table Alphabeticall*, the first English Dictionary compiled in 1604, a year after Williams's birth, by Robert Cawdrey. A crafty lexicographer, Cawdrey included words such as "paradise," which he defined as a "place of pleasure" and "lumber" which, he explained, meant "old stuff." Wilderness in its seventeenth-century usage was perhaps too new a word for Cawdrey to notice and record.

But the word bubbled up from Williams's unconscious and spilled onto the pages of *A Key into the Language of America* (1643) — his bold and innovative masterpiece — at a critical moment in his own life. On a ship halfway between the Old World and the New World, he looked back at America, where his future lay, and ahead to England, where he'd come of age as a young man. He was going home to persuade parliament to grant him a charter for his colony. Writing *A Key* by a "rude lamp" he realized that he had been reborn in the wilderness. The wild had rubbed off on him. He was no longer the proper Englishman he had been.

The fact that he spoke Algonquin and could converse with the Indians meant that he was able to hear and appreciate Indian points of view, a rare gift for a seventeenth-century Puritan. When the English described the Indians as barbarians, pagans and savages he reported that they resented the terms and that they hurled them back at the English. "You are barbarians, Pagans wild, your Land's the Wilderness," an Indian exclaims in one of the most remarkable of the thirty or so poems in *A Key into the Language of America*. That's the kind of Double Consciousness that made the language and the culture of the New World distinctly American.

Two hundred years after Williams, Indians would say much the same thing: whites were wild; civilization was the wilderness. In *Land of the Spotted Eagle* the Indian author, Luther Standing Bear, wrote, "We did not think of the great open plains, the beautiful rolling hills, and winding streams with tangled growth, as 'wild.' Only to the white man was nature a 'wilderness' and only to him was the land 'infected' with 'wild' animals and 'savage' people. To us it was tame." Standing Bear added, "When the very animals of the forest began fleeing from his approach, then it was that for us the 'Wild West' began." The English word "civilization" irked Standing Bear and he noted that it had "not added one whit to my sense of justice; to my reverence for the rights of life; to my love for truth, honesty, and generosity."

In seventeenth-century New England, no one understood the political power of language more than Williams. At the height of his intellectual prowess, he probably would have agreed with Francis Jennings, the twentieth-century American historian and author of *The Invasion of America: Indians, Colonialism, and the Cant of Conquest*, who noted that words such as "civilized," "uncivilized" and "savage" were used as weapons in the cultural war that was fought between settlers and the indigenous people. They were "created for the purposes of conquest rather than the purposes of knowledge" and they evolved from centuries of warfare in Europe, Jennings explained. Writing in the 1970s, in the midst of the War in Vietnam, he argued that Americans had not given up the "cant of conquest."

Roger Williams was a savvy linguist and propagandist and the first poet to write with the voice of an American. He preceded Anne Bradstreet (1612-1673), his contemporary, who has been called the "first true poet in the American colonies." Bradstreet wrote more poetry than Williams, though like him she used the wilderness as a trope. "He that walks among briars and thorns will be very careful where he sets his foot, and he that passes through the wilderness of this world had need ponder all his steps," she wrote.

In the foreword to a collection of her poetry, the poet and critic Adrienne Rich points out that "the landscape, the emotional weather of the New World are totally absent" from Bradstreet's poems. Rich also notes that, "much has been written, by white American male writers, of the difficulties of creating 'great literature' at the edge of wilderness, in a society without customs and traditions." Williams didn't fret about his situation on the edge; he jumped right in, conscious that he was one of the first Europeans to set foot in the wilderness of the New World.

The image of setting one's feet down in a strange land quickly developed into a trope. In 1634, at about the same time that Williams went into the wilderness of what would become Rhode Island, a Jesuit priest, Andrew White, arrived in Maryland and wrote, "we cannot sett downe a foote, but tread on strawberries, raspires, fallen mulberrie vines, achorns, walnuts, saxafras etc: and those in the wildest woods."

Unlike the furtive explorers John Smith, Henry Hudson and Robert Juet, Williams settled down in the woods and enjoyed life there. "I have been oft glad in the wilderness of America, to have been reproved for going in a wrong path, and to be directed by a naked Indian boy in my travels," he wrote. When he sat down with pen and paper to write about the wild he had fun *with* the wild, though at heart he was not a fun-loving fellow. A tragic figure — perhaps the first European in New England to fit that description — he was pulled toward the Indians and toward the English, too.

TURNING THE WORLD UPSIDE DOWN

Williams left nearly all his possessions behind him when he first set foot in the woods, though as a good emissary from the Old World he also brought British values with him into the wilderness. As a pioneer and as a scout, he provided the Puritans with vital information that helped them defeat the "wild Americans" in two major military conflagrations — the Pequod War of the 1630s and King Philip's War of the 1660s — in which hundreds of Indians were slaughtered, their villages set on fire and burned to the ground. King Philip's War and the Pequod War were principally the products of English aggression, though the Indians fought to save their land, their culture and their lives. Not surprisingly, given the fact that whites have written the history books, the Indians have received most of the blame.

Williams knew that the story was more complicated than the English military commanders insisted. He didn't exonerate the Indians, but he knew that Europeans played a major part in

fomenting trouble. Two hundred years after Williams, William
Faulkner refused to blame any single race or group for the destruction of the big woods in Mississippi. For Faulkner, the history of
the wilderness was cyclical. As he explained it, the French dispossessed the Indians who were dispossessed by the Spanish who
were dispossessed by the French, who were in turn dispossessed by
the Anglo Saxons. For Faulkner, the history of Mississippi was the
history of America writ large. No one was innocent.

In the seventeenth century, the English invaded and occupied
Indian territories, took Indians hostage and violated their sacred
spaces. They kidnapped natives, such as Squanto, and transported
them to Europe where they learned European languages and borrowed European ways. Squanto returned to America, greeted the
Pilgrims in 1620 and taught them basic survival skills. Perhaps the
English didn't appear strange to the Indians of Massachusetts after
all. Squanto had observed them on the other side of the Atlantic.

In *Of Plymouth Plantation*, William Bradford noted that
Squanto spoke "broken English" and was a "special instrument
sent of God." He was "profitable" to the Pilgrims. As nearly every
schoolboy and girl knows, the Pilgrims wouldn't have endured their
first New England winter without Squanto and his fellow tribes-
men, though Bradford never acknowledged Indian generosity.

Like Bradford, Roger Williams attributed a great deal to
God, though he also credited human beings as the makers of
history. Curious about the Indian past and about the origins of
Indian society, he concluded, on the basis of the Bible, that the
Indians were a lost tribe who had wandered off course. He vowed
to bring them back into the fold of the church, though not under
threat of punishment. Forced conversions of Indians were antithetical to the spirit of Christianity, he argued.

No Puritan wrote as insightfully about Indians as Williams
and no one wrote as warmly or kindly as he, though he also believed

that they were doomed to be defeated by the English. Long before James Fenimore Cooper wrote lyrically about dying Indians and doomed tribes in *The Last of the Mohicans*, Williams wrote about the last of the Pequod and the Narragansett. One might borrow Joseph Conrad's memorable comment about Henry James and apply it to Williams: "Nobody has rendered better, how to drape the robe of spiritual honor about the drooping form of a victor in a barren strife." Williams draped the robe of spiritual honor about the drooping form of the Indians as they went down to defeat in the wars for control of New England.

In his letters, Williams anguished about his own trials and tribulations. "I set the first step of any English foot into these wild parts, and have maintained a chargeable and hazardous correspondence with the barbarians," he wrote at the age of 51, with three more decades of wilderness living still ahead of him. Proud of his life in the woods, Williams also resented what he regarded as his exile. He had been "banished" and "driven" into the forests, he complained, and then "debarred from Boston, the chief mart and port of New England." The result was "the yearly loss of no small matter in my trading with the English and natives." Profoundly spiritual and in quest of religious freedom, he didn't conceal the fact that he also conducted business, though he insisted that he would not trade, as other Puritans did, in whiskey and guns.

A Christian mercantalist, he embodied the best and the worst of seventeenth-century England: revolutionary fervor and restoration formalities; religious tolerance, even for Turks, Jews, and Pagans, as well as religious fanaticism. In the *Bloudy Tenent* (1644), a screed about intolerance, he played with the metaphors of the garden and the wilderness and noted that, "A false religion out of the church will not hurt the church, no more than weeds in the wilderness hurt the enclosed garden." He hated Catholics and Catholicism and urged relentless warfare against the Pope and "the Anti-Christ," a rough beast that, he insisted, preyed on innocent Christians.

Like the iconoclastic Anne Hutchinson (1591-1643) — a friend who believed women could preach as well as men and that everyone could commune directly with his or her own God — Williams was persecuted for his beliefs. But he had advantages she didn't have: he was male, a minister and a personal friend of colonial Governor John Winthrop. Hutchinson's judges described the meetings in her home as "disorderly" and "without rules." In their eyes she was rambunctious, and that kind of behavior from a woman the Puritans couldn't abide. Governor Winthrop called Hutchinson an "American Jezebel." Accordingly, the Puritan fathers ordered that she be "banished out of our liberties," seemingly unaware that liberty might thrive as much if not more in the wild as in the town.

Banishment to the wilderness was as harsh a punishment as any in seventeenth century New England, save hanging and burning. From the Puritan point of view, no good Christian would want to live among Indians and beyond the sanctified community. As the poet and critic William Carlos Williams noted in *In the American Grain*, the persecuted Puritans persecuted their own. They had "nothing of curiosity, no wonder, for the New World — that is nothing official — they knew only to keep their eyes blinded," Williams wrote, though he also noted that the Pilgrims created "the first American democracy."

In his biography of Hawthorne, Henry James noted that the Puritans employed almost the same weapons on their "inward and outward enemies...the flintlock and halberd against the Indians, and the cat-o'-nine-tails against the heretics." A bullet from a rifle was far more lethal than a lashing from a cat-o'-nine tails, though James's point about the Puritans is well taken. They punished their fellow Puritans as well as the pagan Indians. When witchcraft became an issue they used fire and burned Englishmen and women to death.

MATHER'S MADNESS

Williams and Hutchinson were both pivotal figures in their society. They were both marginalized in early Puritan literature and history especially in Cotton Mather's (1663-1728) magnum opus, *Magnalia Christi Americana*, in which he mentions Indians only in passing as "grim savages" who had "not much less of terror in them, than if they had been so many Devils." In *Magnalia*, Mather praises Columbus, Sebastian Cabot and Henry Hudson and elevates the New England colonial fathers. Mather knew how to flatter men in power and how to puff himself up, too. In almost every respect, he was the antithesis of Williams. Perhaps the first self-promoting American author, he wanted fame far beyond the provincial towns of New England.

"Tis COTTON MATHER that has written all these things," he informed readers at the start of *Magnalia*. The Puritans had an "errand in the wilderness," he insisted. He, too, had a self-appointed errand: to spread his own words and magnify his own importance. Perhaps no one was more pompous than he in early eighteenth-century New England. "Alas, I may sigh over this Wilderness, as Moses did over his," he wrote. Mather even rewrote the Ten Commandments. In "The Negro Christianized" (1706) he instructed African Americans to "show all due respect unto everyone" and to say: "if I have a master or mistress, I must be very dutiful unto them."

For Mather, the Devil took on the form of Indians armed with bows and arrows. Like Young Goodman Brown in Hawthorne's short story of the same name, Mather was haunted by ghosts and demons, though he rarely faced his own, preferring to project them onto others. When he noticed his own laziness, he called himself a "a tame Indian."

In his official portrait, he looks like a proper Englishman, though under his English wig he was an immoderate man. In his book on the "wonders of the invisible world," he advises readers never to be alone. He knew first hand the dangers of living without the company of others. The Devil fell on "our Lord" when "he was alone in the wilderness," he reminds readers. He advises them that, "by being too solitary, we may lay our selves too much open to the Devil; Woe to him that is alone."

INTELLIGENCE AGENT IN THE WOODS

The picture that Williams painted of himself is of a man alone at sea, alone in the wilderness and alone in a "lusty" canoe paddling across unknown waters toward unknown woods. He was indeed a solitary figure. Among the earliest European critics of colonialism in the New World, he pointed out that the English love of wealth made them no purer than the Spanish. "All Europe's Nations and England more or less, and in a sordid and bloody devotion, did sacrifice to that golden image, so many thousands, yea millions of the inhabitants," he wrote. "It is incredible how many millions of mankind were there destroyed."

As a utopian, Williams saw the potential for a New Canaan in New England. But as a dyed-in-the-wool Calvinist he saw the New World as a "dunghill" that duplicated the worst of the Old World and prevented pilgrims from making progress toward salvation. In one of his most memorable passages, he noted that "The wilderness is a clear resemblance of the world, where greedy and furious men persecute and devour the harmless and innocent as the wild beasts pursue and devour the hinds and roe." In his eyes, history was a spectacle in which desperate men attacked and slaughtered the weak and the innocent — and nothing could be done to stop it. Still, he tried to bring justice into the woods and to protect Indians. On one notable occasion, he apprehended a band of European desperados who murdered Indians, took their possessions and as fugitives fled into the forest. At times, he stood up for the Indians.

Into *A Key Into the Language of America*, Williams poured all of his passion and knowledge of Indian life. Page after page, he listed words in English along with the same words in Narragansett. Scholarly, as well as personal and even autobiographical, *A Key* devotes whole chapters to Indian government, religion and money. The Indians were, in Williams's eyes, potential Christians because they worked as hard as the English, told the truth, observed punctuality and excelled as commercial traders.

Indian music and dance was freer and more refreshing than English music and dance, he insisted. In Indian villages, he exclaimed, there were no beggars and no poverty. The English had no legitimate reason to feel superior to them, he insisted. "Boast not proud English, of thy birth & blood, / Thy brother Indian is by birth as good," he wrote, as though delivering a sermon.

Williams was fascinated with nakedness and naked human bodies. He learned to say, "I am naked" in Narragansett and to feel comfortable in the presence of naked men, women and boys. Moreover, he wondered why clothes were obligatory among the English and not among the Indians who seemed comfortable without them.

On the subject of warfare he was refreshingly honest. "Their wars are far less bloody and devouring than the cruel wars of Europe," he wrote in *A Key*. "When they fight in a plain, they fight with leaping and dancing, that seldom an arrow hits, and when a man is wounded, unless he that shoots follows upon the wounded, they soon retire and save the wounded." Christ was a peacemaker, he pointed out; wars took as heavy a toll on Christians as on anyone else.

In *A Key*, he comes back to warfare again and again. "There is a slaughter," he wrote and added ominously, "the Pequod are slain." Williams didn't provide the details of the slaughter, though hundreds of Pequod, many of them women and children, were massacred in 1637 at Mystic, Connecticut. The Pequod village was burned to the ground by English troops under the command of John Underhill (1597-1672) who wrote about the carnage in *News from America* (1638), five years before *A Key* appeared in print. Underhill demonized the Pequod as "insolent" and "blasphemous." Other Puritan military commanders, including John Mason and Leift Lion Gardener, demonized them, too.

At times, Williams could be as virulent as Underhill and the other Puritan military leaders. Despite his friendship with Narragansett Indians and his impassioned sermons about the need for Christian love, he soon came to depict the Indians as bloodthirsty savages and to exaggerate the threat to his own life. "Three days and nights my business forced me to lodge and mix with the bloody Pequod ambassadors, whose hands and arms, me thought, wreaked with the blood of my countrymen, murdered and massacred by them on Connecticut River, and from whom I could nightly look for their bloody knives at my own throat also," he declared. No one cut his throat, shed any of his blood or poked a knife at his throat, but he held onto those gruesome images.

In *News*, Captain Underhill provided his own reasons for the Puritan war against the Pequod. The Indian fort at Mystic, he wrote, was situated, in "a place of very good soil, good meadow, divers sorts of good wood, timber, variety of fish of several kind, fowl in abundance." He added, "It hath a fair river, fit for harboring of ships, and abounds with rich and goodly meadows and fertile soil." Better to be in English than in Pequod hands, Underhill concluded.

Williams was as close as anyone else in New England to the slaughter at Mystic save for the soldiers themselves. He made it his duty to gather information and to weigh its veracity before passing it on to the military authorities. Long before the birth of the Office of Strategic Services (OSS) during World War II or the Central Intelligence Agency (CIA) in the aftermath of the war, Williams worked as a kind of intelligence agent. Indeed, he called himself an "intelligencer" and communicated regularly with the Indians who were loyal to the English and who provided him with information about the Pequod warriors. Using trusted messengers he dispatched news to the authorities in Boston who forwarded it to Captain Underhill who in turn mapped his military campaign. Underhill's attack on the Pequod was no sudden raiding party of the kind launched by Juet and Hudson a quarter of a century earlier, but a carefully calculated assault that was meant to inflict the greatest pain and distress to the greatest number of people. Underhill authored a reign of terror against the Pequod.

Williams suggested when and where the attack might be launched. He urged the troops to bring sufficient powder and shot to overcome the Indians and he provided a hand-drawn map of the Pequod fort at Mystic that showed where the Indians were most vulnerable. He didn't want the troops to murder women and children, though Underhill and his men rejected his plea. "We burnt and spoiled both houses and corn in great abundance," Underhill wrote after one day's warfare. The next day he added, "burnt their houses, cut down their corn, and destroyed some of their dogs."

Though Williams served as the eyes and the ears of the colonial authorities during the Pequod War, he was an odd man for the job. After all, the colonial authorities, including John Winthrop, had expelled him as an undesirable alien. "I was unkindly and un-Christianly, as I believe, driven from my house and land and wife and children, (in the midst of a New England winter, now almost thirty-five years past) at Salem," he wrote. "I was sorely tossed, for fourteen weeks, in a bitter winter season, not knowing what bread or bed did mean."

Still, it was with his help that Underhill and his soldiers won the battle at Mystic. Hundreds of tribal members were slain at Mystic, as Williams noted in *A Key*, but they weren't all slain. Survivors fled into the woods, regrouped and continued to fight the English and to resist what they regarded as the British invasion of their territory. Williams wanted English soldiers to pursue them and apprehend them so that they wouldn't regroup and "turn wild Irish."

Puritan warfare against the Pequod lasted for more than a decade. In *Moby-Dick*, Melville borrows the name "Pequod" for Captain Ahab's doomed whaling ship. "Pequod, you will no doubt remember, was the name of a celebrated tribe of Massachusetts Indians, now extinct as the ancient Medes," he explained. Even as late at the 1850s, the Pequod War still haunted Americans.

As he grew older, Williams grew increasingly bitter and disillusioned; he concluded that all Indians were "wolves endowed with men's brains." Still, he was against blatant atrocities such as "dismembering the dead" and against the enslavement of the Pequod. He tried to walk a fine line between a just peace on the one hand, and a righteous war on the other hand, and more often than not he betrayed his better instincts.

In *A Key*, he provided the Algonquin words for two of the most powerful phrases in the English language: "I love you," and "I will kill you." Sadly, he prefigures Joseph Conrad's fictional character Mr. Kurtz in *Heart of Darkness* who initially wants to bring light and civilization to the natives in the Congo, but is soon persuaded that the best policy is to "Exterminate the brutes."

Williams enjoyed the company of the Puritan revolutionary (and author of *Paradise Lost*) John Milton, with whom he conversed in Latin, Greek, Hebrew, French and Dutch. He also rubbed shoulders with Oliver Cromwell, whom he called a "mighty bulwark of the Protestants." A continental thinker whose ideas were fed by the European tradition of dissenters, outcasts and martyrs, Williams admired Jan Huss, the Prague priest who was burned at the stake in the fifteenth century. He revered John Wycliffe, the fourteenth-century theologian who risked his life by translating the Bible into English. Then, too, he praised the eleventh-century sect of Berengarians who challenged the authority of the Catholic Church and the hegemony of the Pope long before 1517, when Martin Luther launched the Protestant Reformation. Those early Christians rebels against orthodoxy shaped Williams's unconventional ideas about the wilderness, the beauty of the Indians, and the primitive simplicity of Jesus Christ, whom he described as "that green and innocent tree."

Like the dissenters and martyrs he admired, he planted the seeds for an American tradition of nonconformity and freedom. "The foundation of civil power lies in the people," he insisted. To settlers eager for land, he insisted that they had to pay Indians a fair price because the land belonged to them and not to the King of England. To congregations and their ministers, he opposed oaths, tithes, wages and salaries. To the timid foes of change, he noted that "Paul and all true messengers of Jesus Christ" — whom he aimed to emulate — were "esteemed seducing and seditious teachers and turners of the world upside down."

But even the heretical Williams had orthodox English beliefs. During King Philip's War in the 1670s, he urged the military commanders to quell the Indians "as wolves that assault the sheep." If the Indians died in combat so be it; it was the wish of the Lord, he insisted. "God killeth, destroyeth, plagueth, damneth none but those that will perish," he wrote. "Destroy and cut off the barbarians, or subdue and reduce them," he urged in 1675.

He also decried the Puritan failure to create a paradise in the New World. "This land, our poor colony, is in civil dissension," he bemoaned. In his gloomiest moods he saw the "common shipwreck of mankind" along with "calamities and revolutions," "wars, pestilence, famines." To the end of his days, he was deeply divided. He continued to speak out "against oppression" and for freedom of the press. He insisted that no one — not "papists, Protestants, Jews, or Turks" — be "compelled from their own particular prayers or worship." The soul mattered, he insisted, not "children's toys of land, meadows, and cattle."

Selfish individuals jeopardized the "ship of common safety," he exclaimed, and he predicted that the "common trinity of the world, profit, preferment, pleasure" would dominate "in this wilderness." Still, he moved toward a kind of pastoral ideal that sounds uncannily like Thoreau. What he wanted most of all, he told John Winthrop, was "a dinner of green herbs with quietness" and "peace with all men."

Looking back at his early life in the woods, he wrote that God had stirred "the barbarous heart" of the Narragansett chief, Canonicus, and that he "loved me as his son." He had given to the Indians, he insisted, "whatever they desired of me as to goods or gifts." He seemed to forget the part he played in the wars against the Pequod and against King Philip and his tribe.

After his death in 1683, Williams and his work were largely forgotten. He was too complex a thinker to be a popular writer, too much concerned with theological matters, and too critical of settlers who wanted land, money and status to be a favorite of latter-day Puritans such as Cotton Mather. "We are but strangers in an inn, but passengers in a ship," Williams wrote. He added, "and though we dream of long summer days, yet our very life and being is but a swift short passage from the bank of time to the other side or bank of dolefully eternity." After decades in America, he felt like an alien in an alien land. "Long exile in America, have rendered me now a stranger," he wrote near the end of his life.

MARY ROWLANDSON & CAPTIVITY NARRATIVE

By comparison with Williams, Mary Rowlandson (1636-1711) — the wife of a minister and the mother of two children — was a trivial seventeenth-century writer, but she caught the popular imagination in *A True History of the Captivity and Restoration of Mrs. Mary Rowlandson* published in New England a year before Williams died. Not surprisingly, it became a best seller because it played on Puritan fears of the wilderness and the Indians. For Rowlandson, the English were great; God was even greater. In her emotionally charged book she depicts the Indians as "infidels" and as "cruel and barbarous savages," though she also says that not once did an Indian offer "the least abuse of unchastity to me, in word or action." What's memorable about her book isn't forgiveness or compassion, however, but rather revulsion for the Indians and disdain for the "vast and the desolate wilderness." Born in England and brought to New England as a child, she didn't love the land any more than Cotton Mather did.

Mary Rowlandson gave New Englanders what they wanted: an inspiring tale by a wife and mother who survived hell as a captive of the Indians. Her husband paid her ransom; she was released and reunited with family and friends. Her narrative and others that depicted Englishmen and women who were held prisoners by Indians came to be called "captivity narratives." Rowlandson's was the first of a great many that would pour out of the Puritans in the next hundred years. The names and dates changed. The themes remained the same. John Smith described his own captivity, but he didn't develop the captivity trope.

All through the seventeenth century, the Indians of New England didn't retreat meekly into the woods, though 5,000 Indians — roughly forty percent of the total Indian population — died in King Philip's War. Indians defended their culture, language, land and identities. Looking back, they knew what had been taken from them and what they had lost. They spoke eloquently and memorably. "Our fathers had plenty of deer and skins, our plains were full of deer, as also our wood, and our coves full of fish and foul," Miantonomi, a Narragansett Indian chief, exclaimed. He noted that the English "having gotten our land, with scythes cut down the grass, and with axes fell the trees; their cows and horses eat the grass, and their hogs spoil our clam bank, and we shall all be starved."

In the 1670s, the Catholic missionary Chrestien Le Clercq recorded the comments of a savvy member of the Micmac tribe who didn't accept the French narrative about France, their colonial enterprise and the Indians of North America. The anonymous, eloquent Micmac rejected the French notion that France was a "terrestrial paradise" and that the New World was a "barbarous country." It wasn't barbarous to the Micmac, he insisted. Moreover, the Indian wanted Le Clercq and the French to know that his tribe found everything they needed without "anxieties" and that they were "infinitely more happy" than the explorers and settlers from the Old World. He would rather subsist, he argued, on a diet of moose, beaver, fish and waterfowl than on the monotonous French diet of cod, bread, wine and brandy. Not only that, he insisted that he also felt "compassion" for the poor French settlers who presented themselves as the masters but who were no better off than "valets, servants and slaves."

CHAPTER 3

AMERICAN REVOLUTIONARIES

Philip Freneau, Thomas Jefferson,
Thomas Paine & Washington Irving

PURITANS IN RETREAT

I n the Age of Reason, freethinkers and radicals broke the Puritan stranglehold on New England. The Age of Anxiety dissipated. "Their phantoms, their wizards, their witches are fled," the poet and revolutionary, Philip Freneau, exclaimed. Perhaps the most anti-Puritanical of early American poets, his statement is part wishful thinking, part fact. The Puritans lost ground in New England, though their descendants carried Puritan ideas into the West where they were reinvented as settlers and colonists clashed with Indians for hundreds of years.

In the Age of Reason, Cotton Mather's "sacred geography" gave way to an overtly political landscape popularized by the pamphleteer Thomas Paine, who wrote famously in *Common Sense,* "These are the times that try men's souls." Paine's "souls" weren't the same as Mather's. All through the years of the American Revolution, romantic poets liberated the wilderness from the Bible and from Calvinist pulpits and recast the Earth as Mother Nature, a beneficent deity with a friendly face and a bountiful figure ready to show humanity how to give birth to an egalitarian society.

The shift from the wilderness to Nature with a capital N began in the eighteenth century and flowered in the 1820s and 1830s. Ralph Waldo Emerson, the preeminent American Transcendentalist, translated European romanticism into ideas and images familiar to his fellow citizens. He went on promoting revolutionary ideas long after the War of Independence had concluded. "If there is any period one would desire to be born in, is it not the age of Revolution?" Emerson asked in his 1837 Harvard oration "The American Scholar" that was subsequently published as an essay. Emerson instructed his audience, "We have listened too long to the courtly muses of Europe." He added "we will walk on our own feet, we will work with our own hands; we will speak our own minds." American Nature undermined Europe's courtly muses.

Born in Boston in 1803, two hundred years after Roger Williams, Emerson initially adopted old-school strategies; he studied and then taught for seven years at the Harvard Divinity School and served briefly as a pastor in Boston. In 1832, he resigned his post, went to Europe, met Coleridge, Wordsworth and Carlyle, came home and took up the life of a public speaker and essayist who commanded a large following. "Things are in the saddle /And ride mankind," he wrote in his "Ode, Inscribed to William H. Channing." With passion and eloquence, Emerson appealed to the conscience of Americans who were burdened by possessions in the new commercial society of material goods produced in factories and transported by railroad and ship around the nation and the world.

Emerson's genius derived in part from his decision to write, not about the howling wilderness, but about Nature. He did that eloquently in his 1836 essay "Nature" in which he evoked

Coleridge and Goethe, elevated "Reason" above all other human faculties, and called for a new day defined by "Justice, Truth, Love, Freedom." Emerson sounds as though he was prepared to storm the barricades. In "Nature," he mentions "woods" and "wilderness" without allowing them to grow out of control. He couldn't ignore them completely. They were American landmarks. "In the woods is perpetual youth," he wrote in his characteristically ebullient voice, as though, like Huck Finn and his creator Mark Twain (whom he met near the end of his life) he didn't want to grow up or grow old. The wilderness didn't frighten Emerson. Rather it provided the sort of solace and healing that were especially needed, he argued, in an era when things were in the saddle and rode mankind. "In the wilderness, I find something more dear and connate than in streets or village," he mused.

Unlike Thoreau who liked to go Indian in a Harvard sort of way, Emerson mostly ignored Indians. He also removed most of the thorns and barbs from the woods that were close to his Concord home and that had escaped the woodsman's axe and the railroad tracks. Moreover, Emerson broke Nature into small pieces that might be held in the hand of a child. So, for example, when he described Nature he didn't focus on "mighty" trees as Whitman would do in "Song of the Redwood-Tree" or on the "great star... in the western sky," as Whitman did in "When Lilacs last in the Dooryard Bloom'd" but rather on "the acorn, the grape, the pine-cone, the wheat-ear, the egg, the wings and forms of most birds, the lion's claw, the serpent, the butterfly, sea-shells, flames, clouds, buds, leaves, and the forms of many trees, as the palm."

The forms Emerson found in Nature mattered to him, and, even when he wrote about the ferocious King of Beasts, he presented only a small part: a claw and not the whole lion. In his long list of small items, he included the serpent, not the snake, and invited readers to think of the Garden of Eden and its innocent amorous couple, Adam and Eve, who crept inevitably into the literature of the United States and were reborn as mythic figures in the American cultural landscape. A democratic couple in Cooper's novels, the transcendentalist's beloved Adam and Eve would have been unrecognizable to Cotton Mather.

Even Nathaniel Hawthorne, the descendant of Puritans, conjured up a blissful Garden of Eden in *The House of the Seven Gables* (1851). Eden seemed possible to Hawthorne if only greed, envy and ambition didn't ride mankind. "What we call real estate," one of his characters explains, "is the broad foundation on which nearly all the guilt of this world rests." Human nature wasn't evil, only the institutions which human beings created, he believed. Emerson, too, despised real estate and warned that houses would supplant pastures and that whole villages would appear where no one had ever lived. In *The House of the Seven Gables*, Hawthorne's young lovers learn to appreciate a "wilder grace" and to recognize the "strange beauty" in wild flowers. At the end of the novel, Phoebe and Holgrave, both of them the descendants of Puritans, transfigure the earth and make it "Eden again."

In the late eighteenth century, Americans made a religion of Nature — natural laws, natural rights and natural liberties — and rejected the artificialities of the aristocracy and the royal court. In Thomas Jefferson's thinking, "natural works" and "the wisdom of nature" could do no wrong. The wilderness was not to be feared and avoided but directly confronted. Moreover, the word "wilderness" itself sounded obsolete to Paine and Jefferson. They replaced it with the phrase "Back-Lands."

It would not be until the twenty first century that environmental activists redefined crucial terms and rephrased the dialogue about the interactions between Nature and humans. Faced with unprecedented environmental degradation, they argued for the "Rights of Nature," the "Rights of Mother Earth," "Earth Justice" and "Wild Law." That last concept probably would have boggled Jefferson's mind.

The ideals of the Age of Revolution spread to African Americans. Olaudah Equiano (c. 1745-1797), the author of the first slave narrative and an abolitionist, too, described his experiences on both sides of the Atlantic: his love of freedom and his passion for books, including the Bible and Milton's *Paradise Lost* in whose pages he saw a reflection of his own captivity. Equiano depicts the slave masters that beat him as "wild," "wicked" and "mad." Of the Indians, he explains, they are "in point of honesty, above any other nation I was ever amongst." For decades after *The Interesting Narrative of the Life of Olaudah Equiano* (1791) was published, American slaves would echo his sentiments: they would sooner "die like a free man, than suffer...like a slave."

Soon after the triumph of the revolution, settlers from the thirteen original colonies, along with newly arrived immigrants from Europe, pushed into the woods that King George III placed off limits. In Kentucky and Ohio and along the Mississippi, pioneers like Daniel Boone (1734-1820) turned their eyes away from Europe and toward the West. With plebian axes, they assaulted forests. In the act of leveling the wilderness and clearing open spaces a great deal of the American national character was forged. As Lewis Mumford (1895-1990) noted in his seminal work, *The Golden Day: A Study in American Literature and Culture* (1926), it was "with pioneering" that "America ceased to be an outpost of Europe." Curiously, Mumford wasn't a partisan of frontier society. Famous for *The Culture of Cities* (1938) and *The Highway and the City* (1963), he noted that "the pioneering impulse was "compulsive and almost neurotic" and that "the movement into backwoods America turned the European into a barbarian."

In the Age of Reason and the American Revolution, American patriots looked across the Atlantic and regarded European tyrants as barbarians. In the Declaration of Independence, Jefferson complained that King George III "has excited domestic insurrections amongst us, and has endeavored to bring on the inhabitants of our frontiers, the merciless Indian Savages." One of the first tasks of the new government, as Jefferson saw it, was to survey the woods, turn them into bite-sized parcels of land with exact measurements, deeds and price tags. He insisted on branding the continent, naming nearly every square foot and expanding to the Pacific.

During the American Revolution, the tree evolved into a political symbol and cultural icon. The Sons of Liberty, who demanded independence from England, congregated at a real tree in Boston that they dubbed the "Liberty Tree." Loyalists cut it down hoping to stamp out insurrection, but "Liberty Trees" sprouted throughout the colonies and rebels gathered under their branches to plot and conspire. After the British were defeated militarily and the newly independent United States emerged on the stage of history, Jefferson captured the spirit of the age when he wrote that, "The tree of liberty must be refreshed from time to time with the blood of patriots and tyrants. It is its natural manure."

In *Common Sense*, the English-born pamphleteer Thomas Paine (1737-1809), borrowed an image from the wilderness experience and wrote, "One man might labor out the common period of his life without accomplishing anything. When he felled his timber he could not remove it. But four or five would be able to raise a tolerable dwelling in the midst of a wilderness." Moreover, when settlers wanted to build a structure to house their government, Paine wrote that they would only have to find "some convenient tree under the branches of which the whole colony may assemble."

A child of the Age of Revolution, Paine also belonged to an English radical tradition that posited a mythical state of Nature in which there were no social classes and no glaring inequalities. In this earthly paradise, Paine reasoned, there were no lords and no ladies. "Through all the vocabulary of Adam there is no such animal as a Duke or a Count," he wrote in the *Rights of Man* (1791), his defense of revolution. For Paine, the point was to resurrect the foundations of the ancient, inviolable Eden in which citizens were not oppressed by kings or lords. It was essential, he explained, to escape from "counting-houses," "custom-houses" and "workhouses" and live and work in the great outdoors. "We have more land than we can cultivate," he wrote. "Our natural situation frees us from the distress of crowded cities and from the thirst of ambitious ones."

The presence of the Back-Lands and the absence of Old World restraints created the conditions for the kind of grassroots democracy that the American historian, Frederick Jackson Turner, would describe in a series of landmark essays at the end of the nineteenth century. For Turner — whose heroes were frontiersmen, wilderness warriors and American icons such as Roger Williams, Thomas Jefferson, Andrew Jackson and Abraham Lincoln — the frontier was the locus of American history. Moreover, unlike Lewis Mumford, Turner thought that the frontier was cradle, crucible and "gate of escape from the bondage of the past." It was also, he argued, "the meeting point between savagery and civilization" and the place where democracy, nationalism and the American self were forged.

Poet of the Revolution, Philosopher of the Forest

Jefferson and Paine expressed the American passion for freedom in elegant prose, but it fell to their contemporary, Philip Freneau (1752-1832), to record in poetry more thoroughly than anyone else in his generation the seismic shifts in consciousness that took place before and after the revolution. Decades before Emerson told Americans that they had listened to the courtly muse of Europe for too long, Freneau declared his independence from European models and called upon his fellow Americans to follow his example. Like Emerson, he also sang the praises of Nature and idealized the forest as an alternative to the crowded city.

The son of French Huguenot immigrants and a college friend of James Madison — the fourth U. S. president — Freneau experienced life as a Washington, D.C. insider and also as a backwoods outsider. Widely known in his own time as both the "poet of the revolution" and the "philosopher of the forest," he was among the first American writers to see that philosophers might draw inspiration from forests as well as from cobblestone streets and castles.

Freneau loved squirrels, blackbirds, daffodils and buffalo. He detested ministers, priests and manufacturers. "There is not a sight in all the walks of men that gives me half the disgust as that of a Christian Clergyman rolling in his coach, swelling with pride and impertinence, associating only with princes, nobles and the wealthy of the land," he wrote. Moreover, he preferred the countryside with its blacksmiths, farmers and Indians to the nouveau riche and the landed aristocracy.

Born in New York and raised in New Jersey, Freneau embraced almost all of the radical causes of his own "fantastic" century, as he called it. In 1776, after he graduated from college, he settled in the West Indies where he wrote poems with ironical titles such as "The Beauties of Santa Cruz" in which he depicted an island blighted by slavery. Like John Keats, he could not be happy, he realized, while there was a "world oppressed." Then, too, like Keats (1795-1821), who authored the concept of "negative capability," Freneau held "opposite, contradictory thoughts" in his head "without an irritable reaching after fact and reason."

Freneau fused convictions with passions. He was the opposite of the Irish revolutionaries that William Butler Yeats would write about in his 1919 poem "The Second Coming" who "lack all conviction" and overflow with "passionate intensity." Like a fragile leaf attuned to the minute reverberations in a forest, Freneau opened himself to the winds of controversy that blew across America, produced more than 500 poems (all of them carefully rhymed), and 1,100 prose pieces including essays and short stories. His themes were romantic, but his forms were often neoclassical and he heaped praise on Pope, Addison and Dryden, the poets of an earlier age. For all his classical style, however, he struck his enemies as a dangerous man. A "rascal," George Washington called him, while his friends saw him as an advocate for justice and the Rule of Law. Jefferson noted that when President John Adams aimed to deport aliens and prosecute journalists for sedition, Freneau "saved our constitution which was galloping fast into monarchy."

Colonial history Freneau knew as deeply as Cotton Mather, though he rewrote the Puritan past, casting the early colonists as bigots who burned witches at the stake and who executed Quakers for their beliefs. As for Mather himself, Freneau dismissed him as a "musty" fellow who spewed "nonsense."

In a poem he entitled "The Pamphleteer and the Critic," and in an essay entitled "The Sick Author," he offers portraits of himself as an American artist in a nation without a tradition of writers, without patrons of the arts and without appreciative audiences of the sort that existed in Europe. Like Paine, Freneau aimed for a world in which "man shall man no longer crush." He was hopeful that the world might be changed for the better, and yet he also knew that the world was far more powerful than any individual. "The world at last will have its way/ and we its torrent must obey," he wrote in "To an Author." In "To a Night-Fly Approaching a Candle" (1797), he describes an insect scorched by fire, then turns his thoughts inward and imagines "the insects of mankind" driven by "ambition" and seduced by power. To his readers, he cautioned, "If you are wise in time retire." He followed his own advice, abandoned politics and journalism, though he never gave up poetry.

He was aghast when the New York-born satirist, Washington Irving, fled from his native land and lived in Europe as an ambassador for the United States. In the poem "To a New-England Poet" Freneau spoke to and commiserated with an unnamed, impoverished Yankee author who remains at home, and who contrasts himself with the illustrious author of "The Legend of Sleepy Hollow" and "Rip Van Winkle." Freneau wrote, perhaps enviously, "See Irving gone to Britain's court / To people of *another* sort." He added, "He will return with wealth and fame,/ While Yankees hardly know *your* name."

Freneau anticipated a great deal of nineteenth-century wilderness writing, as when he described the grandeur and grace of American trees: cedar, apple, oak, alder and pine. Later generations would probably call him a "tree-hugger." In 1790, he was outraged when he learned that the trees of New York City were soon to become an endangered species. The city passed an ordinance that stated that after June 10, 1791 "no tree was to stand within the city limits."

"An iron age is all our lot," he exclaimed with bitterness in "The Landlord's Soliloquy." He added, "Trees now to grow, is held a crime." The poem was widely read and led to the suspension of the act. By the 1790s, he had already written ardent poems to trees he loved, such as "The Dying Elm." He also lamented the passing of rural places and honored "the labors of the swain" — an idealized fellow whom he lifted from the pages of romantic poetry. Honest manual labor had much to recommend it, he insisted, though he thought of the woods as a place to loaf.

He denounced the empires of Britain and Spain, the European quest for New World gold, and the annihilation of the Indians, but he also urged the creation of an American empire on the banks of the Mississippi. "Empires rise where lonely forests grew," he wrote rapturously. In "On the Emigration to America

and the Peopling of the Western Country," he urged strangers
from Europe to settle on "wild Ohio's savage stream."

Romanticism went hand in hand with the imperial imper-
ative, as T.S. Eliot and others observed. Reverence for nature
and idealization of the Indian didn't prevent poets, novelists and
politicians from dreaming of the Westward expansion of the
American Republic. It didn't inhibit them from urging the creation of cities and the development of commerce along the banks
of the Mississippi and all through the west. In the United States,
romanticism enjoyed a long literary life. It touched Philip Freneau,
James Fenimore Cooper, Lydia Maria Child, Catharine Sedgwick,
Walt Whitman, Herman Melville, Henry David Thoreau, Ralph
Waldo Emerson, Emily Dickinson and Nathaniel Hawthorne.

It took the Civil War to undermine it, as it took World War I
to undermine the Victorian sensibility in England, and even then
it reappeared in new garb. The language of romanticism —with
words and phrases such as "sylvan scenes" and "swains" — could
sound stilted, or it could ring true with precise images of raging
rivers and rugged mountains that captured both the beauty and
the terror of the natural world. American Indians played an essential role in the narrative of romanticism. Had they not existed,
poets and novelists would have had to create them, if only to cast
them as doomed and dying aristocrats of the forest.

In "The Dying Indian," Freneau imagines how an Indian
might look at the "tall and ascending woods." He couldn't think
about Indians without also thinking about dying and dead Indians
as in "The Indian Burying Ground." In "The Indian Student;
or Force of Nature," an Indian rejects the white man's "learned
degree" and exclaims, "Where Nature's ancient forests grow/ I
must go to die among my native shades." Freneau projected his
own feelings on an idealized Indian. In the ironically entitled,
"The Indian Convert," the Indian narrator rejects Christianity

and the Calvinist minister who officiates in a church where there's "nothing to eat and but little to steal." As he leaves the congregation, the Indian, says, "Farewell, I'm not of your mess."

As a revolutionary, he had learned that change was inevitable. Nature would go on; human beings would perish. Even in the harshest wilds, he found reason to delight in life. In a late poem entitled "Winter," he wrote that "there are joys that may all storms defy,/The chill of Nature, and a frozen sky." In 1832, at the age of 80, he was caught in the midst of a blizzard only a short distance from home, lost his way and froze to death in the cold white snow.

NEW MEN IN THE NEW WORLD

It would take three decades after the conclusion of the American Revolution for the novel in the United States to become distinctly American. And yet from the beginning, hybrid works such as J. Hector St. John De Crèvecoeur's *Letters from an American Farmer* (1782) and Gilbert Imlay's *The Emigrants* (1793) carved out literary territory apart from Europe. Today, they might be called creative nonfiction. Crèvecoeur and Imlay both realized that the path to a new literature independent of the Old World lay in the West.

Letters from an American Farmer and *The Emigrants* both borrow the format of the epistolary novel popularized in England by Samuel Richardson and in France by Jean-Jacques Rousseau and Choderlos de Laclos. Crèvecoeur and Imlay both adopted a tone of intimacy and provided moral lessons to readers about the metamorphosis of "the American," whom Crèvecoeur (1735-1813) famously describes as a "new man" in a land where "all nations are melted into a new race of men." As an advertising copywriter, he hit all the right notes.

Crèvecoeur and Imlay both fled from the eastern seaboard into the woods. Later, they would flee from the woods and reappear on the streets of Europe where they traded on the mystique of the frontier. For Crèvecoeur, the "extended line of frontiers" — not the cities on the Eastern Seaboard — was the place where one could see "America in its proper light." Both men carried a distinct whiff of the woods about them; they were also both involved in the revolutions that took place on both sides of the Atlantic. They never met, though their paths might have crossed. Fabulists and fabricators they both fictionalized their own lives. Born Michel Guillaume Jean de Crèvecoeur in France in 1735 and naturalized as John Hector St. John in New York, Crèvecoeur took up farming and writing and married an American woman. During the revolution he was arrested by the British as an American spy, detained and then released.

In 1813, he died in France, though in *Letters* he gives the impression that he's wedded forever to the wilderness. D. H. Lawrence called him a "liar" who posed as a pioneer who fraternized "with the Children of Nature, the Red Men, under the Wigwam." In fact, as Lawrence points out, Crèvecoeur returned to France, wore the latest fashions and presented himself as a "literary man."

In *Letters*, the frontier provides Crèvecoeur with one setting, the South another and Nantucket and Martha's Vineyard a third. Of the Indians, Crèvecoeur writes, "They are all gone. They have all disappeared either in the wars which the Europeans carried against them, or else they have moulded away, gathered in some of their ancient town." Crèvecoeur also felt genuine compassion for African-American slaves and urged their emancipation. For the most part, he didn't idealize them as he did the Indians, whom he depicted as near-perfect creatures: "the undefiled offspring" of the woods who are "more closely connected with nature" than the Europeans.

Crèvecoeur noted that the political revolution in the wilderness brought about the destruction of Indian tribes, and at the same time turned immigrants into "civilized savages" or "white-skinned pagans" as one might call them. Thousands of Europeans fled into the woods and became Indians, he insisted, because the "social bonds" among the Indians were "far superior to any thing to be boasted among us." In forests, Crèvecoeur claimed, human beings could be genuinely free because there are "no aristocratic families, no courts, no kings, no bishops." Like Nathaniel Hawthorne and Henry James a century later, Crèvecoeur was keenly aware of the things that America lacked: the "poverty of materials" as Cooper called it. He was one of the first Europeans to list the institutions missing in the United States: "ancient amphitheaters," "gilded palaces" and "great manufacturers employing thousands."

The revolution that's invisible in *Letters* is the eighteenth-century industrial revolution with its factories, slums and poverty that made the wilderness look like paradise. Crèvecoeur noted that in the wilderness "there is room for everybody." He anticipated the American historian, Frederick Jackson Turner, who insisted in 1901 that in the wilderness there was a flowering of "equality, freedom of opportunity" and a "faith in the common man."

If fiction brought news of the American frontier to the Old World, so, too, newspapers brought information to readers about frontiersmen such as Daniel Boone, the most famous backwoodsman who carved out the "Wilderness Road" in Kentucky and built a fort and settlement at Boone's Station. With axe and gun, Boone helped to break the back of Kentucky forests and, not surprisingly, word of his exploits traveled far and wide, though the further it traveled the more mythological his exploits became.

His appearance on the stage of American history couldn't have been better timed. Seemingly out of nowhere, he became a kind of patron saint to settlers as they fled from the Eastern seaboard and plunged into forests. Boone showed them the way, though the more they followed him, the more he fled from them. He was "doomed," one of his biographers observed, to run from the very civilization that he carried with him. Shades of Gorky's outlawed pioneer. Near the end of his life, he went to the Ozarks and began life as a pioneer all over again, as though he might turn back the hands of time and live forever in an untrammeled wilderness.

Self-reliant and self-motivated, he knew how to survive and even thrive in the wilds. He loved to hunt, but he wasn't solely a hunter. He delivered powder and ammunition to settlers, worked for surveying parties, fought in the militia, served as a magistrate and held court under a "Justice Tree." He had a wife and a family to support and took his familial responsibilities seriously. Unlike Roger Williams, he wasn't a minister or a God-fearing member of a church; he rarely if ever attended religious services. Moreover, unlike Williams, he was not a fugitive from justice forced into the forests to avoid prosecution and imprisonment.

All around him, delinquents, dissidents and the disorderly populated the frontier. Timothy Dwight, the President of Yale, complained about the "foresters, or Pioneers" who were unable to adjust to society. "Under the pressure of poverty, the fear of gaol, and the consciousness of public contempt," he wrote, they "leave their native places, and betake themselves to the wilderness."

In *Virgin Land: The American West as Symbol and Myth*, a seminal text that looks at the pantheon of frontier heroes — Boone, Fremont, Kit Carson and Buffalo Bill — the historian, Henry Nash Smith, noted that by about 1815 there was a veritable cult of Daniel Boone that had been in the making for decades. Nearly everyone wanted a piece of him and he soon enjoyed more fame in America and in Europe than any other American between 1800 and 1850, save for Benjamin Franklin, George Washington, Thomas Jefferson and James Fenimore Cooper. Boone was the embodiment of the "new man" and the "western pilgrim" that Crevecouer depicts in *Letters from an American Farmer*.

If American novelists were sorely tested to create original works of fiction it was in part because the reality of the wilderness outdistanced the literary imagination. When *The Adventures of Col. Daniel Boon* [sic] was first published in 1784, Boone was already fifty years old and still an active hunter. The book's title page proclaims, "written by himself," though the text suggests tampering by an invisible, unidentified editor or more.

From the very start, Boone was mythologized by a host of writers, including himself, though he never embellished his life as intensely or as outrageously as Davy Crockett did his. Boone could read and write, though his spelling was erratic. His ethics were erratic, too. According to *The Adventures*, he "burned to ashes" five Indian villages and "spread desolation through their country." *The Adventures* also explains that the Indians felt "affection" for him and that the Shawnee initiated him into their tribe as one of their own.

Boone's brief narrative offers real surprises, as when he says that when alone in the wilderness he would have been "disposed" to "melancholy if I had further indulged the thought." Occasionally, he resorts to Puritan clichés, such as "the howling wilderness" and adopts Puritan points of view, as when he notes that the mountains are "so wild and horrid that it is impossible to behold them without terror." He was also a child of romanticism, and, in the spirit of the English poets, he lauded the "sylvan pleasures" of the woods and depicted them as "a second paradise."

A trickster, Boone knew how to evade Indians and hide in the woods. Unlike Mary Rowlandson, no one had to rescue him or pay a ransom to the Indians when they captured him and held him prisoner. He rescued himself and won his own freedom. The optimism of the new Republic infused Boone, and, as an action hero with democratic sentiments, he was admired by both patriotic Americans and European romantics. In his epic poem, *Don Juan*, Lord Byron fictionalized Boone's exploits in the "wilds of deepest maze" and glorified him and "the free foresters" who lived "beyond the dwarfing city's pale abortions."

Timothy Flint (1780-1840), a New England-born novelist, graduate of Harvard, and a descendant of Calvinists, met Boone in 1816. He drew on his memories of the frontiersman for an 1833 biography in which he depicts the Kentucky backwoodsman as a son of nature and as a Christ-like human being sacrificed on the cross of the wilderness for the redemption of the American nation itself. "It was necessary" for Boone to "precede" settlers into the wilderness, Flint explained, and to "prepare the way for the multitudes who would soon follow." The multitudes were right behind him. Writers and artists followed him, too, tracking him down and imagining the lives that he could or might have lived.

FLÂNEUR OF THE PRAIRIES

Washington Irving linked Boone to Homer's *Iliad* and described him as "the Nestor of hunters" and as a man of "sylvan honor and renown." In *A Tour of the Prairies*, his quaint memoir of the West, Irving meets an old hunter who reminded him, not of the real-life Boone, but of the fictional hero of James Fenimore Cooper's frontier novels, "old Leatherstocking." After his initial literary success in the 1820s, Irving rubbed shoulders with the rich (the fur trader and real estate mogul John Jacob Astor) and the powerful (President Martin Van Buren). But he began his career as a subversive author who made fun of the rich and the famous. Born three decades after Freneau and a full generation before Emerson, Washington Irving (1783-1859) wanted Americans to be inspired by European muses. Fittingly, he was

the first American author to win critical acclaim in Europe as well
as in the United States.

In his seminal essay, "The Art of Book-Making," published
in *The Sketch-Book* (1819), Irving notes that to make a new literature, one has to have access to an old literature. New writers, he
insists, are inevitably "predatory." They take "the beauties and the
fine thoughts of ancient and obsolete authors" and recast them
to "flourish and bear fruit in a remote and distant tract of time."
That method worked for him, though even when he preyed on
European traditions he Americanized them.

To explain the creative process, Irving offered an image of
the wilderness that put him squarely in the company of American
writers. "In the clearing of our American woodlands," he wrote,
"where we burn down a forest of stately pines, a progeny of dwarf
oaks start up in their place." Much the same happened, he insisted,
in the forest of literature. "Authors beget authors," he wrote, and
urged readers "not, then, to lament over the decay and oblivion
into which ancient writers descend; they do both submit to the
great law of nature."

For Irving, the United States was "necessarily an imitative"
nation and had to "take examples and models, in a great degree,
from the existing nations of Europe." To write "Rip Van Winkle"
he borrowed from European folktales, though the characters and
the settings are distinctly American. From the start of his career,
Irving wrote about the "wild retreats" of the Catskill Mountains.
The nineteenth-century English novelist Charles Dickens praised
him for his descriptions of Catskill trees and crags, and in turn
Irving praised Dickens for his insights into the "villainy" that
"besets the everyday haunts of society."

Landscapes play vital roles in Irving's early stories, "Rip Van
Winkle" and "The Legend of Sleepy Hollow," published in *The
Sketch Book* under the name Geoffrey Crayon. Irving created half

a dozen memorable characters: Rip, the Dutchman who sleeps through the American Revolution; Ichabod Crane, the superstitious Puritan school teacher terrified of forests and the darkness of night; Brom Bones, the chivalrous horseman and Byronic hero; and Katrina Van Tassel, the coquettish daughter of a prosperous Dutch landowner.

Noah Webster, the author of the first American dictionary, would have described the landscapes in Irving's early stories as "wild" in the sense that they're untamed and strange. The fictional community of Sleepy Hollow harbors "wild and wonderful legends," including the legend of a horseman without a head, reputedly the ghost of a Hessian soldier who fought and died on the side of the British in the American Revolution. Irving played fast and loose with history and insisted that there were "pioneers of the mind" as well as pioneers of the wilderness.

In "The Legend of Sleepy Hollow" and "Rip Van Winkle," he conjures up a community of snug, smug Dutch farmers, their wives and children, plus an array of "buxom lasses." By the time he wrote about Rip, Irving had mastered the art of satire. He lampooned the seventeenth-century Dutch settlers in *A History of New York from the Beginning of the World to the End of the Dutch Dynasty*, which was published under another pseudonym: Diedrich Knickerbocker.

Irving wrote well under pseudonyms — Jonathan Oldstyle was yet another — because they allowed him the literary freedom he needed to divagate from fact to fancy, protect his own privacy, and promote himself and his books. Under his own name and pseudonyms, too, he specialized in the exploration of beginnings: the discovery of America in his biography of Columbus; and the birth of the American republic in his biography of George Washington. He also chronicled the birth of John Jacob Astor's American dynasty.

In "The Legend of Sleepy Hollow," one of the earliest American ghost stories, Irving aimed to dispatch Puritanism to the nether world as quickly as the Headless Horseman drives Ichabod Crane from his home where he reads Cotton Mather, and from his schoolroom where he adheres to the maxim "spare the rod and spoil the child."

When it came to the Puritans, Irving didn't have a tactful word to say. "I have no relish for Puritans either in religion or politics, who are for pushing principles to an extreme and for overturning everything that stands in the way of their own zealous career," he wrote. Nor did he relish the extremists and zealots among the early Dutch settlers who, he wrote in his history of New York, were "like good Christians…always ready to serve God, after they had first served themselves" and who aimed to "ameliorate" the conditions of the Indians "by giving them gin, rum, and glass beads." It took genius to make fun of genocide.

In "Rip Van Winkle," the central character works (or is it plays?) harder as a storyteller than as a manual laborer. He doesn't toil on his farm, doesn't attend church and doesn't adhere to the rules of matrimony, an institution he thinks of as "tyranny." Few nineteenth-century American writers were more antithetical to matrimony than Irving. He thoroughly enjoyed bachelorhood and boasted that, "Marriage is the grave of Bachelors intimacy." Unlike Irving, Rip doesn't care about patriotism or the president of the county. He doesn't mind that his own children are "as ragged and wild as if they belonged to nobody." The crucial years of his life are spent asleep in a forest where "everything was strange." When Rip wakes and returns to his village, Irving observes that, "The changes of states and empires made but little impression on him."

Thoroughly un-American in a prankish way, he's a foe of the Puritan work ethic and a deserter from the social contract who is "disloyal to civilization," to borrow Adrienne's Rich's apt phrase.

Like his creator, he disdains the institution of marriage.

In "The Legend of Sleepy Hollow," Irving takes readers behind Icabod Crane's façade and explains that he wants to marry Katrina for "the rich fields of wheat" that she will inherit from her father. Crane gazes at "domains," translates them into "cash" and imagines "the money invested in immense tracts of wild land, and single palaces in the wilderness." He escapes from Sleepy Hollow, defeated by the terrors of the Headless Horseman and the figments of his own wild imagination. Still, he enjoys a new life, Irving explains, as a successful lawyer, an elected official, a newspaper reporter and judge.

Puritans, Irving realized, might have been driven out of New England towns, schoolrooms and pulpits, but they reinvented themselves and continued to shape community values. Puritan power had not vanished. In the United States — where public opinion could doom a promising literary career and political controversy could destroy an author — it would be prudent, Irving believed, for authors to offer disclaimers about their motives. Indeed, in "The Legend of Sleepy Hollow" he appends a "Postscript" in which he offers double and triple interpretations of his tale, all equally absurd. When an old gentleman in Manhattan complains that the story is "extravagant" the narrator replies, "As to that matter, I don't believe one-half of it myself."

During Irving's lifetime, literary critics wrestled with his enigmatic personae. Richard Henry Dana Sr., the lawyer, poet, and critic, suggested that there were two Washington Irvings: one "masculine — good bone and muscle"; the other "feminine — dressy, elegant, and languid." Irving published his masculine stories under the Knickerbocker pseudonym, Dana observed, and the feminine stories under the Crayon pseudonym.

In Europe — where he lived from 1815 to 1832 and again from 1842 to 1846 — his feminine side flowered, though he also made his reputation there as "a man from the wilds of America." In the mid-1830s, he wrote and published three nonfiction books about the frontier — *A Tour of the Prairies* (1835), *Astoria* (1836), and *The Adventures of Captain Bonneville* (1837) — in which he showed readers that he had not forgotten his native land. A flâneur of the prairies, much as he had been a flâneur on the boulevards of Europe, Irving wandered across the West and gazed at wide-open spaces through the eyes of an American expatriate. When he heard the sound of the wind in a forest, he was reminded of an organ in a Gothic Cathedral and, when he saw Western landscapes, he thought that they only need "the battlements of a castle…to rival the most ornamental scenery of Europe."

In *A Tour of the Prairies*, the best of his frontier books and a forerunner of the Western, Irving creates a colorful cast of characters who contribute to lawlessness, as well as to law and order, with a little help from the rifle — which he called the "invariable enforcer of right or wrong." Irving was thrilled to ride horseback, hunt, sleep and eat in the company of "trappers, hunters, half-breeds, creoles, Negroes of every hue" and with "the non-descript beings that keep about the frontiers, between civilized and savage life."

Karl Marx's description of bohemians in *The 18th-Brumaire of Louis Bonaparte* (1852) is equally colorful, though unlike Irving, Marx was aghast at the crew of "vagabonds, discharged soldiers, discharged jailbirds, escaped galley slaves…the whole indefinite, disintegrated mass." Ironically, the German police who spied on Marx described him in their reports as a "bohemian." An ocean and a continent separated his degenerate bohemians from Irving's lusty frontiersmen. What they had in common was their marginalization by bourgeois society, though they also served as the avant-garde for the bourgeoisie. Where frontiersmen wandered, merchants were likely to follow. Where bohemian artists gathered, bankers were sure to congregate. American writers would soon regard Marx's metropolis as a wilderness and view its urban vagabonds as no less wild than the wildest creatures on the frontier. Americans writers, including Melville, would share Marx's notion that progress was a "hideous pagan idol…who would not drink the nectar but from the skulls of the slain."

Irving also understood the hideousness of progress. He read about Indians and wrote about them sympathetically in his history of New York and in an essay on King Philips's War in which he described King Philip himself as a "military genius" who was defeated in battle but "not dismayed" and "not humiliated." It was an important distinction, though few writers in the nineteenth century made it. On the American prairies, Irving had his first real contact with Native Americans. He was honest enough to realize that, "The Indians that I have had an opportunity of seeing in real life are quite different from those described in poetry."

They were "keen observers" of nature and society, and, like the most literary European gentlemen they were capable of "criticism, satire, mimicry, and mirth." Life on the prairie made Irving feel lonely, melancholy and gloomy, though he enjoyed looking at the stars in the night sky and delighted in watching the antics of prairie dogs, the vast herds of buffalo and honey bees that he described as the "heralds of civilization." On the frontier, the most ominous sound Irving heard wasn't the sound of the "howling wilderness," but "the sound of the axe" and the crash of falling trees. So, *A Tour of the Prairie* is a hymn to the death of the American forest.

CHAPTER 4

CONTINENTALS

Lewis, Clark & Sacagawea

THE CAPTIVITY NARRATIVE REDUX

The American captivity narrative that Mary Rowland-son created in the 1680s usually featured a white female abducted by Indians and carried into the woods against her will. Cotton Mather expanded the genre a decade after Rowlandson in *The Captivity of Hannah Dustin* — and that was just the beginning. More than two hundred years after the publication of the first captivity narrative the genre was still going strong, though readers might not have been aware of its deep roots and its longevity. Novelist Alan LeMay brought it into the twentieth century in two westerns, *The Searchers* and *The Unforgiven*, both made into movies, the first directed by John Ford, staring John Wayne as the quintessential searcher and Natalie Wood as the white girl abducted by an Indian named Scar. Something about captivity and the captivity narrative has long fascinated freedom-loving Americans. Something about the national character prompted Americans to cast themselves as the victims of Indians and at the same time as lovers of freedom and justice who have had to take revenge.

The female captive, whether an actual person or a fictional character, was usually saved by fellow Christians from pagans, as in the frontier novels of James Fenimore Cooper. But sometimes the captive and hostage didn't want to be saved from the "savages" who, it turned out, had civilizations of their own, families and spirituality, too. Eunice Williams (1696-1785), the daughter of a New England minister, married an Indian, joined his tribe, became Marguerite Kanenstenhawi Arosen, and by almost all accounts lived happily with her husband away from the rigors of Puritan society. The New England novelist Catharine Maria Sedgwick fictionalized Eunice's story in *Hope Leslie,* published in 1827 but set in the 1640s.

Indians also abducted and held as a prisoner Eunice's father, John Williams, who wrote candidly about his experiences in *The Redeemed Captive* published in 1707, twenty years after Rowlandson and nearly a hundred years before the explorers Lewis (1774-1809) and Clark (1770-1838) plunged into the wilderness and remade the captivity narrative, in which they featured themselves as two explorers in the thrall of the North American continent. Their voyage into the psychological wilderness was as dramatic as their geographical expedition. Moreover, the information that they recorded about their inner journeys is as crucial for understanding the impact of the continent on their thinking and feeling as the facts that they gathered about the flora and fauna were invaluable for science.

Seemingly inseparable, Lewis and Clark were only together for a brief period of time, and even then they weren't always together or of one mind. Clark was older and perhaps wiser; he made the journey with far less anxiety than Lewis, who thought that the only way to cross the American continent was to will himself across, as though his legs alone wouldn't carry him. "I now begin to be apprehensive that I shall not reach the United States within this season unless I make every exertion in my power," he wrote ominously, on the last leg of his homeward bound journey in July 1806.

A romantic figure, an enlightenment thinker and a government agent, Lewis carried elements of Puritanism in his head. In May 1806, at a pivotal moment in the journey that President Jefferson commissioned, he described the Bitterroot Mountains as a "dreary wilderness" and explained that he was afraid to "get bewildered" and lose his way, along with his baggage, horses and all-important journals, which Jefferson had instructed him to write and to guard against danger. Afraid of losing time, losing his identity, and his written record of the journey, he held on to the journals as though his life and his own self depended on them.

Lewis's co-commander, William Clark, was cut from nearly the same cloth. Both Virginians born in the 1770s, and both slave owners unopposed to the westward extension of slavery, Captain Meriwether Lewis and Second Lieutenant William Clark were too young to have fought in the American Revolution and yet not too young to reap the benefits afforded by the new nation. An odd couple, indeed, as odd a couple as Cooper's Natty Bumppo and Chingachgook — or Melville's Ishmael and Queequeg — Lewis and Clark took turns playing *the* authority figure on the journey. Clark was only a second lieutenant while Lewis was a captain and his superior, though they kept rank a secret and presented themselves as equals to the men in the Corps.

Sons of men who fought the British and the Indians in the War of Independence, Lewis and Clark and the men of their generation felt that they had to protect frontiers against attacks from without and guard the citadels of power from internal foes. Their sentiments echoed the old Puritan narratives about savage

Indians outside the community and New England heretics inside it. Lewis and Clark carried no Bibles in their outstretched hands and raised no crucifixes above their heads. Tomahawks and pistols were more their style than scripture. To the Indians, they offered neither Catholicism nor Protestantism, but rather the religion of civilization and a patriotic furor so hot it burned. Love of country replaced love of Christ.

The singer/songer Stevie Wonder might have had Lewis and Clark in mind when he wrote, with help from Michael Sembello, the lyrics to "Saturn," a meditation on the evils of Western expansion. Wonder must have been thinking of the archetype to which Lewis and Clark belonged when he took on the persona of an Indian and wrote the lines: "We can't trust you when you take a stand/With a gun and Bible in your hand/And the cold expression on your face/Saying, Give us what we want or we'll destroy."

Jeffersonian Republicans as far as party labels go, and eager proponents of Jefferson's trinity of life, liberty and the pursuit of happiness, they were Indian haters and Indian lovers, too, as they make abundantly clear in their journals. They lauded Indian "ingenuity," "civility" and "dexterity" and yet like the Puritans, who fought against the Pequod and Naragansett, Lewis and Clark used the words "uncivilized," "savage," and "treacherous" to denigrate Native Americans. Clark called the Lakota Sioux the "vilest miscreants of a savage race," a phrase not calculated to win friends among the Sioux. On one occasion, he drew his sword against them and would have used it, too, until Black Buffalo, a Sioux warrior, interceded and invited the women and children of the tribe to met the white men.

Like Lewis, Clark kept one foot in the age of the Puritans. Adopting the allegorical habit of the New England settlers, he looked at a beached whale on the coast of the Pacific and thanked "providence for directing" it to him and to the Corps of Discovery

"to be *swallowed by us* instead of *swallowing of us* as Jonah's did."
With the continent behind them and no longer inside the belly
of the beast, the Corps of Discovery rested and waited in no rush
to turn around and complete their mission. Going back, they
learned, was emotionally and psychologically harder than going
away. On the outward-bound journey they were less familiar with
the terrain than on the homebound journey, but the trek from
West to East unnerved them, especially Lewis.

From the vantage point of the twentieth century, the two men
look like outdoorsmen, budding naturalists and incipient colonial-
ists, as well as primitive hunters and gatherers who felt they were
entitled to hunt and gather everything that crossed their paths.
They went into territory where they weren't beloved, borrowed the
customs of the natives and imposed their own. They hunted deer,
antelope and buffalo that they saw in herds of more than ten thousand, or so Clark reported. On the march across the continent, they
began the century-long killing spree that resulted in the decimation
of species. Game was so abundant and seemed so "tame" that members of the party "clubbed them out of the way."

Everyone in the Corps — there were more than thirty members of the permanent party — had his or her own individual
journey. Some had several journeys: visionary, pedestrian, poetic
and prosaic. York, an African-American slave, didn't have the
same experience as his white master, William Clark. Lewis was in
his head much of the time. Going west, he enjoyed a trip to paradise that ended with the idyllic Nez Pierce Indians. Going east, he
suffered a trip to hell that ended with the death of two Blackfoot
Indians. No Indian killed or wounded a single white man in the
8,000-mile epic journey of the Corps of Discovery — and that
probably wasn't an accident. The Indians had far more poise and
self-control than the members of the Corps. They were at home.
Lewis and Clark were in the wilderness.

Over the course of the twenty-eight-month-long expedition that started in 1803 — the same year as the Louisiana Purchase — and that ended in 1806 — the year Webster published his *Dictionary* — Lewis, Clark and company were never taken prisoner by Indians and never held against their will, though they were afraid they would be. Enemies seemed to lurk behind every tree. Still, they never felt freer than in the wilds and in many ways they never enjoyed life more. *Boudin blanc* tasted as good if not better in the woods as in Washington, D.C., and so did stews, ragouts and truffles. "This white pudding we all esteem one of the great delicacies of the forest," Lewis exclaimed of the *boudin blanc*. The wilderness provided an endless pantry and an immense lumberyard ripe for pillaging.

In 1805, perhaps *the* pivotal year for the Corps, Lewis and Clark breathed a sigh of relief when they reached the Pacific. Success, which Clark spelled "suckcess," was theirs at last. (Throughout this chapter, I have corrected his and Lewis's atrocious spelling rather than inflict it on readers.) "Great Joy," he exclaimed when he saw what he thought was the sea. In fact, he only spied a tip of Grays Bay, an estuary twenty miles from the coast. Soon real joy arrived. Joseph Whitehouse spoke for the Corps itself when he noted, happily, that, "we are at the end of our voyage to the Pacific Ocean."

With the Clatsop tribe in what is now Oregon, Clark wrote that he was treated "with extraordinary friendship" and served delicious food: cockle shells along with a syrup made of dried berries. The Indians of the Pacific Northwest treated the white men who arrived in their world with much the same hospitality that the Indians of New England had extended to the Pilgrims two hundred years earlier.

Jefferson warned Lewis and Clark to be wary of Indians, and as obedient citizens they took his advice seriously. In their journals, they told themselves repeatedly that Indians — all Indians — were dangerous, even when they met Indians who obviously weren't dangerous. Breaking away from Jefferson's narrative took time, space and conscious thought and even then it proved to be challenging. They wanted to like the Indians, but nearly everything they were told about them prevented frienship.

In the era of Lewis and Clark, men and women held captives of Indian tribes weren't always white. Indians captured and held other Indians. Captives were nearly always female, perhaps because women on the Great Plains and in forests often had more cultural capital than men. Frontier women usually worked harder than men, made and reared babies and preserved oral traditions that made them valuable to the societies in which they lived. And yet historians, novelists and artists often pushed frontier women to the sidelines. Even when the German-born artist Charles Wimar painted a scene that he entitled "The Abduction of Daniel Boone's Daughter by the Indians" (1853) he didn't mention her name. That abduction was significant for Wimar because Boone was her father. Eunice Williams didn't write about her captivity or become a household name in the early eighteenth century. Her father did. No American woman became a national hero in the first half of the nineteenth century, though women lived heroic lives. The giants of nineteenth-century folklore, from Paul Bunyan to Pecos Bill, were usually supersized men.

No one on the expedition wrote much about York, Clark's captive and slave, or about Sacagawea, the Corps' interpreter and guide and the indispensible agent for its survival. Sacagawea had a riveting story to tell or be told. Part I might read: taken prisoner while still a young girl by the Hidatsa, then transported to their territory, and turned into a virtual slave. (Fortunately for Lewis and Clark she remembered the way her captors took her.) Part II: as a mother and wife, she merged her individual journey with the epic of the "most famous exploring party in American history," as the Pulitzer Prize-winning author, Eric Foner, calls it. Lewis and Clark made Sacagawea famous. But she made them famous, too, by bringing them and their companions across the Rockies, then all the way to the Pacific and across the Rockies on the way back.

In the Indian world she was as famous as Lewis and Clark were in theirs. Sacagawea's father had been the chief of the Shoshone; her brother ascended to that position and helped the Corps by selling horses that enabled them to reach the Columbia River and the coast. Sacagawea was as much of an insider in her brother's world as Meriwether was an insider in Jefferson's. She was perhaps the *last* of her kind in a century in which Indian warriors — Sitting Bull, Crazy Horse and Geronimo — defined tribal life even as disease, warfare and assimilation eroded it. Lewis and Clark were the *first* of their kind, the fathers of a tribe of imitators who competed with rival tribes of whites who pledged their allegiance to Daniel Boone, who moved ever westward, and Davy Crockett ("King of the Wild Frontier") who went to Washington, D.C. as a Congressman and who died at the Alamo in Texas during the war that saw the United States gobble up Mexican territory.

THE JOURNEY & THE JOURNALING

The two co-commanders produced riveting journals in which they linked their own individual stories to the story of the continent. Writing supplies weren't a problem, even thousands of miles from Washington, D.C. They brought reams of paper, pens and ink. Supplies of whiskey and tobacco ran out before writing materials. Neither Lewis nor Clark were trained journalists, but they looked carefully and listened closely, tasting and smelling the world around them, and writing, writing, writing until they improved. Lewis's advice to himself — to write down "the first impression of the mind" — worked well for him, Clark and the other journalists in the Corps. Kerouac gave himself much the same advice when he voyaged across the continent.

Lewis urged the men to record "passing occurrences...as shall appear...worthy of notice" — which gave them free reign to write about their bowels and their brains, their agony and ecstasy. The men in the Corps wrote about nearly every possible subject, though they didn't describe everything they might have described. While the journals provide a wealth of information they also leave out information; why for example Lewis went for months without writing in his journal and then wrote frantically for days. The journals don't explain his metaphors and his word choices, either, that were consistently striking; he described the tour as a "peregrination." Indian women were "tawny damsels." The Rocky Mountains were "stupendous." The verb he uses to describe his interaction with the continent itself was "penetrate" which sounds sexual. The writers in the Corps — "the writingest explorers of their time," historian Donald Jackson called them — produced some of the best nineteenth-century American wilderness writing.

Lewis and Clark drew pictures of birds and plants and aimed to please their readers, including Jefferson, a captive audience of one, by appealing to eighteenth-century sensibilities and by court-ing the wave of romanticism that caught them up in its energies. In their own narratives, they cast themselves as heroic American citizens beholden to members of no other nation except their own and yet curious about the Indians who loved their nations, too, as they recognized. Day after day, week after week, they chronicled the impact of North America on their own consciousness, at the same time that they used language to categorize the wild, define it, shape it and Americanize it. To Indians they met across the country, Lewis and Clark handed out medallions with images of

George Washington and Thomas Jefferson, and, while the Indians accepted them, they didn't prize them highly.

They named rivers after Jefferson and Madison, buried one of their own, Sergeant Floyd, their only casualty, and named the place where he died in August 1804 "Floyd's Bluff." Floyd was court-martialed and lashed in punishment, but the Corps thought of him as a stalwart member and wanted him to be remembered. Clark carved his own name and "July 25, 1806" on the face of a rock. He also borrowed the nickname, "Pomp" from Sacagawea's son, Jean Baptiste, and fixed it to a landmark in what is now Montana. Reading the names — Hungry Creek, Independence Creek, and Cape Disappointment — that they gave to places says a lot about their states of mind and the condition of their bodies.

Lewis insisted that he told the truth to the Indians, even when they didn't want to hear his truths. He lied to the Indians, too, then turned around and told the Indians that white men never lied. To Sacagawea's brother, Cameahwait, he said that, "among white men it was considered disgraceful to lie or entrap an enemy by falsehood." Jefferson instructed Lewis specifically to persuade the Indians of the "innocence" of the expedition and to gather information about them so that they could "civilize" them.

They were to find a waterway across the continent "for the purpose of commerce," the president explained. Along the way they eluded Spanish soldiers sent to arrest and detain "Captain Merry," as they called Meriwether Lewis, who moved swiftly to elude them. Captivity by the agents of the Spanish crown was more likely than captivity by the Indians. The Spanish minister to the U.S., Carlos Martinez de Yrugo, thought he knew what made Jefferson tick. He was a "lover of glory," he insisted, who wanted "to perpetuate the fame of his administration" by extending the U.S. to the Pacific.

Lewis wanted fame, too, and might have won it for any

number of achievements as diplomat, soldier, trader and writer. He struggled to keep all of his many hats on his head and to prevent his head from imploding under the pressure of the opposing voices that told him to be all things to the Indians: friendly and suspicious, duplicitous and sincere. Jefferson was his role model and Jefferson was a complex politician who could be generous and kind as well as shrewd and sinister. The president himself didn't have first-hand knowledge of Indians, but he had a good idea of how to terrify and manipulate them.

It was "essential to cultivate their love," Jefferson wrote, and to persuade them that "we have only to shut our hand to crush them." When a group of Indians arrived at the White House in January 1806 at about the same time that Lewis and Clark were homesick on the Pacific, Jefferson told them that the whites were "as numerous as the leaves on the trees," that the white men in Washington D.C. were their new "fathers" and that the United States did "not fear any nation."

With Jefferson as his mentor, role model and employer, it's not surprising that Lewis spoke to the Indians from both sides of his mouth, tenderly as well as terrifyingly. On April 21, 1806, he wrote in his journal that he told the Indians that he "had it in my power at this moment to kill them and set fire to their houses, but it was not my wish to treat them with severity provided they would let my property alone." No wonder the Indians complained to Jefferson that his agents had "raised their tomahawks over our heads" and that they "do not keep your word."

The Indians also told Jefferson that the "words you put in his mouth" — meaning Lewis's — sounded hollow, as for example when Lewis told them he was going to "restore peace and harmony among the natives." How could they believe Jefferson's "beloved man" when he carried guns, revered guns and promised to sell guns to warring Indian tribes?

MERIWETHER LEWIS'S INNER JOURNEY

Grandiose and apocalyptic, a man of property and an "obedient servant" of the president, as he called himself, Lewis meant to
teach Indians to respect his own private property, not to touch or
take his things, especially his weapons and his dog, Seaman, either.
Lewis could be adamant and generous, smiling and frowning. His
profound mood swings, which he dutifully recorded in his journals
like a patient tracking an illness, intensified the kinds of philosophical dualities that are reflected nearly everywhere in his writings.

Lewis was a perfect candidate for a psychological study by a
nineteenth-century alienist. In his biography of Lewis, the military historian, Stephen Ambrose, calls him "a manic-depressive."
He was not the first to diagnose him. Jefferson noted, during the
course of Lewis's stay in the White House when he worked as his
private secretary, that he suffered from "depressions of mind" and
from "hypochondriac affections," though he also praised Lewis
for his "fidelity to truth" and his ability to maintain "order &
discipline."

Jefferson recorded his memories and impressions of Lewis in
a biography written for the first published version of the journals.
No doubt about it, Jefferson was impressed with Lewis, his family,
his military record, and his boyhood adventures that he probably
heard from Lewis himself.

"When only eight years of age," the president wrote, "he
habitually went out in the dead of night alone with his dogs, into
the forest to hunt the raccoon & opossum." Then, too, as Jefferson's
secretary, Lewis weathered political storms, performed well under
pressure, understood that Congressional funding had to be kept
secret and that the expedition itself had to be carried out clandes-
tinely. Jefferson's Washington enemies ridiculed his $10 million
dollar purchase of Western real estate. A Federalist newspaper in

Boston noted that Louisiana was "a great waste, a wilderness unpeopled with any beings except wolves and wandering Indians." Those words sound as though lifted from William Bradford's *Of Plymouth Plantation*. Linguistically not much had changed in two hundred years, though Lewis meant to change it and change it he did in his journals with romantic passages about nature that replaced traditional Puritan language about the howling wilderness.

Lewis had more going *for* him than against him, Jefferson concluded; he was "intimate with the Indian character" and "habituated to the hunting life." The president provided him with a crash course in political science and sent him to experts to learn medicine, zoology and botany. Lewis was a fast learner and did his best to ready himself, though the real wilderness was nothing like what he expected. Still, he did his best not to disappoint Jefferson, or his own mother.

Even when Lewis was down, he gave the two of them the impression that he was up. He wrote to the president from the wilderness to tell him that he had "never enjoyed a more perfect state of good health" and that everyone in the Corps was "in good health." He presented a smiling face to his mother, Lucy Marks, who had remarried after the death of her first husband, Meriwether's father. "We have experienced more difficulty from the navigation of the Missouri than danger from savages," he wrote her in 1805. He was soon to change that story in his journals.

In *Undaunted Courage*, Ambrose concludes that Lewis was "the perfect choice" for the job in large part because he "knew the wilderness as well as any American alive during his day, including Daniel Boone." Granted, Lewis was familiar with the wilderness in parts of Virginia and Kentucky. But the wilderness beyond the upper reaches of the Missouri — and in the snow-capped peaks of the Rockies — wasn't the same as the wilderness East of the Mississippi that Boone had explored and that made him a skilled woodsman, hunter and trapper. Like Boone, Lewis had, Ambrose writes, "the frontiersman's faith in the rifle."

That faith protected him and also endangered him and the Corps. Lewis turned to rifle and pistol when he might have turned to the spoken word or to sign language, especially near the end of the journey when he gave up verbal communication and turned more readily to bullets — a story he narrates in his journals in the manner of an action hero battling Indians. "I reached to seize my gun but found her gone," he wrote in July 1806, when he was both manic and aggressive. He added, "I then drew a pistol from my holster and turning myself about saw the Indian making off with my gun." Reinforcements arrived and Lewis instructed his men "to fire on" the Indians if they tried to stampeed their horses. Dangers mounted, violence flared and two Blackfeet were soon dead.

In the East Room of the White House, where he lived in close quarters with Jefferson, Lewis looked like the perfect man for the job, but in the wilderness among Indians, he found himself in an unheroic narrative he couldn't control. Off the map and perhaps out of his own mind, he had trouble coping day to day. The extremes of the weather, a near-death experience in the Rockies, and the anxiety-producing encounters with Indians all pushed him to extremes he had never known before. They made him far more manic, more depressed and more violent than he'd ever been. Moreover, his mood swings colored the ways that he looked at the wilderness as friend and as foe and at the Indians as allies and adversaries in the battle to control North America.

After he came back from the wilderness, he tried to compose himself so that he could devote himself to "the composition of his travels." But the "cold and hunger of which I shall ever remember" — as he put it — had taken a toll on him. He had literally and figuratively taken a bad fall. He tumbled forty feet down a hillside and was nearly crushed to death by his own horse — a vivid incident he recorded in his journals. At the same time, he took an emotional tumble. Lewis, the idealist and Jeffersonian who wanted to "further the happiness of the human race," failed to further his own personal happiness. The "dreary wilderness" that stalked him in the Rockies became a part of his inner landscape and contributed to his suicide at a hotel in Tennessee where he stopped for the night on October 11, 1809.

In his room and in a state of delirium, Lewis shot himself twice with two pistols and stabbed himself with a knife. Before his last act of self-destruction, he explained that he was afraid that his journals would fall into the hands of the British and that they would be used against the Americans. Then, too, Lewis reportedly said that "he had killed himself to deprive his enemies of the pleasure and honor of doing it." What also might have prodded him to do the deed were the attacks that the publisher David McKeenhan made on his credentials and his standing in the community. McKeenhan published Patrick Gass's journal in 1810. Gass's was the first journal by any member of the Corps to appear in print; it scooped Lewis and irritated him, too, as did McKeenhan's wounding accusations. "You were not a man of science," McKeenhan wrote. "You were not a man of letters." Lewis was, McKeenhan charged, a man of "insatiable avarice."

Gilbert Russell, an American soldier and the military commander at Chickasaw Bluff in Tennessee, described Lewis's last days, including his "derangement of mind." By today's standards, we'd probably say that Lewis suffered from post-traumatic stress disorder (PTSD). The wilderness traumatized him. Study the journals knowing he committed suicide and they read like a long suicide note in which he tried frantically to talk himself out of his depression and to put himself back on the road to sanity.

Jefferson thought that the wilderness provided Lewis with a kind of "tonic" — to borrow the word Thoreau used to describe the healing powers of the wilderness. "During his Western expedition the constant exertion which that required of all the faculties of body & mind, suspended these distressing affections," Jefferson wrote. Granted, the wilderness distracted and entertained Lewis, but it also stirred him up.

One might borrow Joseph Conrad's harrowing description of Kurtz in *Heart of Darkness* to understand Lewis. "The wilderness had patted him on the head," Conrad wrote. "It had taken him, loved him, embraced him, got into his veins, consumed his flesh, and sealed his soul to its own by the inconceivable ceremonies of some devilish initiation." A newly minted U.S. colonialist, Lewis meant to bring enlightenment ideals into the wilderness and to show off the civilized goods that he and the Corps hoped to sell the Indians, along with American values, including "chastity." The Indians were far too unchaste for him, though the fact that the men in the Corps weren't chaste didn't trouble him. They were innocent sons of Adam in the garden of the West; Indian Eves seduced them, and through "amorous contact" infected them. They were to blame, not his own boys.

The sexual encounters were among the least of his worries. What was especially troubling was the sight of white hunters and trappers penetrating the continent without government permission or approval. Even before he and Clark returned to Washington to meet Jefferson and to be feted, wined and dined, their expedition inspired citizens to plunge into the wilderness, trap beaver and make their fortunes. On the way down the Mississippi, they encountered fur traders on the way up. Lewis knew, as Jefferson also knew, that to develop the territory commercially, they had to move the Indians out of the forest and to segregate them from whites. No easy feat.

It's no wonder that Indians — not all but many — didn't trust Lewis and didn't trust Clark and Jefferson, either, who lied when it was expedient and told the truth if and when it suited them. Clark lay down the law — "not to take any thing belonging to the Indians even their wood" — and then broke the law, took wood and other possessions. Lewis stole a canoe from Indians when he could just as easily have bought it. He had the money; the Indians were prepared to sell it. A prisoner of his own culture most of the time, he didn't try to look at himself through Indian eyes, not even the kind of imaginary Indian eyes that Cooper would create in the Bumppo novels and that might have helped him on his journey. Rarely if ever did Lewis see Indians as they saw themselves. Moreover, he just didn't see or understand Sacagawea. "If she has enough to eat and a few trinkets to wear I believe she would be perfectly content anywhere," he wrote, perhaps half-wishing he might not be unhappy with his own lot in life.

SACAGAWEA'S SACRED JOURNEY

Using wits, guns, tobacco and whiskey and with lots of beginner's luck, the Corps survived before Sacagawea joined the party. For months in advance of their fortuitous meeting with her, Lewis, Clark and the Corps knew they had to pay close attention to changing environments and keep accurate records in their journals. After she joined the Corps, it changed, though she didn't give orders or tell anyone what to do. It helped that she carried her baby with her most of the time she was with Lewis and Clark and that she was already married, though Lewis dismissed her husband, Charbonneau, as "a man of no peculiar merit." In 1839, at the age of 80, he showed up alone at a fort, poor and penniless, unknown and unappreciated and asked for assistance. That kind of narrative of the old man defeated by the wild rarely showed up in American chronicles of the West.

When Sacagawea was near, Lewis tended to be less hot-headed and less paranoid, though not always. The minibattle with the Blackfeet took place in July 1806, not long before she left the Corps. Whether Lewis killed an Indian or not isn't clear. He doesn't claim credit in his journal nor does he provide enough details to label him a killer. For a moment or two, shooting an Indian might have felt exhilirating, though it probably would not have rebounded to his glory with Jefferson.

Clark and Sacagawea didn't take part in the incident with the Blackfeet. They had parted company with Lewis, the whole group splitting up into four separate parties, each exploring on its own, a sign that the Corps was confident about itself, or perhaps that it had slowly come undone. Separated from Clark, Lewis promptly landed in trouble with the Blackfeet who tried to steal a prized horse and a beloved gun, or so he claimed.

"I shot him through the belly," Lewis wrote in his journal as though crafting a narrative about the Wild West with guns, bullets, gunslingers, Indians and horses. Lewis depicted the wounded Indian as he "fell to his knees...raised himself up and fired at me, and turning himself about crawled in behind a rock." He had learned to tell a story with suspense and crucial details. "He overshot me, being bareheaded I felt the wind of his bullet very distinctly," he wrote. Soon after that encounter, Lewis was shot and wounded in the butt, not by a hostile Indian, as he initially suspected — only an Indian would shoot him, he thought — but by one of his own men, accidentally or perhaps accidentally on purpose. As an authority figure he must have elicited resentment.

Moreover, in yet another violent encounter with Indians, he set fire to their shields, bows and arrows that he collected from a battlefield. He left "about the neck of the dead man" one of the medals he'd given the Indians as a token of friendship. The medal sent a message of war, not peace, enmity and not amity: "that they might be informed who we were," Lewis wrote. He had stepped over the line and become as savage as any "savage."

Sacagawea probably would not have been surprised by Lewis's turn toward violence, though she carried no guns, didn't use them and practiced a kind of wilderness quietude. Matriarchal scholars would probably call her the heroine of the war party, though Lewis and Clark never did. She kept no journal, left no written records and no artifacts. Still, Lewis and Clark's journals — which helped to turn her into a cult figure in the twentieth century — show that she played a significant role in the expedition. In the published journals that now run to thirteen volumes, Sacagawea isn't much more than an extended footnote. Lewis called her "the Indian woman" without recourse to her name. On at least one occasion, he turned her into an abstraction and described her as a "poor object."

If Lewis was the Corps' Achilles and wounded hero, Clark its Ulysses and conquering hero, York was a black Sisyphus who pushed the rock of his own bondage uphill every day. Sacagawea was Gaia, the Earth goddess. The Corps recognized her spiritual powers and called her "Bird Woman" and "Snake Woman." In their journals, Lewis and Clark spelled her name "Sah-ca-gah-we-a." The American poet, Erika Funkhouser, argues that she was unique because she was a woman in a man's world and because she knew that in order to survive "you go inside." But Lewis and Clark went inside, too, as did the other men — Ordway, Floyd, Gass, and Whitehouse — who kept diaries that reflect their personal lives and the collective life of the Corps.

As primitive recording devices, the journals provided a proscribed space in the seemingly limitless wilderness where they could explore the interior world of the self, write down their impressions, float their hopes, and test and perhaps exorcise their own fears, especially the abiding fear of hunger. The more one reads and rereads the journals the more they seem to be about food: who ate what in the wilderness and what the food, both raw and cooked, that they ate says about the relationships between whites and Indians. Increasingly Lewis and Clark ate like Indians, without becoming Indians and without giving up the desire for a "repast of civilization."

"A man had like to have starved to death in a land of Plenty for the want of bullets," Clark wrote. Bullets obsessed him and obsessed Lewis, though his manta was "hunger" along with "anxiety and fear." He continually thought of the Indians as "treacherous." Lewis, Clark and the whole Corps felt that they had to be "on our guard" the whole time. For thousands of miles they rarely relaxed.

"We all believe that we are now about to enter the most perilous and difficult part of our journey," Lewis wrote in July 1805. A perilous leg nearly always lay ahead. Dangers unfolded, darkness gathered and hunger became excruciatingly painful. A hungry Jeffersonian pilgrim in the wilderness of the world, Lewis discovered what it felt like to go without food and what it felt like to make little if any progress. Occasionally, he felt that he had to make a tactical retreat or "a retrograde march." Going backwards depressed him; the long march home felt like a forced march that he knew he had to make and didn't want to make.

Initially, Jefferson thought the men would sail home from the Pacific, but that was not to be. They sighted no ship, though English and American ships had in the past anchored off the coast. Lewis never fully accepted the grim thought that he'd have to walk thousands of miles home. Sacagawea may have shared his dark thoughts — she seems to have felt empathy for him — though she never said. Surrounded by men who didn't understand her or her culture, but who bonded with her nonetheless, as she bonded with them, Sacagawea exhibited an uncommon kind of quietude. Giving birth to her son, Jean Baptiste, endeared her to Lewis, who served as her doctor and who prescribed everything from opium to a concoction made from dried rattlesnake skin.

Clark relied on her and thanked her unambiguously, though like Lewis he often regarded her as a kind of abstraction. "The Indian woman," he wrote in his journal, "has been of great service to me." He and Lewis both called her their "pilot" and described the expedition as a "voyage" and as a "tour." They named a river after her, but that wasn't unusual. Their nomenclature was predictable. Lewis named one for a cousin; Clark, who worked tirelessly to make his map accurate, wrote down dozens of names for the rivers they christened, including one for Judith Hancock, the Virginia woman he would marry.

Sacagawea wanted to move swiftly and so did they, though they also knew when to stop, rest, reconnoiter and when to hold a democratic election in which York and Sacagawea voted, along with everyone else in the Corps, about where to build a fort and spend the winter. They knew, too, to celebrate Christmas, New Year's and the Fourth of July, in part to maintain their connections to the past and to the future. The present gave them an awful beating, but they were willing to take it most of the time, and to prove that if the Indians could live in the cold and snow they could live there, too. Social Darwinians before the Social Darwinians of the nineteenth century, the Corps illustrated two competing ideas: the survival of the fittest in the struggle for food and power; and the necessity for cooperation between all parties if survival were to take place. Lewis and Clark coevolved with Sacagawea, or devolved as she evolved. After the tour, she dressed as a white woman while Lewis dressed up in an Indian costume.

Even as a "child bride," as Lewis called her, and as a teenage mother, she knew how to survive in extreme conditions. Historians say she walked at the head of the Corps not only because she could read and interpret the landscape better than anyone else, but because she provided a cover for the heavily armed military expedition that didn't mean to start a war, but that was prepared to defend itself by any means necessary if attacked. The Corps boasted an arsenal with the most up-to-date weapons — pistols, rifles and a cannon that swiveled and could fire in any direction — that they dangled in front of the Indians as so many new toys. No wonder the Indians wanted guns.

Sacagawea protected the Corps from warfare, captivity and death, though not with guns and bullets. Guns had a life of their own in the wilderness. Before long, it wasn't clear to anyone in the Corps who started the cycle of fear, or how it would end. In the wilderness of fear, the Corps and its entourage of Indians became a kind of dysfunctional family with secrets about sex, parents and their own oddities, such as Lewis's hypochondria and Clark's preoccupation with the Indian customs for the burial of the dead.

Erika Funkhouser argues that Sacagawea's journey took her home and enabled her to be reunited with the Shoshone. But like everyone else on the journey, she also ventured away from home so that she might one day go home. Sacagawea found roots and connections almost anywhere, though she never had a map, except the map in her head, and never wrote anything down, as did Lewis and Clark, an activity that spooked the Indians and sparked their fears. The written word was nearly as strange as the white men themselves.

Ecologically literate, Sacagawea took the Corps to the Yellowstone River, which led the men to the Columbia that in turn brought them to the Pacific. When they didn't rely on her and on other Indians to guide them they often lost their way, lost valuable time and were assaulted by fatigue — the enemy inside that Dr. Benjamin Rush, their medical adviser, warned them against before they left the East.

ECSTASY & AGONY

At times, Lewis thought Indians were not far removed from the condition of animals, as when he watched a group of men eating the uncooked guts of a deer. "I really did not until now think that human nature ever presented itself in a shape so nearly allayed to the brute creation," he wrote. With a sense of "pity and compassion," he looked down at the "poor starved devils" and felt both a sense of attraction and repulsion, much as he was attracted to and repelled by the "tawny damsels" that he sexualized far more explicitly than any seventeenth-century Puritan.

Moved, too, by the seductive body of the continent with its nurturing "bosom," as he called it, Lewis felt an attraction to the earth that the Puritans would have called heretical and might have punished with exile. He could be a naturalist at play in a world without a deity, except perhaps Nature herself. Along the Missouri River, he was impressed by the white cliffs made of sandstone and noted that, "as we passed on it seemed as if those scenes of visionary enchantment would never have an end." He might have been a Coleridge hallucinating on opium, which he carried with him as medicine and administered as need be. Soon afterwards, while scouting on his own, he spied the Great Falls of the Missouri and wrote that they were "the grandest sight I ever beheld." God had no place in his cosmology; there was no deity to pray to and no devil to denounce.

Lodge Lewis and Clark in the seventeenth century and they're in the same league as Anne Hutchison and Roger Williams: outcasts and iconoclasts. Perhaps only misfits — unmarried men without children, willing to withstand intense physical pain — would go into the wilderness for years. Clark's orders were to recruit the "best woodsmen & hunters," not the best scientists. An apologetic Jefferson explained that he could find no qualified scientists to undertake the journey. "These expeditions are so laborious & hazardous, that men of science, used to the temperature & inactivity of their closet, cannot be induced to undertake them," Jefferson wrote in 1806 in response to public criticism of the men he'd chosen to lead the Corps. Lewis, Clark and everyone else on the expedition not only roughed it, but also thought of roughing it as a patriotic duty. They would show the world that they could rough it better than anyone else. No wonder the nation waited expectantly in 1804, 1805 and 1806 for news of the Corps and its mission. In the White House, Jefferson waited expectantly and assumed that every American citizen shared his anxiety.

He thought of Lewis and Clark's expedition as a kind of Wild West show that they "performed" daily and nightly by "order of the government of the United States." Even "the humblest of citizens had taken a lively interest in the issue of this journey" and "looked forward with impatience for the information it would furnish," Jefferson wrote. He exaggerated, though it's fair to say that *he* was impatient for news of the enterprise. Jefferson helped to create the legend of Lewis and Clark that preceded their return to the East and that followed them for decades. In 1806, they were greeted and treated as conquering heroes. Washington Irving met them and was astounded. Speakers extolled them for going where "the footsteps of civilized man" had never gone before and for "uniformly" respecting the "rights of humanity." The image of civilized men stepping into the wilderness and then stepping out of it gained renwewed life. On their return, they were saluted with the toast, "To victory over the wilderness."

Out of the wilderness, in step with civilized men again and working for the federal government, Lewis and Clark took on new careers. Clark assumed management of Indian affairs in the West, where he belonged, and where he moved Indians around, often against their will, though his paternalism earned him the

reputation as a frontiersman soft on Indians. Jefferson appointed
Lewis the governor of Louisiana, a place where he didn't belong.
At first, he thought that the territory was ungovernable. Feuds
and factions divided communities.

JEFFERSON'S JOURNEY

According to Jefferson, Lewis "wore down animosities and
reunited the citizens again into one family." He had less success
with himself, unable to stop his downward fall into madness and
self-destruction. When he committed suicide, he left a trunk full
of papers, but no manuscript ready for publication and not a single tidy, polished page to show an editor. Jefferson was embar-
rassed; he sent a letter to the Prussian naturalist and explorer
Alexander Von Humboldt (1769-1859), apologizing for the
absence of Lewis's book. Then he did everything in his power to
make sure that, in the absence of the Corps' two co-commanders
— Clark in the West and Lewis in his grave — the project would
be completed. If Jefferson was the "author" of the expedition, as
Lewis called him, he was also the midwife for the book.

By the time they arrived in reader's hands in 1814, the journals were greatly mutilated and brutally edited in a manner that
robbed them of their authenticity. Someone had seen fit to serve
as a ghostwriter and added passages to the text that made it sound
priestly. It might have been Nicholas Biddle, the President of the
Second Bank of the United States and the project's shepherd, or
else Paul Allen, who received credit on the title page as the person
who "prepared" the text for publication. Biddle, Allen or some
unknown and acknowledged author inserted the sentence, "It is
not unworthy to remark the analogy which some of the customs
of those wild children of the wilderness bear to those recorded in

holy writ." That passage, with its echoes of the Puritans and its allusion to the Bible, doesn't sound as though it comes directly from Lewis or Clark.

Not surprisingly, there was no stampede for the book and no one made money from the publication, either. Victory over the wilderness in the wilderness was the order of the day, not reading about it in the comfort of one's home. Jefferson's profile of Lewis didn't make the work a best seller, either. The title itself gave away the story and didn't leave room for mystery or intrigue. It went on far too long: *History of the Expedition under the command of Captains Lewis and Clark to the Sources of the Missouri, thence Across the Rocky Mountains and down the River Columbia to the Pacific Ocean.* The book soon went out of print and Lewis and Clark faded into the national unconsciousness. Strange as it may seem, given current fascination, they were largely forgotten.

For nearly one hundred years, the journals went on a journey without a map. They bounced around from hand to hand, printer to printer, editor to editor, and then all the way to President Madison who didn't have the same attachment to the work and its authors as his predecessor in the White House. For much of the nineteenth century the journals were lost. Then, in the 1890s, they turned up in the archives of the American Philosophical Society. In 1904 and 1905, Reuben Thwaites published an eight-volume edition with misspellings and typographical errors that accurately mimicked the originals. The Lewis and Clark cottage industry shifted into gear.

Teddy Roosevelt helped matters when he created the Lewis and Clark National Monument and declared the journals, which he first read as a boy, a national treasure and much better than *Gilgamesh.* "Few explorers who saw and did so much that was absolutely new have written of their deeds with such quiet absence of boastfulness and have drawn their descriptions with such complete freedom from exaggeration," he insisted. By Roosevelt's time, the myth of Lewis and Clark, which they'd co-created one hundred years earlier, took on continental proportions.

Now and then, an artist or writer poked a hole in the myth of the two men that also served as a myth about the heroic origins of the United States. The Corps spelled "the beginning of the end" for Indians, William Least Heat-Moon, the author of *Blue Highways*, says in Ken Burns's documentary about the expedition. He adds, "We went downhill after Lewis and Clark." Increasingly, whites (such as Roosevelt), who identified with Lewis and Clark, wanted to set foot in territory where no white man had been before. Lewis and Clark were strange heroes for the age of Teddy Roosevelt's imperial adventures and yet perhaps they were perfect heroes, too, and set the stage for empire.

Like many colonists in foreign lands, Lewis and Clark tried to insulate themselves mentally and physically from the continent they penetrated. They drank hundreds of gallons of alcohol, devoured tons of meat, and smoked hundreds of pounds of tobacco until they smoked it up and turned to the bark of the trees to smoke. Lewis and Clark became American archetypes: rough, ready and rowdy members of a gang of men led by an Indian woman.

CHAPTER 5

PIONEERS

James Fenimore Cooper's Wild Literary Ride

In the 1790s a curious fellow named William Strange wandered from a survey party in West Virginia, and, with his last ounce of strength and surprising presence of mind, carved into the bark of a tree, a rhyming couplet that went, "Strange is my name & I'm on strange ground/and strange it is I can't be found." His bare bones and his rifle were found in the woods in 1795 near a creek now known by his name. Mr. Strange may have been the only lone surveyor to die in the wilderness, but he was not the only American to lose himself in the woods. Pioneers and explorers habitually found themselves bewildered and bedeviled, turned around and tempted by terrible thoughts.

Strangers in a strange land, Americans scrambled to find their bearings and shed their abiding sense of themselves as alien creatures terrified and amazed by the bigness and the majesty of the continent. The literature of the new nation helped to provide them with a sense of place even as it reflected its unsettled and unsettling character. No one provided a more colorful or more compelling

map of the wilderness than James Fenimore Cooper and no one
in the United States from about 1820, when he began his career as
a writer, until 1851, the year he died, had a wilder literary career.
A pathfinder and pioneer, he made the myths that made America
and he ploughed the field of wilderness fiction for others to follow.

In his bestselling novels, many of them still in print, strangers
meet strangers in woods and on prairies. They might as well be on
a distant planet light years from home. Against all odds, they forge
enduring friendships, defy the elements, defeat their enemies and
stitch together outposts of civilization. That's the official story that
Cooper tells. He also offers a contrapuntal narrative of gloom and
doom, individual death and environmental destruction. Indeed,
Cooper had the genius to take the strange, alien quality of the
American landscape and couple it with eye-popping scenes of violence and a subtext of interracial sexuality. His vast body of work
reflected the national character of the United States in the first half
of the nineteenth century. Cooper's novels were popular because
they were new and news and because they mimicked the collective experience of Americans. Moreover, they enabled the reading
public to feel victorious in the war for control of the continent and
at the same time to maintain a sense of humility.

Cooper didn't set out to write fiction for readers around
the world. He began more modestly as a localist who fashioned
worlds from his own adventures on land and at sea, from his wide
reading and from his close observations of human behavior in cities and in the countryside. What he knew best was the geography,
history and legend of Upstate New York. In a series of novels that
came to be called the *Leatherstocking Tales* he invented a landscape
as mythical as Faulkner's Yoknapatawpha County that appealed
to the French, the English and the Russians. While they probably didn't care a hoot about the real Cooperstown or the actual
meanderings of the Susquehanna River, they were fascinated by

the dance that Cooper choreographed between the wild and the tame, the savage and the civilized.

As famous before the Civil War as Mark Twain would be famous afterward, Cooper was a looming presence in the United States and Europe, too, though his literary reputation faded fast after his death, and as a generation of new American writers from William Dean Howells to Mark Twain replaced him. In 1936, Ernest Hemingway ignored Cooper entirely when he put together his short list of great American novelists that included Henry James, Stephen Crane and Mark Twain. (His contemporary, F. Scott Fitzgerald, focused less on American literature; Scott included only two American writers on his list of required reading: Theodore Dresier and Dashiell Hammett. Nearly everyone else was French, English or Russian.)

In what sounds like a snit, Hemingway insisted that Twain was the father of modern American literature, that *Huck Finn* was *the* Great American novel and that there was "nothing as good since." Few comments about American literature have been as frequently quoted and few have been as misleading. The fact is there is no one Great American Novel, just as there's no Holy Grail and just as there is no one single Great Russian Novel or French Novel. Hemingway also insisted that "politics, women, drink, money, ambition" destroyed all American writers. That comment says as much about Hemingway's own passions as it does about any other author or about the whole tribe of American writers. Cooper didn't drink or play the role of Casanova, but money, ambition and politics played havoc with his literary career and he found himself isolated from the reading public that once adored him.

Born in 1789 to an elite, prosperous family with deep roots in America, Cooper grew up reading novels, playing games in the woods, and rebelling against his patrician father, a judge and a Congressman. Fenimore's voyages as a sailor and his sightseeing in England taught him the ways of the world and prepared him for his role as chronicler of American institutions and social types. By birth and breeding, he enjoyed the comforts and the leisure that enabled him to pursue a literary career and to stick with it through failure as well as success. At the same time, he had a constitution necessary for hard work and the business savvy to ride the market economy in which writing, like farming and manufacturing, was yet another way to make money. Perhaps more than any other writer of his time, Cooper begs to be situated in his era as literary nationalism took root and as writers beat the drums of patriotism for the United States.

INDEPENDENTLY DEPENDENT

Noah Webster of *Dictionary* fame, insisted that, "America must be as independent in *literature* as she is in *politics*." He enjoined Americans: "unshackle your minds and act like independent beings." He was not the last to call for an American cultural revolution from mother England. Herman Melville — the scion of a failing merchant family turned sailor, turned novelist — condemned "literary flunkeyism" and insisted that "mediocrity at home" should be praised before "genius abroad." To his voice, others added theirs.

Edgar Allan Poe, the hypnotic poet and haunting short story writer, called for a "Declaration of War" to throw off the "yoke" of the British and liberate Americans from the "sin of colonialism." Henry Wadsworth Longfellow — the author of *The Song of Hiawatha* (1855), his faux tale of an Indian warrior — advised American poets to write "from the influence of what they see around them, and not from any preconceived notion of what poetry ought to be."

It was easier for Longfellow to say what American cultural independence ought to look like than it was to take on the hard work of hammering out a new independent literature itself. To write *The Song of Hiawatha*, his long narrative poem, he borrowed from the Finnish epic, *Kalevala*. Moreover, as American authors including Washington Irving recognized, original works couldn't be created on demand or by decree.

Adherence to the spirit of liberty expressed in the Declaration of Independence and the Bill of Rights helped immensely, Melville insisted. It gave him permission, he wrote, to be more candid even than Shakespeare, who, he wrote, "was not a frank man to the uttermost." Melville would out Shakespeare Shakespeare in *Moby-Dick*, the megafiction that turns into a Shakespearean tragedy enacted in the wildness of the sea and on the theatrical deck of the Pequod.

The Bill of Rights and the Declaration of Independence weren't the only powerful forces afoot in the land. There was also an unwritten Declaration of Conformity that was obvious to the French writer, Alexis de Tocqueville, who noted in *Democracy in America* (1835) that there was "a sort of censorship" that ran parallel to "license of speech in all things." Americans — supposedly the freest and most democratic people on the face of the Earth — were afraid to speak lest they invite the wrath of friends and neighbors. Like Melville and de Tocqueville, Cooper praised American democracy, and yet nothing provoked his ire more than the tyranny of public opinion and the rule of conformity in the United States that he attributed to the unbridled power of the press. "The American is compelled to submit to a common rule," he complained. "The American...eats when others eat; sleeps when others sleep." His countrymen moved in lock step with the crowd and were guilty of what he called "moral cowardice."

Noah Webster was far less independent of English writers and the English language as spoken and written in England than he let on. In fact, he borrowed heavily from Samuel Johnson's landmark *Dictionary of the English Language* (1755), which included the words "wilderness," "wild," "wildfire," "wild-goose chase," and "wilding," which he defined as a sour, wild apple. He also featured the word "wildness" — which he defined as "rudeness" and "disorder."

A century later, Thoreau would reinvent and redefine "wildness" as a nature writer and as an anarchist of the woods who defended John Brown as sane, moral and good. "In wildness is the preservation of the world," Thoreau famously exclaimed. He didn't mean, as Johnson did, rudeness and disorder, but rather the kind of disciplined and yet exuberant living that he carved out in his own life apart from the "mass of men" who led "lives of quiet desperation." In *Walden* (1854) he argued that wildness would enable men to break away from "the pace" of their companions and to follow "a different drummer." It was all about nonconformity.

In his American dictionary, Webster listed the nouns "wilderness" and "wild" along with the verb "wilder" that, he explained, meant to be lost in "an unknown or pathless tract." That word, which long ago went out of fashion, would describe the sad story of the lost surveyor, Mr. Strange. It also fits the preeminent pioneer, Daniel Boone, who admitted that he had been "bewildered" in the woods, though he also boasted that he had never been truly lost.

Like his English predecessor, Samuel Johnson, Noah Webster defined the wilderness as "a tract of solitude and savageness." Wilderness meant loneliness, though American writers usually populated forests and woods with settlers, scouts and soldiers. No one, except perhaps Thoreau and his spiritual descendant, John Muir, wanted to wander alone. Curiously, Webster's definition of the wilderness wasn't just an approximation of Johnson's. In fact, his own words were mostly an exact copy of Johnson's. Still, Webster didn't merely repeat his English progeniteur. He also broke new ground. To

Johnson's definition of wilderness, he added more than half a dozen synonyms of his own: "not tame," "turbulent," "savage," "fierce," "licentious," "loose," "fickle," "strange" and "fanciful." In America, the word "wilderness" went wild. As a place, a state of mind, and as a behavior, it could be almost anything and everything.

Webster didn't stick to Standard English in his *Dictionary.* He included Indian words such as "tomahawk" as noun and verb and "wigwam," which he defined as an "Indian cabin." Before long, those two archetypes — the wigwam and the cabin — entered American literature, as in William Gilmore Simms's collection of stories about the backwoods, *The Wigwam and the Cabin* (1845-46).

After the War of 1812, when the Americans defeated the British military once again, writers in the United States began to follow a more independent literary course. That meant writing about American landscapes, even if only along the Hudson, as Irving did in "The Legend of Sleepy Hollow" and "Rip Van Winkle." Writing independently also meant writing about the "Back-Lands" as James K. Paulding, a forerunner of Cooper, did in his 1818 epic poem, *The Backwoodsman.*

Paulding spoke in two different voices: one sweet, as when he wrote, "O! Nature! Goddess ever dear"; and the other snarky, as when he wrote that the Indian "mind was like the forest that he rov'd,/ Dark, gloomy, rayless, rugged, unimprov'd." His sentiments weren't new; Cotton Mather had expressed no less vitriolic comments. Paulding's literary form wasn't new, either. A copycat, he imitated English lyrical poetry.

New innovative literary movements, such as realism and then naturalism, took longer to take hold in the United States than in England and France, in part, scholars have insisted, because Americans were apprehensive about fiction and the imagination. In *American Renaissance*, Matthiessen described the phenomena as "cultural lag." Eighteenth-century styles "lingered in America," he noted, decades after they had vanished in England. "Traces" of "formalism," he added, made Cooper "seem stilted in contrast with the easy naturalness of Scott." Still, what seemed like cultural lag to some appeared to be avant-garde to others. For Lawrence, the classics of nineteenth-century American literature plumbed the extremes of human consciousness and anticipated French modernism and futurism.

English Imagination, American Fancy

About England and the English, Cooper rarely offered unqualified praise. On a tour of Great Britain, everyone seemed smug and everything seemed to be in "perfect order." By his standards, perfect English order was far too orderly. Still, Cooper was usually wary of disorder and suspicious of the lure of the imagination, which Samuel Taylor Coleridge, the chief English aesthetician of the age, defended as a magnificent human faculty that "dissolves, diffuses, dissipates in order to recreate." Probably no terms are more helpful for an understanding of the differences between early nineteenth-century British and early nineteenth-century American literature than imagination and fancy. While Cooper didn't have a theory of the novel or a formal aesthetics, he entertained strong ideas about the function and purpose of art in America, for Americans, by an American. Form and content, beauty and truth, place and character were meant to mimic one another.

Not surprisingly Cooper didn't accept Coleridge's spirited endorsement of the imagination, though he met Coleridge at his home and found him "a picture of green old age; ruddy, solid." The author of "Kubla Khan" and "The Rime of the Ancient Mariner" — as well as an opium-eater and for a time an ardent revolutionary

— tested Cooper's patience and politeness. After their brief meeting, Cooper reported that Coleridge made remarks in "bad taste," though his own good taste prevented him from repeating them. Notoriously, he censored himself even as he complained about censorship.

Stubbornly, Cooper refused to abandon "fancy" and to embrace the imagination, though his own imagination took hold of him in his 1835 novel *The Monikins,* in which he depicted a society of aristocratic monkeys, and in his 1843 novelette, "Autobiography of a Pocket-Handkerchief," in which the handkerchief herself tells her intimate story. Melville would have called the idea of a talking handkerchief a "wild conceit."

Other Americans shared Cooper's distrust of the imagination. Jefferson had what might be called a vivid political imaginatio. In *Notes on the State of Virginia,* he observed that the work of the author, musician and abolitionist Ignatius Sancho (1729-1780) — who was born a slave and who became a freeman — was "incoherent and eccentric." Jefferson described Sancho's work as a "meteor through the sky." He also complained about the work of the African American poet, Phyllis Wheatley, (c.1753-1784) who was born a slave and who learned to read and to write about what mattered most to her: slavery and freedom.

Jefferson compared Sancho's poetry to the fiction of Laurence Sterne, the author of *Tristram Shandy,* the quirky English novel that was published between 1759 and 1767. Sterne intentionally jumbled chronology and deconstructed the form of the novel itself. It spoke well of Jefferson that he was familiar with *Tristram Shandy* and yet he couldn't work up an iota of enthusiasm for Sterne's work or for Sancho's, either. He scolded Ignatius Sancho because he "affects a Shandean fabrication of words" and because "his imagination is wild." Jefferson wished that his work had undergone "a process of sober reasoning" before publication. In a continent that seemed formless, borderless and inchoate, Americans craved order and cast doubts on the disorderly power of the imagination.

Like Jefferson, Cooper was intolerant of anything that smacked of Shandean fabrication, though unlike Jefferson he turned primarily to the heart, not to the head, to feelings not reason. One doesn't travel far in Cooper's world without encountering sentiments, sentimentality and copious tears from both men and women. Moreover, while he rejected the rage for facts that seemed to rise up all around him in America, he borrowed historical facts when they suited him, embellished them, and inserted them in narratives in which he tried to blend the real and the make-believe, fact and fancy, the wild and the tame.

For example, Cooper borrowed the "facts" of Daniel Boone's murky life, at least as he understood them, then used them to make his own frontier fictions credible. In his five-part *Leatherstocking Tales*, Cooper created his one truly memorable character, Nathaniel Bumppo, a mythical hero to rival Daniel Boone. He dispatched Bumppo into the west, he explains in *The Prairie*, because Boone went west. He depicts Bumppo as an old man eager to live far from the crowd because Boone lived far from crowds. The resemblances between Boone and Bumppo are striking, indeed.

Pioneers, hunters and warriors, they know forests intimately well. Both have strong ties to Indians, both rescue white women from Indians, both move further and further west, and both are romantics and naturalists. The first name, Nathaniel, seems to be derived from Daniel. Then, too, the name Bumppo looks as though it might have been adapted from Boone. Along with Boone, Cooper and his protagonist, Bumppo, achieved a kind of cultural revolution that influenced at least two generations of American writers, both men and women, schoolboys and schoolgirls. In far-off Nottingham, England, D. H. Lawrence came of age reading the Bumppo novels. "I think this wild and noble

America is the thing that I have pined for most ever since I read Fenimore Cooper, as a boy," he wrote.

BUMPPO'S WAY

The publication in 1823 of *The Pioneers* — the first full-fledged American work of fiction about the wilderness — touched the heart strings of readers and writers alike, and presaged a promising future for the thirty-three-year-old author who had already published two novels. On the morning it appeared in bookstores, it sold 3,500 copies. The twenty-one-year-old novelist, Lydia Maria Child, read it instantly and fell in love with it. *The Pioneers* inspired her to write her first novel, *Hobomok* (1824), in which she gushed, "American ground is occupied." She went on to say, "'The Spy' is luring in every closet – the mind is every where supplied with 'Pioneers' on the land, and is soon to be with 'Pilots' on the deep."

The Spy was Cooper's second novel: an ambitious tale about the American Revolution in which the author tried to occupy a middle ground between revolutionaries and royalists. *The Pilot* appeared a year after *The Pioneers*. Child didn't mention *Precaution*, Cooper's first novel, an imitation of Jane Austen's *Pride and Prejudice* and *Persuasion*. Cooper signaled the message of his book in the title itself: "precaution." Passion, the imagination and "unlicensed and indiscriminate reading" waylay the heroine, Jane Mosley. *The Pilot*, which Cooper subtitled "A Tale of the Sea," features a fictionalized version of John Paul Jones, the American sailor and hero of the revolution. Cooper went back and forth from land to sea, wilderness trails to ocean currents. He also published, under the pseudonym "Jane Morgan," a collection of short stories entitled *Tales for Fifteen: or Imagination and Heart* that suggest that the open heart is superior to the heady imagination.

With the publication of *The Pioneers*, Cooper popularized and Americanized the word "pioneer" and the image and the idea of the pioneer, too. (The old French word, *pionier*, meant "foot soldier sent out to clear the way.") Before long, "pioneer" would be on nearly everyone's lips, including those of James Russell Lowell, the Harvard professor and poet, who cofounded with Robert Carter in 1843 the monthly literary magazine, *The Pioneer*, whose mission it was to advance the culture of the new nation. Lowell's and Carter's *The Pioneer* published the pioneering Poe, Hawthorne, Jones Very and John Greenleaf Whittier, the Quaker-born abolitionist, newspaper editor and poet influenced by Robert Burns.

The pioneer as a distinct American social animal fascinated Europeans. In *Democracy in America*, Alexis de Tocqueville wrote that, "he is a very civilized man who, for a time, submits to living in the wilderness of the New World with his Bible, hatchet, and newspapers." De Tocqueville omitted the all-important rifle that no pioneer, backwoodsman or hunter would be without. A whole school of poets wrote hymns to pioneers, including Whitman in "Pioneers! O Pioneers!" that harkens back to Cooper in lines such as "Come my tan-faced children,/Follow well in order, get your weapons ready." Whitman could be as intoxicated on the wine of Manifest Destiny as any patriot.

From 1823, when *The Pioneers* was published, until 1828, when he set sail for France, Cooper held sway over the American literary scene though his contemporary, Catharine Sedgwick, provided competition in novels such as *Hope Leslie*. By the end of the nineteenth century, Cooper's reputation was punctured by Mark Twain's 1895 essay "Fenimore Cooper's Literary Offenses," but it wasn't flat out destroyed. In an era of increasing global expansion and the clash of civilizations, readers turned to Cooper for news from the edge, the frontier and the wilderness battlfield.

Big-city critics rebuked the fledgling novelist and also forgave him his flaws. Honoré de Balzac (1799-1850) in France and William Gilmore Simms (1806-1870) in South Carolina — which boasted a thriving regional literary culture of its own — both found flaws in Cooper's fiction, though they also commended him for writing about the wilderness. "Cooper is illogical," Balzac wrote in *Paris Review* in 1840. He added, "He proceeds by sentences, which, taken one by one, are confused, the succeeding phrase not allied to the preceding." True enough. Reading Cooper can feel like trudging through a thicket, though his novels also arrive at bright clearings. Balzac noted without equivocation that Bumppo would "live as long as literatures last." He also described Bumppo as "a magnificent moral hermaphrodite," by which, I think, he meant that he combines the morality of the savage with the morality of the courtier.

Balzac was right. Bumppo's morality reeks of contradictions and ambigutities. Moreover, Bumppo lives on as the great grandfather of the popular American hero. Contemporary audiences may not recognize his outlines in the hulking figures who animate blockbuster movies and pulp fiction, but he's there nonetheless as the hunter who's hunted; the pursuer who's pursued; the masked man who disappears, reappears and disappears; and as the assassin who kills for country, family, and for his own honor. Bumppo guaranteed that the hero's return would be an essential chapter in the American narrative.

In Cooper's day, the illustrations to the *Leatherstocking Tales* added to their popularity. Thomas Cole (1801-1848) — the English-born founder of the Hudson River School of landscape art — provided sketches for *The Last of the Mohicans* that helped make the novel a success. In 1825, two years after the publication of *The Pioneers*, Cole took a steamship up the Hudson, hiked into the Catskills, and began to paint dramatic scenes of the landscape that told stories with line, color and form. "The most distinctive, and perhaps the most impressive, characteristic scenery is its wildness," Cole wrote of the United States. He lamented the passing of the wild, and yet like Cooper he assumed that the end of the wilderness marked the opening of the door to progress.

In "A View of the Two Lakes and Mountain House, Catskill Mountains, Morning," Cole depicts a denuded landscape that suggested the devastating hand of man, though no man or men appear in the scene. Then, too, he painted allegories on the rise and fall of empires, depicted haunting ruins to evoke the past, and rendered spectacular images of clouds, skies and sunsets meant to lift the spirit. Together Cole and Cooper constituted a cultural movement that brought together the Hudson River School of landscape artists and the poets, novelists and journalists who belonged to Cooper's own New York club, the Bread and Cheese.

In the twentieth century, movie directors brought Cooper to the screen and introduced several generations to his "palefaces" and "redskins" as he called them. As recently as 1992, the British actor Daniel Day-Lewis brought Bumppo to life in *The Last of the Mohicans*, the most popular and the most violent book in the series. More than any other element, including the sentimental portraits of female characters and the grotesque representations of the Indians, it's Cooper's violence that's troublesome today, though his contemporaries weren't bothered by it. Neither Balzac, nor William Gilmore Simms or George Sand — yet another enthusiastic Cooper fan — complained about the ritualized slaughter that takes place in the Bumppo novels.

In a long essay about Cooper published in 1842 in *Magnolia*, Simms noted that the same "defect" appears in every Cooper work: "In truth, there is very little story." Indeed, Cooper's narratives trail off, fall apart and pop up again. Still, Simms agreed with Balzac that Cooper was a genius and that Bumppo was an immortal literary figure. "The ordinary writer, the man of mere talent, is compelled to look around him among masses for his material," Simms wrote. Not Cooper. He "concerns himself with one man, and flings him upon the wilderness." With Simms and with Edgar Allan Poe, who also reviewed Cooper's work, wilderness literary criticism emerged as a field of study. "Life in the Wilderness…is one of intrinsic and universal interest, appealing to the heart of man in all phases," Poe wrote in 1843, though he didn't explain why.

The accolades didn't stop with Poe and Simms. The French novelist and critic George Sand observed in an 1856 essay that, "America owes almost as much to Cooper as to Franklin and Washington; for if these great men created the Union, by skill in legislation, and force of arms, it was Cooper, the unassuming storyteller, who broadcast the news of it across the seas by the interest of his tales."

Cooper's patriotism helped to secure his popularity in the United States, though after he abandoned the United States and became an expatriate, he lost readers at home. His grand literary gamble didn't pay off commercially, though he didn't stop writing in Europe. Surprisingly, his reputation revived after Twain's double-barreled assault on his work. *Studies in Classic American Literature* gave Cooper a big boost when it appeared in 1923, just as Americans were beginning to resurrect and critique the early literature of the Republic.

In 1923, on his "savage pilgrimage" across America, Lawrence hoped to find Cooper's lost world and instead found himself disillusioned. "I used to admire my head off: before I tiptoed into the Wilds and saw the shacks of the Homesteaders," he wrote. Cooper irritated Lawrence no end; he called him the "National Grouch" and a "gentleman in the worst sense of the word." Still, he praised him as the author of the "myth of the essential white America" and the creator of a mythic figure who is "an isolate, almost selfless, stoic man, who lives by death, by killing."

What Lawrence never says is that Bumppo *only* kills Indians not white men. It seems like Lawrence's blind spot. In *The Last of the Mohicans*, the novel that anticipates Joseph Conrad's novella *Heart of Darkness*, Bumppo exclaims, apropos the Iroquois, "Extarminate the Varlets!" [sic]. Kurtz will echo Bumppo when he writes, "Exterminate the brutes." In *The Last of the Mohicans*, Cooper's hero circles a bloody field of dead and dying Iroquois warriors. To make sure they won't rise up to fight palefaces another day, he thrusts his knife into "senseless bosoms...as though they had been so many brute carcasses."

Conrad knew Cooper as intimately as Lawrence knew him, and, while he was drawn primarily to his stories of the sea, his comments about them apply equally well to his wilderness fiction. "He loved the sea and looked at it with consummate understanding," he wrote in 1898, a year before publication of *Heart of Darkness*. He added, "In his sea tales the sea interpenetrates with life...it is always in touch with men, who, bound on errands of war or gain, traverse its immense solitudes." Conrad might have been thinking of Bumppo when he wrote those last words.

In the aftermath of the killing spree in *The Last of the Mohicans* it's not easy to empathize with Bumppo, but he's worth dissecting because he's the American archetype of the killer of Indians: agent of genocide and poster child for the wilderness, too. Bumppo goes on killing Indians in *The Prairie*, *The Pathfinder* and *The Deerslayer*, the last book that Cooper wrote and published in the series, and that for accuracy sake ought to be renamed *The Indian Killer*.

The Pioneers is the only novel in which he doesn't kill Indians. In *The Deerslayer*, Bumppo is younger than in any other book and at the start of his life as a killer. The key scenes in the novel take place between Bumppo and Judith Hutter, "The Wild Rose," who asks him a question to which she already knows the answer: "Do you really love war…better than the hearth, and the affections?" Given his code of honor as a knight of the wilderness, he can't give a simple yes or no answer. All that he can say is, "we can never marry" which is precisely what Miss Hutter doesn't want to hear. Bumppo loves war more than he loves peace, love, marriage and women. He'd rather be in the bosom of the wilderness than in the arms of a woman, and while Cooper doesn't disapprove of him, he doesn't entirely approve of him, either. He's a bit of a mess.

Balzac's two-word phrase, "moral hermaphrodite" probably suits Bumppo as well if not better than any other single phrase, though Lawrence is also spot-on when he says that Bumppo "lives by death, by killing" and that he embodies the "myth of the essential white America." But Bumppo isn't only a killer; he's also a naturalist who cleaves to the woods as a boy might cleave to his mother. A strange case of arrested development, he's a child who never becomes an adult, though he's more adult than most of the other characters in the novels.

A philosopher, a poet, an avenging angel, an American Adam and a Tarzan of the forest, he's also an existentialist who stares into the "blue void of space." Morphing is his modus operandi. Moreover, his dualities reflect the contradictions of a democracy morphed into an empire that made war on Indians and on the wilderness, and at the same time swooned over the beauties of Nature and rhapsodized, as Cooper did, about noble savages with names like Chingachgook, Uncas, Magua, and "Hard-Heart," whom the author calls "an Apollo-like person." Bumppo befriends Indians and exterminates Indians. He sheds their blood in war and sheds tears with them when the killing fields are sated.

FATHERS & SONS, MOTHERS & DAUGHTERS

Ever since the 1970s, when feminist literary critics went hunting for Cooper, he has been eased from the Pantheon of American literature, though not expunged entirely. What Twain stated in 1895, American women academics tried to finish. The reaction against Cooper was inevitable, given the fact that for decades his novels were required reading. As H. L. Mencken (1880-1956) noted as late as 1931 in an introduction to Cooper's *The American Democrat*, "college tutors…boil sophomores in the *Leatherstocking Tales*." When the gender of college teachers and tutors changed, reading lists changed, and so did Cooper criticism.

Nina Baym anatomized Cooper in her 1971 essay, "The Women of Cooper's Leatherstocking Tales." Later, in her role as editor, she gently excised much of his writing from the *Norton Anthology of American Literature*, including more women, African Americans and Native Americans who had been ignored. Volume "B" in the eighth edition of the Norton anthology, which covers the years 1820-1865, runs to 822 pages and embraces American writers of nearly every gender, ethnic group and social class. A big soup of a book, it suggests the cultural diversity of American novels, stories, essays and poems, but what they all add up to isn't clear. American literature, Nina Baym and her coeditors seem to say, is up to each and every American. We're all independently minded readers and critics.

At least Baym read and reviewed Cooper's work before she cut him down to size. Ann Douglas seems to have given his novels a cursory glance. How else to explain her comment in *The Feminization of American Culture* that, "Thoreau, Cooper, Melville and Whitman wrote principally about men, not girls and children, and they wrote about men engaged in economically and ecologically significant activities."

Those four male authors — Thoreau, Cooper, Melville and Whitman — deserve more than splashdash treatment. Douglas also might have explained what she meant by "ecologically significant activities." In 1977 when her book first appeared, the word "ecology" had only begun to enter the working vocabulary of environmentalists, though the German scientist Ernst Haeckel (1834-1917) coined it in 1866 when Melville and Whitman were still alive and still writing. One might call Melville and Whitman ecologists in the sense that they explore the interactions between species, both human and animal, and their environments. They were fascinated by what we would call ecosystems; they emphasized both the creative and destructive forces unleashed by human beings on land and at sea that disrupted whole species. Thoreau could rightly be called the first American ecologist. He aimed to simplify his life and to leave as small and as light a footprint on the Earth as possible. Before Thoreau presented his philosophy of woods and fields in *Walden*, Natty Bumppo expressed an early iteration of the ecological point of view. A conservationist, he would surely disapprove of Ahab's hunting practices and might urge the crew aboard the *Pequod* to turn the ship around and head for home.

While Melville didn't include women characters in *Moby-Dick*, he created in *Pierre* (1852) a cast of distinctive women — Isabel Banford, Lucy Tartan, Delly Ulver and the protagonist's mother. Moreover, Melville wrote with an eye on female as well as male readers — for Sophia and Nathaniel Hawthorne.

Cooper situated women in all the Bumppo books. He also helped to feminize American culture first by publishing a collection of short stories under the name Jane Morgan, second by taking his mother's middle name, Fenimore, and adding it to his own, and third by creating feisty women characters. In *The Prairie*, Cooper explains in an aside to readers that the history of the American frontier abounded with "many tales of female hero-ism." Nineteenth-century women writers including George Sand and Maria Edgeworth, the Irish novelist, raved about his work. If we look at it through their eyes he doesn't seem onerous.

His women are not all alike, though Baym insists they are, echoing the nineteenth-century poet and critic, James Russell Lowell, who wrote of Cooper in *A Fable for the Critics*, "The Women he draws from one model don't vary/All sappy as maples and flat as a prairie." Cooper's cast of frontier women was drawn from at least half a dozen different models: his mother, wife, and daughters, and from the helpmates, coquettes and queens he encountered in Shakespeare, Byron and Sir Walter Scott. Indeed, his fictional women belong to a literary sisterhood: Judith Hutter and her half-mad sister, Hetty, in *The Deerslayer*; Mabel Dunham, the only eligible white female on the frontier, in *The Pathfinder*; Esther Bush, an "Amazon" and a "Sybil" in *The Prairie*, along with the Creole heiress Inez and the independent young woman, Ellen; Cora and Alice, the two sisters who are "flowers...never made for the wilderness" in *The Last of the Mohicans*; and Elizabeth Temple, the city girl in the provinces in *The Pioneers*. Cooper had to include Elizabeth: he put his own perspective, or at least one of them, into her character.

True enough, Cooper was a patrician, a patriarch and a paternalist. He embodied the dominant culture of his own day, along with the values of Jacksonian Democracy, which touted the common workingman, but not the common workingwoman who toiled in New England mill towns and longed for the beauty of the woods she left behind her. Like the Jacksonians, Cooper didn't make room in his democracy for the slave on a Southern plantation, nor the Indian uprooted and driven at gunpoint into the West. He doesn't seem to have known that African Americans were also pioneers, that they lived on the frontier and battled Indians.

James P. Beckwourth (1798-1866) tells part of that story in his memoir, *The Life and Adventures of James P. Beckwourth: Mountaineer, Scout and Pioneer, and Chief of the Crow Nation of Indians* (1856). Born a slave and freed by his master who was also his father, Beckwourth settled in Missouri and worked as a trader, scout and guide. He used many of the same words and phrases to describe the West that white writers used: "howling wilderness," "wild west" and "wild children of the forest." In his memoir, he boasted that, "with five hundred men of my selection I could exterminate any Indian tribe in North America."

For all his cultural blinders, Cooper genuinely aimed to create characters that speak for nearly every segment of the society. Indeed, he represented immigrants from Europe, slaves from Africa, wealthy girls like Elizabeth Temple, and poor girls like Louisa Grant who observes, "It is sometimes dangerous to be rich." Attentive readers can always find at least one character in a Cooper novel who offers a dissenting voice and goes against the grain, although Cooper was often afraid to allow the dramatic conflicts in his novels to lead to real fissures. As he noted in *Precaution*, "Books are, in a great measure, the instruments of controlling the opinions of a nation like ours. They are an engine, alike powerful to save or to destroy." Engines and technology didn't offend him, nor did the idea of literature as a tool to control public opinion. A patrician on the page as well as in public life, he kept a tight reign on his characters and didn't allow them to collide violently with one another unless they were palefaces and redskins. Only then could they battle one another.

All of the Bumppo books express contrary voices, probably nowhere more articulately than in *The Pioneers*, a paean to the vanquished wilderness that Cooper remembered from his own boyhood in Cooperstown, the frontier settlement founded by his father, William, a conservative judge and a Federalist who detested

Jefferson. In *The Pioneers*, Cooper introduces Bumppo as an old man on the last frontier of upstate New York. "Only forty years have passed since this territory was a wilderness," Cooper writes in the novel's introductory paragraph, reminding his audience of the revolution in the forest that had taken place in their own lifetime.

He wanted readers to look back and to see the progress that had been made in Upstate New York and by analogy across the whole continent of North America. At the same time, he wanted readers to recognize the environmental degradation that had occurred in less than half a century. A spokesman for civilization and for the wilderness, too, he was split down the middle. It wasn't that he couldn't make up his mind, but that he was of two minds and two hearts.

Autobiography inspired his art, most notably in *The Pioneers*, the novel in which his own contrary views find expresion in the two main characters: Marmaduke Temple, a law-and-order Judge and a feudal-style landlord inspired by Cooper's stern father; and Nathaniel Bumppo, the cunning outlaw, based on Daniel Boone and on the old white hunters that he remembered from his youthful days in the woods where, as his sister Hannah noted, he grew up "very wild." The conflict between Temple and Bumppo fizzles by the novel's end, but for a time it draws much of its energy from the real tug-of-war that took place between James Cooper, the son who played in the open air, and William Cooper, the father, who insisted that the boy buckle down indoors and study.

Fenimore's father ruled with an iron fist, while his mother, Elizabeth, allowed her son to reign freely in woodland haunts. She bent her will to his will, or so he noted in the 1840s, when he first acknowledged his gratitude to her. But there are more than personal conflicts behind the adversarial relationship between Bumppo and Marmaduke. As a young man, Cooper detested Thomas Jefferson, whom he saw as a kind of French hooligan pretending to be an upright American citizen.

Then, in the early 1820s, his views underwent a radical shift. He came to see Jefferson not only as a gentleman, but also as a great statesman. The purchase of the Louisiana Territory, Cooper insisted, was the "greatest masterstroke of policy that has been done in our times." In *The Pioneers*, Bumppo is a Jeffersonian who believes in natural rights and natural laws, though one might also call him a civil libertarian. Bumppo expresses his ideas freely, exercises the right to bear arms and opposes unreasonable searches and seizures.

He's an embodiment of the First and the Fourth Amendments to the Constitution. Freedom of speech is near and dear to him. Even in the wilderness, he insists that he has a right to privacy and that his simple hut is as inviolable as another man's castle. His sometimes foe and opponent, Judge Temple, is a Federalist who believes in strict enforcement of laws, especially his own, and in the virtue of authority, also his own.

Cooper accords the two characters equal respect for much of the novel. Significantly, he introduces both of them in the opening scene of chapter one, which takes place on the border between the town and the wilderness. The judge appears in a sled along with his daughter and their Negro servant Agamemnon. Bumppo emerges from the depths of the wilderness with his fellow outcasts, Indian John, also known as Chingachgook, and Oliver Effingham. Judge Temple accidentally shoots Effingham, an aristocrat posing as an Indian. His buddies, Bumppo and Chingachgok, come to his rescue. The French novelist Alexandre Dumas would present a similar trio of characters in *The Three Musketeers* (1844).

Critics, such as James Grossman — the author of a first-rate appraisal of Cooper's work — have argued that Bumppo was meant to be a minor character and that only slowly and gradually did he outgrow the limited role that the author initially assigned him. Much the same criticism has been made about Captain Ahab

in *Moby-Dick*. Scholars insist that Ahab became a more promi-
nent character as Melville developed his story. Indeed, the captain
of the *Pequod* doesn't appear until chapter 28, which is entitled
simply, "Ahab" in which Melville writes, "Reality outran appre-
hension; Captain Ahab stood upon the quarter-deck." Unlike
Ahab, however, Bumppo is a major character from start to finish.

He reappears in four novels after *The Pioneers* while Temple
vanishes at the end of that novel. Bumppo also appears in the
pages of *Eve Effingham* where the main character, an American
Eve who belongs to the patrician class, explains what readers
know from the moment that Bumppo appears on the scene in
The Pioneers: "the day of the Leatherstocking is over." Indeed,
he's a ghost of wilderness past. Not surprisingly, given Cooper's
romantic predilections and his affinities for the sentimental novel,
he characterizes his hero as a social animal endangered by the
disappearance of the wilderness itself. Given his attachment to
his hero, it's not surprising that he refused to allow him to die.
Yes, Bumppo breathes his last breath and is buried in *The Prairie,*
the third book published in the series, but he comes back in *The
Pathfinder*, the fourth book in the series, as alive and vital as ever.

In chapter one of *The Pioneers*, Cooper makes it clear that
Bumppo is the big man in the story. He mentions Bumppo's
height and build, describes his hair, ruddy complexion, grey eyes,
checked shirt, fox-skin cap, deerskin coat, deerskin belt, deerskin
moccasins and buckskin breeches. He's a man who literally wears
the wilderness and is inseparable from it, though he's also inseparable from civilization. He always carries a rifle he calls "Killdeer"
and a horn filled with powder. As Balzac noted, he's "born of the
savage state and of civilization." He embodies both, not simply
one or the other. What's striking about him in *The Pioneers* is that
he's a man without a future, without descendants and without
property.

Bumppo and Temple both claim to represent what's best for the wilderness. Temple defends economic development, while Bumppo speaks for unfettered freedom, wild life, and an economy based on hunting and fishing. For the judge, the landscape is a commodity; for Bumppo it's a spiritual entity. Both are elitists: Bumppo is the king of the woods; Temple is the king of the town. The founding father of Templetown, Temple looks to the future as well as to the past; he has an eye toward "futurity," as Cooper calls it. "Where others saw nothing but wilderness" he sees "towns, manufactories, bridges, canals, mines" and "all the other resources of an old country."

Temple wants to balance the wild with the mild. In his view, the woods must be protected from ordinary citizens, whom he distrusts and who, he insists, will destroy the wilderness if left to their own devices. Bumppo recognizes the shameful degradation of nature by man. "All the treasures of the wilderness," he insists, "begin to disappear before the wasteful extravagance of man." But he's reluctant to summon the police to protect trees, woods and forest.

Though he's a Jeffersonian and an embryonic ecologist, he's also Puritanical and argues that whites are "sinful" and "wicked," especially when they slaughter whole schools of fish and flocks of birds. He's shocked by the hunting and fishing practices of the townspeople, and irate about the unsustainable practice of maple sugar gathering and the kind of reckless logging by lumberjacks such as Billy Kirby, who chops down trees as though they're toothpicks and then arrogantly strides out of "the prostrate forest like the conquer of some city." Judge Temple is no less irate about the same practices, though he and Bumppo have fundamentally different notions about how to address the problem.

What Bumppo would like is a spiritual resurrection driven by individual choice, not by order of a magistrate or a judge. "Use, but don't waste," he insists in an early iteration of the "wise use" philosophy propounded by Gifford Pinchot, John Muir's rival and the first chief of the U.S. Forest Service. Then, too, Bumppo sounds like the environmentalist and wilderness advocate, Aldo Leopold, when he observes, "Wasn't the woods made for the beasts and birds to harbor in?" Furthermore, he argues that the rule of law ought not to apply to him. "What has a man who lives in the wilderness to do with the ways of the law?" he asks rhetorically. The novel is punctuated by rhetorical questions. After Bumppo confronts the magistrate, Hiram Doolittle, Judge Temple asks him, "Would any society be tolerable...where the ministers of justice are to be opposed by men with rifles?" He follows it with another: "Is it for this that I have tamed the wilderness?"

Bumppo tells the judge, "You've driven God's creatures from the wilderness." Temple counters with two related ideas: "laws alone remove us from the condition of savages" and "on the skirts of society, it becomes doubly necessary to protect the ministers of the law." On the frontier, he insists, it's necessary to enforce the rules and regulations of civilization, lest "savagery" return.

Bumppo remembers an era when the land itself was "a second paradise" and when, as an American Adam, he enjoyed "the wonders of the woods." Temple remembers his first journey into the "silent wilderness" (it wasn't "howling," as it was for the Puritans), when he climbed a tree, saw no houses and no roads and had a quasi-religious conversion. Temple offers a spirited defense of his right to the lands he owns. He sounds remarkably like Cooper's father, William. From Temple's point of view, no one — not the Indians, the Royalists who sided with the British during the revolution, or a lone hunter — has a claim on his property.

Everyone in the book has something pithy to say on the theme of the wilderness that touches everyone's life, even the pinched life of the Judge's brother, Richard, who rebukes Marmaduke for expressing himself wildly on the subject of the wild. The

English-born servant, Benjamin Penguillan, regards the woods as a strange and curious place. "As he had seen all the civilized parts of the earth," Cooper writes, "he was inclined to make a trip to the wilds of America." Elizabeth Temple looks at a stand of trees and sees "endless forests." Bumppo regards the same trees and tells her "these be nothing to a man that's used to the wilderness."

The Pioneers begins with violence and hinges on a series of violent incidents, but it turns into a frontier fairy tale replete with a series of happy endings. Bumppo and Temple join forces and Cooper explains that Bumppo's "rapid movements preceded the pursuit which Judge Temple both ordered and conducted." Cooper wants Bumppo to be "the foremost in that band of pioneers, who are opening the way for the march of the nation across the continent." But he couldn't allow his plebian hero to lead a patrician. He had to place in Judge Temple's hands the power to direct Bumppo in much the same way that a conductor in a symphony would direct the performance of an opera. The metaphor of the conductor fits Cooper as the author of *The Pioneers*, an operatic tale that's set in the open air in which each and every character comes forward and performs his or her aria.

Like the settlers in *The Pioneers*, the unsettled Bumppo has to learn to occupy his own appointed place in both the settlement and in the wilderness. While he must lead everyone else on the cross-continental march across the country itself, he also has to be under Judge Temple's thumb. To borrow one of Cooper's images, he's a "link in the great social chain of the American continent." Every character in the Bumppo novels knows his or her place or is reprimanded and punished for violating it, whether they're lascivious Indians, counterfeiters or coquettes.

Cooper must have known in his heart that Bumppo and Temple couldn't co-exist and that his frontiersman had to go into the forest, while his judge had to remain in the settlement. West is

West and East is West; the twain shall only meet briefly. In town, Bumppo is outclassed by the judge; in the wilderness the judge is outgunned by Bumppo.

Significantly, Cooper affixed to *The Pioneers*, four lines from James K. Paulding's epic poem *The Backwoodsman:* "Extremes of habits, manners, time and, space,/ brought close together, here stood face to face,/ And gave at once a contrast to the view,/That other lands, and ages never knew." Like Paulding, Cooper believed in a literary version of the phenomenon that's come to be known as "American exceptionalism." Only in America, Paulding and Cooper believed, did extremes meet face-to-face without casusing violence. Only in America did extremes provide aesthetically pleasing scenes.

Throughout the *Leatherstocking Tales*, Bumppo — the unattached bachelor — plunges into the wilderness and emerges from it. In each and every book and in incident after incident, he abandons his paleface kinsmen, fights redskins in the forest, and returns to the settlements. He goes away and he comes back, shuttling between the two polarities in his universe, unable to surrender his ties to either node or to the values they represent. Time and again he says, as he does for example in *The Pioneers*, "I crave to go into the woods." He adds, "I'm weary of living in clearings, and where the hammer is sounding in my ears from sun-rise to sun-down."

Cooper echoed his hero's sentiments nowhere more emphatically than in Paris. "Now my longing is for a wilderness," he wrote in a letter in which he outlined his plans for a forest retreat. "Cooperstown is far too populous and artificial for me and it is my intention to plunge somewhere into the forest, for six months in the year, at my return," he explained. "I will not quit my own state, but I shall seek some unsettled part of that."

More than any other place, Paris prompted him to appreciate

the American wilderness. Paris, he insisted, was "the peopled wilderness" and a "vast receptacle of selfishness, of gaiety without heart and vanity without pride." For most of his life, Cooper lived in cities and settlements, though he also saw them as Bumppo did, as artificial worlds that lacked true heart and natural beauty.

At the very end of *The Pioneers*, Bumppo sets out for the wilderness once again. His dogs crouch at his feet as though he's an American Ulysses bound on an *Odyssey* across the trackless tracts of the wilderness. Here, Bumppo stands "on the verge of the wood." He draws his hand across his eyes — to wipe away his tears — then waves an "adieu." (He knows French from the French and Indian Wars.) He pauses for a moment and then enters "the forest." The newlyweds Elizabeth Temple and Oliver Effingham watch him as he vanishes, they think forever. "This was the last that they ever saw of the Leather-stocking," Cooper wrote, hoping that readers would pull out their handkerchiefs and wipe away their own tears.

The wilderness is a kind of fire-breathing dragon that Bumppo must engage with and defeat in battle after battle even as he rescues victims from its jaws. Cooper calls Bumppo the "Liberator," though in *The Deerslayer, or The First War-Path* (1841), he relishes his captivity and, in an ecstasy of masochism worthy of a Christian martyr, he invites his Indian captors to inflict pain on his body and his soul. Not surprisingly, the tone of the novels — with the exception of *The Pioneers* — tends to be dark. Horror follows anxiety, which, in turn, is followed by more anxiety, and then even more horror. And around and around the plot goes. No character can feel safe for long in the *Leatherstocking Tales*, and, like the eternally vigilant comic book hero Superman, Bumppo has no choice but to fight "a never ending battle for truth, justice and the American way."

In *The Deerslayer*, which is probably the bleakest novel in the series, Judith Hutter recognizes that Bumppo is "self-destructive." She doesn't understand that his ordeal and his suffering are necessary for his rite of passage from boyhood into manhood and secular sainthood. "I am your prisoner," he tells his Indian captors. "Act your will." For American democracy to thrive, Cooper suggests, it must be crucified on the cross of the pagan wilderness, just as the hero must prove himself again and again in a series of repeated stations of the cross. If he's Adam and Moses, he's also a frontier Jesus. There's almost always a hostage crisis in the Leatherstocking series, and, while one crisis is resolved, another arrives. Indians — the eternal terrorists of the woods — are never defeated once and for all. The war goes on and on.

At the end of *The Last of the Mohicans*, the English troops help save the half-sisters: the impure Dora, who is the daughter of an Anglo father and a West Indian mother; and the alabaster Alice Munro, who is as pure as virgin snow. Bumppo rescues them twice, though in the last chapter he describes them as "buried in the vast forests." Cooper's answer to the sinister forests that shelter "evil" Indians is defoliation. Remove the leaves and the trees themselves, he suggests, and the Indians will have nowhere to hide. Bumppo defeats guerrilla war by using the tactics of counterinsurgency; he turns the strategies of his enemies against them and uses the woods as his own hiding place and the trees as weapons.

In *The Pioneers*, Cooper heralds "the march of civilization." Near the start of *The Last of the Mohicans*, he celebrates "the progress of the American nation." In *The Prairie*, he explains that the United States has "restored peace to these wild scenes." In *The Pathfinder*, he borrows the language of the Puritans and speaks of "the wonderful means by which Providence is clearing the way for the advancement of civilization across the whole American continent." Deep down, however, Cooper didn't swallow the twin pills of progress and optimism that he dangles before his readers.

Old World history with all its vices unfolded in the New World, he insisted. The ancient Romans were reincarnated as redskins and nearly all the disorders of Europe were revisited in America. Paradise is nearly always lost and diabolical redskins — the "rude and fierce tenants of the forest" — conspire "like their more nurtured brethren of the court and the camp."

When all is said and done, noble savages, Cooper suggests, are no better or no worse than jaded European nobility. Extremes met. Wherever he looked — whether in the wilderness or in the town — Cooper saw the "folly of man." In *The Prairie*, Bumppo complains that, "an accursed band of choppers and loggers will... humble the wilderness...on the banks of the Mississippi." *The Deerslayer* ends on a profoundly pessimistic note that reflects Cooper's world-weariness and growing disillusionment with American democracy. "We live in a world of transgressions and selfishness," he wrote.

No character, certainly not Bumppo, evades catastrophe. At the end of his life, he's further west and further removed from civilization than ever before, but the further west he moves, the further human nature devolves into barbarism. In *The Prairie*, the pioneering family of Ishmael Bush — his wife Esther, and their "seven sledge hammer sons" — roams the Great Plains kidnapping, holding hostages and pillaging. Cooper took the captivity narrative into the West. In *The Pathfinder*, the depraved white hunters Hurry Harry and Tom Hutter scalp Indians for financial rewards and without a sense of remorse. To evade one's conscience, Cooper writes, one must harden it until no human feelings remain.

One might say that Bumppo has a death wish and carries about him the aroma of the grave. Thirteen years after Cooper interred him in the cold pages of *The Prairie*, he brought him back, apologetically, in *The Pathfinder*. "After so long an interval," he admitted, he was afraid "to recall to life" a character whom he had "regularly consigned to the grave." A sense of mortality infuses *The Pathfinder,* the book in which Cooper calls the West "an unpeopled desert" and observes that human beings "affect to search for truth, while in reality we are only fortifying prejudice."

"Life is an obligation which friends often owe each other in the wilderness," Bumppo explains. In fact, Cooper couldn't imagine his hero alone in the wilderness. Bumppo needs the companionship of Chingackgook much as Chingachgook needs him, though they do not "sit night after night around the campfire in the purest domestic bliss," as Leslie Fiedler insisted in his landmark 1948 *Partisan Review* essay, "Come Back to the Raft Ag'in, Huck Honey!"

The only interracial physical affection in the Leatherstocking novels is between the women characters. The men barely touch one another, though in *The Last of the Mohicans,* Chingachgook, the sole surviving Indian in the tribe, stands over the body of his mortally wounded son, and with Bumppo at his side, sheds "scalding tears." Death is a collective fate in *The Last of the Mohicans* — the 1826 historical novel in which Cooper returns to the French and Indian wars of the 1750s and portrays the wilderness as a vast graveyard.

To write *The Last of the Mohicans,* Cooper drew on (largely unreliable) accounts of the battle that took place at Fort William Henry, borrowing what he wanted to create the impression that redskins, not palefaces, slaughtered innocent women and children. "The soil," he wrote, was "fattened with human blood." In his 1828 nonfiction book, *Notions of the Americans,* Cooper observed that "as a rule, the red man disappears before the superior moral and physical influence of the white, just as I believe the black man will eventually do the same." In the Introduction to *The Last of the Mohicans,* he wrote that "the red man has entirely deserted this part of the state," as though Indians departed from New York freely, voluntarily. Then, too, like Jack London, he created Indian characters who accept their own imminent demise as the natural law of the universe. "There will soon be no red-skin in the country," Chingachgook says in *The Pioneers*. How much better, Cooper thought, to have Indians foretell their own end then to have whites brazenly proclaim it. That would be bad manners.

AUDUBON & DE TOCQUEVILLE

John James Audubon (1785-1851), the ornithologist and artist, and Alexis de Tocqueville (1805-1859), the author of *Democracy in America,* shared many of Cooper's views about the wild and the wilderness. De Tocqueville spent just nine months touring the United States. Audubon lived for decades in his adopted country, much of the time wandering through forests, shooting and killing birds and then painting their portraits in his studio.

Audubon and de Tocqueville both wondered why Americans weren't as outraged as *they* were by the spectacle of death and destruction. Both agreed that commerce and the almighty dollar were to blame for the fall of the forests; in America, de Tocqueville insisted, commerce was imbued with "a sort of heroism" that just didn't exist in Europe. "The love of money," he wrote, reigned more supremely in the U.S. than elsewhere in the world. Audubon echoed de Tocqueville. Deer, caribou and all other game were killed for the dollar, he wrote, though he noted Americans also killed for sport.

Audubon's art was ecological; it aimed to preserve the birds of America, many of them, as he knew from his own observations, bound for extinction by "the destroyer, man." In Audubon's celebrated portraits, birds appear to be in their natural settings perched on twigs or branches, as though resting before or after flight. In fact, as he explains in an essay entitled "My Style of Drawing Birds," he shot and killed the birds he painted — sometimes as many as 100 in a day — and then with wires and pins arranged the wings, heads and tails to make them appear "as if full of life." To conjure the wild he first had to kill it. That, too, was an American way.

Audubon also painted vivid portraits in words. In his essays about the environment, he documented awesome beauty and terrible destruction. On the coast of Labrador, he witnessed the wanton theft of birds' eggs and predicted that, "these wonderful nurseries will be entirely destroyed, unless some kind of government will interfere to stop the shameful destruction." That was a novel idea: government protection of the environment. A bold and original thinker, Audubon explained in the essay, "The Eggers of Labrador," that the first people to rue the disappearance of wild animals are often the same people who murder them.

In a hundred years, he predicted, nature would be "robbed of many brilliant charms" and "the timid deer will exist nowhere, fish will no longer abound in the rivers, the eagle scarce ever alight." Gazing dejectedly at the Ohio and Mississippi rivers, he watched the carcasses of dead buffalo float downstream and observed that they had been "murdered in senseless play." Forests were leveled and species decimated nearly everywhere Audubon turned. Moreover, he noted that the white settler "rifles home, food, clothing," and life itself from the Indians — or "aborigines" as he called them — who perished, not from the consumption of alcohol, as many suggested, but from starvation and the loss of the abundant wild life that the white man killed.

Though he was born in Haiti and reared in France, he seemed perfectly at home in the American wilderness, even when he was without human companionship. "La Forêt Audubon," he called himself. In Europe he earned the epithet "the Woodsman from America." Birds were his near-constant companions and his "near-mania," as he described it. He felt an affinity for birds and frequently depicted himself as a bird-like creature; a "winged pheasant," he called himself on one occasion. On another, he wrote, "I stood motionless as a heron."

Audubon's love affair with the forests of America, its birds
and beasts intensified during his lengthy sojourn in industrial
England, especially in "smoky Manchester" with its "noise and
tumult" and the constant "whirring sound of machinery." He
appreciated the "perfection of manners" in English society and
enjoyed the mountains of Scotland where he visited Sir Walter
Scott — America's favorite early nineteenth-century novelist —
but he longed to return to "the forest and feast my eyes on their
beautiful inhabitants." Perhaps because he felt at home in forests,
he empathized with people who were terrified by the wilds. He
understood that "a person bewildered" in a forest might become
easily confused and mistake the trunks of decaying trees for "some
wondrous and fearful being."

In 1821, in the swamps of Louisiana, Audubon met a fugitive
African-American slave, or "Negro," as he called him, and quickly
realized that the wilderness provided him and his family with a
sanctuary outside the plantation. Frederick Douglass painted a
similar picture in *Narrative of the Life of Frederick Douglass, an
American Slave* (1845) in which the woods are the only place
where slaves can express themselves without fear of punishment.
"They would make the dense old woods, for miles around, rever-
berate with their wild songs, revealing at once the highest joy
and the deepest sadness," Douglass wrote. "They would compose
and sing as they went along, consulting neither time nor tune."
Douglass also described the woods as a punishing place where
slaves were "stung by scorpions, chased by wild beasts, bitten by
snakes...suffering hunger and nakedness."

Like Douglass, Harriet Jacobs (1813-1897) depicted her
plight on a plantation and her delight in the woods in her memoir,
Incidents in the Life of a Slave Girl (1861). Writing under the pen
name Linda Brent, she described the institution of slavery as a

"wild beast" and a "vile monster" that preyed on all black people
and especially on black women. For seven years, Jacobs hid from
her white masters in the attic of her grandmother's home, then
escaped from the South and joined abolitionists in the North. In
Incidents in the Life of a Slave Girl, she remembered that slaves
"built a little church in the woods" and that they "had no higher
happiness than to meet there and sing hymns together, and pour
out their hearts in spontaneous prayer."

After Nat Turner's rebellion in Virginia in 1831, planters
across the South outlawed churches in the woods. Then, too, after
Turner's rebellion was crushed, woods and trees increasingly presented African Americans with dual associations. Southern mobs
lynched black men and left their bodies to hang from the limbs of
trees. The legacy of lynching prompted the teacher and songwriter
Abel Meeropol to write and the blues singer Billie Holiday to sing
her best-known song with the ominous title, "Strange Fruit." For
the Black Muslims, Elijah Muhammad and Malcolm X, when he
belonged to the Nation of Islam, the U.S. worshipped at the shrine
of the "blue-eyed devil white man" and African Americans were
held captive in the "wilderness of North America." To find their
own authentic black selves and liberate themselves, they would have
to topple the devil and escape the wilderness, Malcolm X insisted.

In the years before the Civil War, American writers notoriously failed to see slavery as a political and economic system. Then,
too, they rarely empathized with African Americans, though there
were notable exceptions, including Harriet Beecher Stowe, the
author of *Uncle Tom's Cabin*, a masterpiece of melodrama and
propoganda. In 1838, Cooper argued against the abolition of
slavery and predicted the coming of a "war of extermination" in
which whites would eliminate all blacks from the United States.
He wasn't sorry to think that they would all vanish. Audubon
expressed far more empathy than Cooper.

In his essay, "The Runaway," he touts his own efforts to persuade a slave master not to breakup an African American family. But he felt powerless to prevent the decimation of the wilderness and the destruction of the American Indians. In "The Wreckers of Florida," he offers a lament for a murdered Indian and by inference all other slain Indians. "Would that I could restore to thee thy birthright, thy natural independence," he writes. "But the irrevocable deed is done, and I can merely admire the perfect symmetry of his frame."

Audubon disliked the "greedy mills" that devoured the forests and turned trees into lumber, but he saw no way to stop the logging and milling. He envisioned a day when "crowded cities" would rise along the banks of the Mississippi River and when "enlightened nations will rejoice in the bounties of Providence." That attitude was nearly all-pervasive all through America in the nineteenth century.

As an interloper in America, de Tocqueville was more emotionally detached than Audubon, though he was among the most candid and discerning of nineteenth-century travelers. In *Democracy in America,* first published in France in 1835 and in the United States in 1838, he claimed that Americans "perceive the admirable forests that surround them only at the moment at which they fall by their strokes." Europeans were far more appreciative of the "marvels" of the wilderness than Americans, he insisted.

"I never gave in to the temptation to tailor facts to ideas rather than to adapt ideas to facts," he explained. "Sometimes," he wrote, "man advances so quickly that the wilderness re-appears behind him." That was a singularly hopeful sign. Typically, he noted that state governments acted like "companies of merchants formed to exploit the wilderness lands."

In *Democracy in America,* de Tocqueville also describes the continent before the arrival of Europeans when Indians inhabited the "wild woods of the New World" and exhibited an "intractable

love of independence." De Tocqueville plunged bravely into the
woods, and, though he was distressed by the destruction he saw,
he also marveled at pioneer customs and culture, and at American
bravery, innovation and ingenuity. On the frontier, he was taken
aback by the presence and the astounding poise of young women
once reared in "rich dwellings" who lived in simple cabins in the
middle of forests. Then, too, he saw the cabin in the woods as a
microcosm of American society: "a little world" and "the arc of
civilization" that extended across a vast territory.

De Tocqueville was struck by the "profound silence" that
reigned in the wilderness of North America," and, while he was sad-
dened by the destruction he saw, he argued that civilization would
inevitably triumph. Confident, too, that a vital culture would spring
from American soil, he predicted that American authors would write
books with "immense and incoherent images, overloaded depic-
tions, and bizarre composites." De Tocqueville added that "fantastic beings" would issue from the American imagination. Then, too,
"order" and "regularity" would be absent from the literature.

For Audubon, America itself was a fantastic place without
order, without regularity and without a settled quality. In 1820,
he looked back and explained in an essay entitled "The Ohio" that
he could scarcely believe what he saw. The land that had been in
"a state of nature" was "now more or less covered with villages,
farms, and towns, where the din of hammers and machinery is
constantly heard." Woods disappeared "under the axe by day and
the fire by night." Steamboats glided along rivers and the "surplus
population of Europe" aided and abetted the "destruction of the
forest." He wasn't sure, he wrote, "whether these changes are for
the better or for the worse."

What distressed him, too, was that there was "no satisfac-
tory account" in works of fiction about the transformation of the
continent. Why was that, he wondered? American writers were

certainly talented. "Our Irvings and our Coopers have proved themselves fully competent for the task," he insisted. "The movements of their pens" were outdistanced by reality, he concluded.

Audubon seems unreal, as his biographers have noted. In *John James Audubon: The Making of an American*, Richard Rhodes described him as the real Natty Bumppo. Shirley Streshinsky makes much the same comment in *Audubon: Life and Art in the American Wilderness*. Audubon saw himself as a character in a novel and a figure in a sketchbook. When he stopped long enough to divert his eyes from birds and looked at himself, he was startled. With his unkempt hair and unwashed face, he might have been mistaken for Robinson Crusoe, he insisted. The English artist Hogarth might have rendered a striking likeness of him.

CHAPTER 6

REDSKINS & PALEFACES

Robert Bird, Catherine Sedgwick & Lydia Maria Child

THE POVERTY OF MATERIALS

I n 1960, Wallace Stegner, the novelist, environmentalist and author of his famed "Wilderness Letter," looked back at history and concluded that American national character had been forged in the wilderness and that when the frontier ended, the literature of the United States went from "hope to bitterness." With real ire, he noted that Americans had been "the most efficient and ruthless environment-busters in history."American writers chronicled the busting of the environment, and at the same time they revived the wilderness as a hope, a dream and a memory in fiction, poetry and in nonfiction narratives such as Thoreau's *A Week on the Concord and Merrimack Rivers* and *Walden*.

In the nineteenth century, essayists, travel writers and historians joined the chorus of novelists in a literary movement that explored life out-of-doors and in the open air. William Cullen Bryant, Cooper's friend, wrote about Nature with a capital N. In

1834, after a trip to Illinois, he offered his own version of land-scape painting in "The Prairies," a long mournful poem about the "butchered" Indians and the slaughtered bison. The poem ends with an indelible image: "And I am in the wilderness alone."

Cooper consciously and deliberately blazed a literary trail "Westward Ho," to borrow a well-worn phrase used first in 1604, then in an 1832 novel by James K. Paulding and in a 1935 film staring John Wayne. In 1820, the year in which he vowed to become an "American writer" and create "a manly independent literature," Cooper explained to Andrew Goodrich, a Manhattan bookseller, that he wanted to make "American Manners and American Scenes" interesting to American readers. In the open-ing pages of *The Pioneers*, he fulfilled no small part of his prom-ise when he offered a bird's-eye view of rural American scenes: "Academies, and minor edifices of learning" along with "manu-facturing" and "farms" that nestled in the "romantic and pictur-esque" countryside. Cooper also aimed to satisfy Europeans who expected, he wrote, that an American work would show them "churches, academies, wild beasts, savages, beautiful women, steam-boats, and ships." He loved lists. In the Bumppo series he proved that he could write genuine American books that were read at home and abroad. He gave the lie to Sidney Smith's 1820 mocking statement in the prestigious *Edinburgh Review*: "In the four corners of the globe, who reads an American book?"

Curiously, Cooper quickly burned out on American scenes. In *Notions of the Americans*, his first work of nonfiction, he com-plained about the emptiness of American life and the "poverty of materials" — a phrase that would haunt him for years and make him seem like a born complainer. Wearing his high hat, Cooper insisted famously that in the United States, there were "no annals for the historian; no follies…for the satirist; no manners for the dramatist; no obscure fictions for the writer of romance…nor any

of the rich artificial auxiliaries of poetry." In his role as patriarch
and patrician, he felt he was entitled to rag on his own country —
for the good of the country.

Crèvecoeur offered a list similar to Cooper's in his *Letters
from an American Farmer*. Hawthorne and James would provide
their own lists. It was part of the national character to look from
America to Europe and then back again with a sad face and lament
the cultural emptiness in the United States. Independence from
England was well and good, but it also cut off Americans, writers
felt, from the rich soil of English culture and history.

Cooper's list of the items that he suggested were missing from
America has caused so much consternation among cultural critics that it probably makes sense to explain what he did and didn't
mean. He didn't believe that the United States provided no materials for a writer. All through the *Leatherstocking Tales*, he makes it
clear that ample literary materials might be found most everywhere.
In *The Pathfinder*, Bumppo gazes at the woods and says, "These are
our streets and houses; our churches and palaces." America was different and it was also the same; Europe's opposite, twin and double
had equivalents for everything Europe had. Still, in *The Pathfinder*,
Cooper couldn't let Bumppo's voice be the only one on the subject
of American culture and landscapes. A sailor who has journeyed far
and wide looks at the shore along one of America's inland seas and
expresses "disgust at there being no light-houses, church-towers,
beacons, or roadsteads with their shipping."

There were absences on the American horizon, Cooper
allowed, but that didn't translate into European moral superiority to America. In *Notions of the Americans*, he insists that what
made the United States an improvement over Europe was the
blend of "the conveniences of civilized life with the remains of
the wilderness." Overcivilization was in his eyes as noxious as
undercivilization. Moreover, despite his criticism of America as a

nation in which "public opinion" was a "Despot," he enjoyed natural American ways above artificial European customs. When he said that the United States had no "Annals," "follies," "obscure fictions" and "artificial auxiliaries," he spoke ironically. Who would want the artificial and the obscure? Not Fenimore Cooper. His father had written his own annals of colonial history, *A Guide in the Wilderness* (1810), and beat his son into the woods.

"In 1785, I visited the rough and hilly country of Otsego, where there existed not an inhabitant, nor any trace of a road," William Cooper wrote. "I was alone three hundred miles from home, without bread, meat, or food of any kind; fire and fishing tackle were my only means of subsistence." He added, "I laid me down to sleep in my watch-coat, nothing but the melancholy Wilderness around me." That was real wilderness even by Wallace Stegner's 1960's standards. Annals of his father's sort didn't count as real literature for Fenimore Cooper. They were too factual and far less fanciful to satisfy his taste. In his father's narrative there was too much "I": "I visited," "I caught," "I laid me down," and the embarrassing admission, "I was alone."

In June 1826 when he set sail for Europe with his wife and children, Cooper felt he'd already conquered the New World; now, he wanted to conquer the Old World. For Cooper, America represented democracy, the future and independent pioneers, while Europe represented feudalism, the past and deferential knights. America boasted the wild while Europe boasted ruins of former civilizations. The Old World looked ripe for him to plunder. As a writer, he felt that he had as much a right to exploit France, Italy and Germany for materials as did any European. He excavated the European past in three novels that he cranked out in rapid succession: *The Bravo* (1831), set in eighteenth-century Venice; *The Heidenmauer* (1832), set in sixteenth-century Germany, and *The Headsman* (1832), which he placed in eighteenth-century Switzerland.

Once he'd proved to himself and others that he could write about Europe, he grew bored with Europe and Europeans, returned to the United States, and insisted that he would retire from writing. To his South Carolina friend, William Gilmore Simms, he explained, "If I were a young man, I would either transport myself to a part of the world where literature has some rights and is honored or throw away my pen altogether." In another letter, he complained, "We serve a hard master, my dear Sir, in writing for America."

In America in the 1830s and 1840s, he became increasingly conservative and even reactionary. What mattered most to him now wasn't the freedom of the woods or the liberty of unsettled lands, but the rights and privileges that belonged to owners of private property, especially his own. "When property ceases to be protected, the door is open to barbarism," he exclaimed. "Even savages respect these rights." He added that, "literary property... is as much entitled to be protected, as houses, lands, and merchandize."

A stickler for legal details, he concerned himself now with the exactness of copyright law, not with literary distinctions between fancy and the imagination. Now, he meant business. "Unless we have a copyright law, there will be no such thing as American Literature," he wrote. At home after his sojourn in Europe, he hired lawyers and sued newspaper editors who published negative reviews of his books and his own character. In *The Morning Courier* and *New York Enquirer*, James Watson Webb called Cooper "a base minded caitiff who has traduced his country for filthy lucre and from low born spleen." Webb was indicted for libel by the Otsego County grand jury. Reviews of his books lost him a small fortune, Cooper complained. Those same reviews bruised his ego. "We shall bring the press again, under the subjection of the law," he wrote, and sounded very much like Judge Temple and President John Adams, too, who signed the Alien and the Sedition Acts into law.

At his best, Cooper had been *both* a "paleface" and a "redskin," to borrow the two categories that the critic Philip Rahv had borrowed from Cooper and used in a benchmark essay entitled "Paleface and Redskin," published in 1939 in the *Kenyon Review.* For Rahv, there were two schools of American literature: the palefaces who were patricians, highbrow, cerebral and snobbish; and the redskins who were plebian, lowbrow and sentimental. "The national literature suffers from the ills of a split personality," Rahv wrote. The very next year he published a retraction of sorts and explained that, "the contrast between the two archetypal Americans may be said to have been overdrawn."

Anyone who looked closely at Cooper's work would see that he had several personae, as highbrow and lowbrow, gentleman of quiet refinements and frontiersman with sentimental feelings. Near the end of his life, he looked back at his work — more than fifty books — and concluded that in the highbrow, lowbrow Bumppo books he had reached his peak. "If any thing from the pen of the writer," he wrote, "is at all to outlive himself, it is, unquestionably, the series of 'The Leather-stocking Tales.'" Writers, he noted astutely, were not the best judges of their own work, but in this case he judged as well if not better than any reviewer or literary critic in his own day. Until the end, he was attached to Bumppo — as he explained in 1850 to William Cullen Bryant, whose friendship went back to the 1820s when they were budding young writers in New York, tied together by a love of books and by an abiding curiosity about Indians and the wild. "He was contemplating," Bryant would remember, "another Leatherstocking tale, deeming that he had not yet exhausted the character."

When Cooper died in 1851 at the age of 61, America and the American language were not the same as they had been in 1789, the year he was born. Of Cooper, Conrad observed that, "he wrote before the great American language was born."

Cooper himself noted the revolution that took place in the American language in his own lifetime: the words "boss" and "help" replaced "master" and "servant." Behind those linguistic changes were vast social transformations that unnerved him. His ideal nation, he insisted, would be marked by "regularity," "neatness" and "quietude." What he liked least in a society or an individual were what he called extremes and excesses. "The French Revolution led to so many excesses," he fumed.

Relieved that Americans hadn't imitated the French and gone wild in cobblestone streets, he praised his countrymen and women because they demonstrated "an admirable respect for the laws and the institutions of their country." Not always. Slaves, farmers and mechanists had rebelled, resisted and protested their plight, their taxes, their working conditions and their servitude at one time or another, going back to the 1790s and even before. White men would riot in the streets of New York in 1863 in the midst of the Civil War to protest the draft, prompting Melville to write in "A Night Piece" that, "the Town is taken by its rats." Cooper would have felt much the same as Melville. At his best, he was a genuine democrat who recognized that it "was very possible to live in a gilded palace...and still have a strong flavor of barbarity about one and all." At his best, he expressed the secular humanism of his age, as when he noted that, "There can be no true humanity...until man comes to treat and consider man as his fellow."

At his worst, Cooper expressed the chauvinisms, jingoisms and prejudices of his age, as when he noted that African Americans belonged to an "inferior class" and that Indians were "a stunted, dirty and degraded race." For all his emphasis on "futurity," he never saw the advent of the Civil War that would transform the nation, destroy much of the South, and bring unprecedented ecological disaster to the U.S., as Stephen Crane (1871-1900) and other authors recognized. No one expressed it more poetically than Crane. In *The Red Badge of Courage* (1895), he wrote, "Bullets began to whistle among branches and nip at the trees...It was as if a thousand axes, wee and invisible, were being wielded." No axe does as much damage in the Bumppo books as the guns and bullets in *Red Badge.*

HECKEWELDER

Cooper knew more about Indians than he knew about African Americans, though even there his knowledge was limited. In 1827, in Paris, he informed a European duchess that he'd met two Indians on the Great Plains: one "a chief of great dignity"; the other a man who "would have been a hero in any civilized nation." In France, a nation enamored of noble savages, his tales of Indians in the American West stood him in good stead. Cooper's novels might have offered more complex portraits of Indians if only he made advantageous use of John Heckewelder's *An Account of the History, Manners and Customs of the Indian Nations* (1819), perhaps the most reliable account of Indian life in the early nineteenth century. Cooper read the book and chose to ignore it, or else reject almost all the information it contained.

An English-born missionary, Heckewelder (1743-1823) lived with and observed Indians closely for thirty years. At the start of *An Account,* he addresses the reader directly and explains that he means to "rise above the cloud of prejudice" that surrounded Indians. For the most part, he succeeded, though at times, he idealized the "ancient Arcadia" the Indians inhabited before the coming of white men. Cooper reworked the information he found in *An Account,* turning it inside out and upside down. Heckewelder minimized the "bloody wars" between rival tribes and downplayed the cruelties Indians inflicted on one another, though he didn't deny them. He also accused whites of genocide and charged them with complicity in "acts of cruelty and injustice" perpetrated by Indians against other Indians. Cooper refused to accept that perspective.

Cooper might have recognized himself in a memorable and discerning passage in *An Account*. Writing about whites, Heckewelder observed that the "Imagination is immediately at work to paint" the Indians "as a species of monsters, to whom cruelty is an appetite; a sort of human shaped tigers and panthers." In *The Last of the Mohicans*, Cooper describes an Indian who takes a paleface baby from its mother and bashes its head against a tree. He found that incident in Heckewelder. In *An Account*, the killer is a white man and the baby is an Indian. Heckewelder claimed to have heard the story from the killer himself who wrenched the child "from its mother's arms and taking it by the legs dashed its head against a tree, so that the brains flew out all around."

Heckewelder was not alone in defending Indian virtues and exposing white vices. The New England author Lydia Howard Huntley Sigourney recounted Indian legend and history in *Traits of the Aborigines* (1822) and in *Pocahantas and other Poems* (1841) that helped to make Pocahantas as well known as John Smith. The author of nearly seventy books, Sigourney aimed to rewrite the history of the continent and to accord dignity to African Americans, Indians and the landscape itself, in poems such as "Fallen Forests" in which she describes "Man's warfare on the trees." In "The Indian Welcome to the Pilgrim Fathers" Sigourney imagines the initial contact that took place between whites and natives. With both pathos and passion, she addresses the Indians as the "Poor outcast from thy forest wild."

Increasingly, Indians didn't leave it to whites to preserve the historical record. Indeed, they took it upon themselves to record their own annihilation and the destruction of the environment.

One anonymous Indian insisted, "They would make slaves of us if they could, but as they cannot do it, they kill us!" He added that the whites would call an Indian friend and brother and "at the same moment destroy him." George W. Harkin, a chief of the Choctaw, described "the mountain of prejudice" that weighed against the American Indian and the habitual ways that whites "obstructed the streams of justice." There was an image that hinted at the harm to waterways as well as violations of human and civil rights. Jane Johnston Schoolcraft, the daughter of an Indian mother and an Irish father, told and retold Indian legends. She also recounted in both English and Ojibwe the "pain and the sickness" of her native land. William Apess, a Wampanoag from Rhode Island, chronicled his own individual quest for freedom and the decline and fall of his tribe in *A Son of the Forest* (1829). (Not surprisingly, he didn't call himself "a son of the wilderness.") For Apess, whites introduced "the fatal and exterminating diseases of civilized life." By 1829, the evidence against the virus of civilization was overwhelming. Moreover, the attachments to it and to its ubiquitous "things," as Emerson would have called them, and to its "toys," as Williams would have said, were nearly unbreakable.

ROMANCING THE WILD

Cooper's friend and fellow writer William Gilmore Simms wrote about South Carolina history, and not surprisingly, he felt personally offended by Cooper's lament about the so-called poverty of materials in the United States. In an 1842 essay, Simms insisted that creative American writers didn't need an abundance of raw materials from the past or the present, close to home or far away. If writers exercised their imaginations, Simms insisted, they could build mountains out of proverbial molehills. "Possessed of the requisite resources of imagination," he wrote, the fiction writer "needs but a slender skein of raw material...out of which he fabricates the divine and most enduring works of art."

Simms did more than praise the imagination. He also proposed a theory about literature in the United States that put it on an equal footing with English literature. In 1853, in an introduction to his own frontier novel, *The Yemassee*, Simms called the American "romance" a "substitute...for the ancient epic." *Gilgamesh* resurfaced in America. He also argued that it was fundamentally different from the domestic novel as written by Samuel Richardson and Henry Fielding. By "romance" he didn't mean a love story that involved courtship and marriage, though his and Cooper's narratives include amorous relationships between men and women. For Simms and Cooper, the attraction between man and woman was superseded by the attraction between hero and wilderness.

The traditional English novel, Simms explained, confined itself "to the felicitous narration of common and daily occurring events, and the grouping and delineation of characters in ordinary conditions of society." Curiously, George Sand noted much the same quality in Cooper's work. Like Sir Walter Scott, whom she admired, Cooper had the art, she wrote, "of grouping, moving apart, bringing together, and finally reintegrating incidents and characters." For Sand, it didn't matter what label — novels, tales or narratives — one assigned Cooper's work. Moreover, she didn't distinguish between fancy and the imagination. Indeed, she was sure that Cooper had a vivid imagination and that Bumppo was "a creation which raises Cooper above himself." For Sand as for Balzac, it was Cooper's ability to conjure moods and to create enduring characters that made his work stand out. She added that his painting with words brought him into the orbit of the Flemish masters and the school of "literary-landscape painters"— as Balzac had described it.

For Simms as for Cooper, romance as a genre and the wilderness as a unique American place were inextricably entwined. Writers of romance didn't seek "common and daily occurring events," he argued, but rather "adventures among the wild and wonderful." With Cooper's work in mind, Simms insisted that the romance "does not confine itself to what is known, or even what is probable. It grasps at the possible." He also noted that the romance places "a human agent in hitherto untried situations" and exercises "its ingenuity in extricating him from them, while describing his feelings and his fortunes in his progress." Indeed, much of the verve of Cooper's fiction derives from the feelings that well up from inside and sweep over his resourceful hero, whether he's in captivity, in battle or engaged in conversation with a woman. Common, ordinary events — the bedrock of English fiction according to Simms — take place in the Bumppo books, especially when the setting is a settlement not a forest. When Elizabeth Temple engages Bumppo in a conversation about the wilderness they're in a domestic English novel. When she's alone in the forest threatened by a wild beast she's in a romance. Cooper wanted both the American romance and the English novel.

Simms's theory of the romance, while intriguing to readers in the 1850s, might have been lost in the annals of nineteenth-century American literary criticism if it were not for Richard Chase, who revived it more than one hundred years later and gave it renewed currency in *The American Novel and Its Tradition*. "The main difference between the novel and the romance is in the way in which they view reality," Chase wrote. He added that romance "feels free to render reality in less volume and detail." Like Simms, Chase connected the romance to the "borderland…between civilization and the wilderness." To buttress his argument, he turned to Hawthorne, who consciously and deliberately wrote romances and who noted that in the romance "the Actual and the Imaginary may meet."

In *Studies in Classic American Literature,* Lawrence didn't debate nomenclature. His two chapters on Cooper are entitled respectively, "Fenimore Cooper's White Novels" and "Fenimore Cooper's Leatherstocking Novels." In his second chapter on Cooper, he describes *The Last of the Mohicans* as a work "divided between real historical narrative and true 'romance.'" Lawrence added that he preferred Cooper's romances to his historical narratives because they expressed "myth meaning," perhaps the highest praise he assigned to any work of fiction.

INDIAN HATERS, INDIAN LOVERS

In the first quarter of the nineteenth century, women writers adopted and adapted the romance as a genre, which meant that they eschewed the probable, explored the possible, and placed their characters — both male and female — in lawless woods and on raging frontiers. The two major nineteenth-century women writers of romance in the United States — Lydia Maria Child and Catharine Sedgwick — borrowed from the English novel and introduced English characters into American landscapes as though American stories had to include English characters. Child in *Hobomonk* and Sedgwick in *Hope Leslie* feminized the wilderness, domesticated it and at the same time worshipped it as a goddess. By stretching the gendered boundaries of the borderland, they also expanded the reading public to include women.

That their books were popular and then largely disappeared for decades says more about the power of the literary patriarchy in the nineteenth century than it does about their own talent or the seriousness with which they practiced the art of fiction. In the 1830s, the stories that men told one another — and everyone else in the nation who would listen — were largely about white hunters, killers, trappers and explorers who went into the wilderness alone, or in packs with other men. In 1823, the American frontier author Edwin James wrote about an all-male expedition from Pittsburgh to the Rocky Mountains, under the command of Major Stephen H. Long. He noted "a manifest propensity, particularly in the males, to remove westward, for which it is not easy to account." Women removed westward, too, and women writers portrayed their heroism but men stole the show.

Of all the borderland writers of romance, including Cooper and Simms and their literary sisters and contemporaries, Child and Sedgwick, Robert Montgomery Bird (1806-1854) stands out as the outlier in the group. Like the hero in *Nick of the Woods; or, Jibbenainosay* (1837) — his most popular work of fiction — Robert Bird straddled worlds. A doctor, novelist, dramatist and the literary editor of the *Philadelphia North American*, he's perhaps the strangest of the popular American writers of the 1830s. Like Cooper, Bird wanted a manly, independent literature. Like Cooper, he also placed strong male characters at the heart of his narratives and arranged female characters around them like planets orbiting the sun. A native of Pennsylvania and a fierce American patriot, Bird had an axe to grind with Cooper, especially with his portraits of Indians. Cooper's redskins struck him as unreal, inaccurate and even contemptible. It was essential, Bird felt, to show Indians as bloodthirsty savages. He also felt that it was essential to present a white protagonist who avenges white settlers victimized by Indians.

Bird's novel *Nick of the Woods* probably offers a far more damning portrait of the Indian killer than he intended. It also reads like a curious artifact of its time and place: the frontier of the 1830s when white men hunted and killed Indians and the nation wondered if hunting and killing Indians was morally right or wrong, as if debate would solve the issue. The slaughter of

Indians is the *raison d'être* of Bird's novel. The name of the hero says nearly everything about him. "Nathaniel Slaughter" is known to the Indians as the "Jibbenainosay" and to the whites as their savior, "Nick of the Woods."

Far more calculatingly than Bumppo, Slaughter slaughters for the joy of slaughtering. A lone assassin who kills under cover of darkness, he's more sinister than Bumppo, except perhaps the Bumppo who goes to war in *The Last of the Mohicans*. But even Bumppo at his most violent doesn't hate and kill all Indians. He always enjoys the company of Chingachgook. Bird didn't like the very idea that redskins and palefaces might be friends. Slaughter, his iconic protagonist, belongs in the company of the American vigilante who takes the law into his own hands in pulp fiction and popular movies such as *Dirty Harry* starring Clint Eastwood and *Death Wish* staring Charles Bronson.

In a sly preface to *Nick of the Woods*, Bird insists that his novel doesn't merely present "the appearance of truth" but rather "the truth itself." The Indians that he describes in *Nick of the Woods*, he argues, are true to life, not "beautiful unrealities and fictions merely." Bird also explains that his protagonist was based on people he knew who lived "lives of vengeance and 'Indian hating.'" They were, Bird, explains, "solitary men, bereaved fathers or orphaned sons, the sole survivors, sometimes, of exterminated households." In *Nick of the Woods*, Indians initiate violence; whites merely defend themselves against it and seek justice.

At times, Bird seems to parody Bumppo and mock his creator. It was certainly cheeky to call his character Nathaniel. In the 1830s and 1840s, readers would have been familiar with Nathaniel Bumppo. They would have made connections between the two Nathaniels, both of them foresters, both crafty creatures of the woodlands, both men of dualities — though Slaughter has an acute case of a borderline personality disorder. The line that he crosses is the line that divides whites from Indians and men of conscience from men without an iota of remorse or guilt. Unlike Bumppo, who never marries, never has a wife and children, Slaughter is a lone widower mourning the death of his wife and children.

Herman Melville knew both the Nathan Slaughters and the Nathaniel Bumppos of the world. In *Moby-Dick*, he presented in Ishmael a portrait of the white man who loves Africans, Indians and even a cannibal, so much so that he's willing to cuddle up with him in bed. In Captain Ahab, he created a despot and a monomaniac who unifies a polyglot crew and commands them to slay the white whale. The slaughter that Melville has in mind in *Moby-Dick* is the slaughter of the wilderness itself, as embodied in the leviathan of the seas.

In his novel, *The Confidence-Man: His Masquerade* (1857), published six years after *Moby-Dick*, Melville wondered how a killer of Indians could become a hero in fiction. His answer was paradoxical: the Indian hater was also an Indian lover, as ready to embrace and revere redskins as to kill them. Lawrence came to more or less the same conclusion in the 1920s when he said that, "There has been all the time, in the white American soul, a dual feeling about the Indian…the desire to extirpate the Indian. And the contradictory desire to glorify him." He added, "Both are rampant still, today."

The archetypal Indian killer that Melville describes in *The Confidence-Man* is a brooding hulk with wild impulses and crazy desires. He's an Ahab on dry land, or perhaps part Ahab and part Ishmael, a lonely outcast who seeks revenge and a lost soul who wants to embrace his Indian brothers. Melville doesn't explicitly mention Robert Montgomery Bird or his book *Nick of the Woods*, though he seems to have Bird and his novel in mind when he describes the Indian killer as a frontiersman "widowed by a tomahawk." The

Indian killer lives alone in the woods, Melville explains, because
Indian warriors have murdered his wife and children.

In the chapter entitled, "The Metaphysics of Indian-Hating,"
Melville dramatizes the precise moment when the poor, traumatized backwoodsman turns into a vengeful killer. At a campfire,
eating dinner alone, the frontiersman and hunter — a wanderer
"from wilderness to wilderness" — hears tidings about the murder
of his wife and children. Melville describes the man as he "chews
the wild news with the wild meat," carefully digesting both. The
food and the food-for-thought fortify his resolve to seek revenge.
Melville adds, as though eager to drive his point home, "From
that meal he rose an Indian-hater."

The ideas and the language are distinctly Melvillean.
Who else but Melville would turn "Indian Hating" into a
"Metaphysics." Scrupulously, Melville examines the clashing
impulses that wash over his Indian hater, then describes him as
he "hurries openly toward the first smoke, though he knows it is
an Indian's, announces himself as a lost hunter, gives the savage
his rifle, throws himself on his charity, embraces him with much
affection, imploring the privilege of living a while in his sweet
companionship." How absurd! How comic! In the same vein,
he might have imagined a French revolutionary abandoning the
guillotine and embracing an aristocrat.

Melville concludes his reflections with a literary question,
"Where does any novelist pick up any character?" His answer, "For
the most part, in town" because, as he explains, "every town is a kind
of man-show, where the novelist goes for his stock." He suggests that,
"In nearly all the original characters…there is discernable something
prevailingly local, or of the age." Nathaniel Slaughter, aka Nick of the
Woods, aka the Jibbenainosay, belongs to the antebellum American
frontier. Unlike Bumppo, he's never been more than a local figure. A
kind of skeleton in the literary closet, he's a serial killer couched by his

creator as an honorable man. Hollywood movies would elevate the type into a national hero again and again.

CHILD & SEDGWICK GO WILD

Lydia Maria Child's *Hobomok* (1824) and Catharine Sedgwick's *Hope Leslie* (1827) were both inspired by the bravado of *The Pioneers* and the dramatic clashes in *The Last of the Mohicans*. Both women wrote historical novels and morality tales set in the seventeenth century. Both look at the Puritan past through the lens of the present and at the present through the lens of the past. Young and bright and from families of privilege, Sedgwick and Child empathized with outcasts, misfits, captives and fugitives. Not surprisingly, they wrote more subversively than Cooper.

In many ways, they turned his wilderness narrative inside out, much as they turned his redskins and palefaces upside down. Neither Child nor Sedgwick created a frontiersman who hates and loves and slaughters Indians, though they both describe warfare in the wilderness. They both created white women who love, live with and marry Indian men and don't go to hell because they do. Miscegenation didn't terrify Child and Sedgwick as it did Cooper. Revolution didn't terrify them, either. Both expressed ambivalence about the wild: if it entailed freedom and liberty they were for it; if it meant lawlessness and chaos they were against it. Reconciling freedom *from* and freedom *to* demanded all their willpower.

Child published her first frontier novel three years before Sedgwick published hers. She breached the boundary for women writers. Over the course of the next forty years or so Child produced mostly nonfiction works with captivating titles such as *The Evils of Slavery, Cure for Slavery*, (1836), *The Progress of Religious Ideas* (1855) and *The Patriarchal Institution* (1860). She wasn't

afraid to call institutions and men by their rightful names. For
decades, American women learned about domestic economy
from her how-to book, *The American Frugal Housewife* (1833).
A forerunner of Martha Stewart and Arianna Huffington, Child
appealed to poor and working class housewives in both the city
and the country. (The country was a more civilized place than the
frontier.) And while she offered practical advice she also aimed
to subvert and unsettle. "The greatest and most universal error is
teaching girls to exaggerate the importance of getting married,"
she insisted. "And of course to place an undo importance on the
polite attentions of gentlemen."

Child wrote about production as a subject apart from repro-
duction, sex and sexuality. "Rise early. Eat simple food. Take plenty
of exercise," she urged, sounding not unlike Benjamin Franklin's
Poor Richard. "Wash very often." Sedgwick lived by Child's pre-
cepts. She also wrote novels that Cooper praised for their "fine
power of imagination" — though that comment was probably a
backhanded compliment. Like Child, Sedgwick wrote books with
provocative titles — the *Twin Lives of Edwin Robbins* (1832) and
The Poor Rich Man, and the Rich Poor Man (1836) — that convey her double vision and indelible sense of American dualities.
Indeed, doubleness defined her consciousness and her art. Born
in 1789, the same year as Cooper, she joined the cultural and
intellectual revolutions that her contemporaries launched, more
often than not, against their own dour Puritan forefathers.

The author of eight books, all of them published between
1822 and 1837, Sedgwick took writing seriously, exhibited a wry
sense of humor and aimed to write for the whole nation. Her
first book, *A New-England-Tale*, appeared anonymously in 1822.
By the time she wrote her second novel, *Redwood* (1824), she
boasted her own name. A neo-Puritan and an ultra romantic, too,
she took pleasure in the romantic imagination and regarded it as

a weapon that would pierce the "cruel doctrines" of Calvinism. For Sedgwick, the worst thing about Calvinism was that it made her own sisters gloomy. In her candid autobiography, *The Power of Her Sympathy*, she noted that they "suffered from the horrors of Calvinism." She had not allowed herself to be persecuted by it, and for most of her life she was unrelentingly defiant as well as empathetic. "Woman," she insisted, "has an independent power to shape her own course, and to force her separate sovereign way."

As matriarchal as Cooper was patriarchal, Sedgwick's life and work were eclipsed by the patriarchy in the era that followed the Civil War. In the twentieth century, feminist critics rediscovered her and resurrected her lost classic, *Hope Leslie*. Ever since 1987, when it was republished, it has enjoyed a second life. Still, it's probably safe to say Sedgwick isn't as well known as Cooper, Hawthorne and Melville and that over the past hundred years her quintessential female character, Hope Leslie, hasn't captured the imaginations of readers as forcefully as Natty Bumppo, Hester Prynne or Captain Ahab. An idealized, fictionalized version of the author herself, Hope is too good to be true, though she was also a perfectly good character for young women readers in the 1820s, including the women in the Sedgwick family who were brought up to be very good, indeed.

Sedgwick reacted strongly to the seismic shifts in the lives of her sisters. "The first tragedy in my life," she wrote in her self-mocking autobiography was the marriage of her "mother-sister" Eliza to a husband of the old school who was "resolute, fearless, enduring, generous...tender, austere, rigid." Sedgwick belonged to the world of new school thought in New England and gazed with new-school eyes at old-school gentlemen. Another writer probably would have pruned that long list of words that moves from resolute to tender; Sedgwick didn't because she saw the contradictions in nearly everything and everyone, including her brother-in-law. Words rarely escaped her control; she used them precisely, avoided verbiage and escaped the rhetorical excesses that plagued so many nineteenth-century American writers. Like Hawthorne, Sedgwick combined "spontaneity of the imagination with a haunting care for moral problems."

In 1854, Hawthorne wrote to Richard Monckton Milnes, a member of the British Parliament and a patron of the arts, to steer him in the direction of "good American books." Hawthorne didn't leap at the opportunity. He confessed sheepishly, "I sometimes fancy it is a characteristic of American books, that it generally requires an effort to read them; there is hardly ever one that carries the reader away with it; and few that a man of weak resolution can get to the end of."

Hawthorne might have been thinking of *Moby-Dick*, *The Scarlet Letter* or *The Prairie*, all of them weedy novels that forsake the garden for the wilderness. He probably wasn't thinking of *Hope Leslie* when he insisted that readers would have difficulty finishing an American book. Sedgwick's narrative bounces along even with its large cast of outlaw girls such as Hope herself, who are illuminated against the dark backdrop of seventeenth-century New England Puritanism. "Hope Leslie took counsel only from her own heart," the author explains. A teenage female version of Natty Bumppo, she's at home in the woods and among Indians. "Her love for exploring hill and dale, ravine and precipice had given her that elastic step and ductile grace which belonged to all the agile animals," Sedgwick wrote of her rambunctious heroine.

To create Hope, Sedgwick drew on memories of her own childhood and adolescence when she roved the hills and mountains of Connecticut undeterred by tales of savage Indians that made "the stock terror of our nurseries." Sedgwick's parents failed to instill in her a fear of the forests. A genuine lover of nature — "my heart was early knit to it," she wrote in her autobiography

— she was also a trenchant critic of the Puritan work ethic and the routines of the machine age.

Thirty-seven-years old when she wrote *Hope Leslie*, she was still young enough to remember rural villages before they turned into hives of industrial activity. Her heroine, Hope, defies the rule of the machine and speaks for the wildness of youth itself against the conspiracies hatched by old men instinctively opposed to the new simply because it is new. Hope refuses to follow established ways. "I would not be a machine, to be moved at the pleasure of anybody that happened to be a little older than myself," she says.

Sedgwick's heroine is an American girl of the 1820s as well as the 1640s. She's the first genuine literary character in an American novel to identify herself wholeheartedly with the wildness of youth and with young adults like herself, whether they're Indians girls such as Magawisca, or white boys such as her brother Everell, who since boyhood has rebelled against tyranny.

Hope Leslie conjures the innocence of the Housatonic Valley and its fall from paradise. Once the home of "sylvan freedom," the landscape is desecrated by "clattering mills and bustling factories." The past was much pleasanter, Sedgwick writes, when "the axeman's stroke, that music to the settler's ear, never then violated the peace of nature, or made discord in her music." Still, Sedgwick didn't want to return to a primitive past. A member of the party of progress, she reminds readers in *Hope Leslie* that New England society had improved and that nineteenth-century New Englanders rejected the noxious, all-pervasive Puritan idea that the Indians "were the children of the Devil." That was her idea of progress.

Sedgwick praises New England meeting houses, where everyone in the community — mechanics, merchants and ministers — meet "on even ground" and as "one religious family." Then, too, while she denigrates the arrival of the machine, she also describes a peaceful revolution that improved the landscape.

"The forest vanished, and pleasant villages and busy cities appeared," Sedgwick wrote. "The tangled foot-path expanded to the thronged highway — the consecrated church on the rock of heathen sacrifice."

Not a religious writer in Roger Williams's sense of the word, she worshipped at the shrine of American democracy and shared Cooper's idealism about democracy in the New World. Into the mouths of her characters — ordinary Americans gifted with extraordinary eloquence — she put democratic sentiments. One European immigrant observes: "There is a new spirit in the world — chains are broken —fetters are knocked off— and the liberty set forth in the blessed word is now felt to be every man's birth-right."

In *Redwood* (1824), her first novel, published three years before *Hope Leslie*, she praises New England libraries and citizens who make a "fuss" about learning and attend public lectures. With the spread of libraries and the rise of readership, it's no wonder that she boasted, "we live in a country...beyond parallel, free, happy, and abundant."

F. O. Matthiessen doesn't mention Sedgwick or her work in *American Renaissance*, his hymn to our national literature that was published a year before the United States entered World War II, when democracy was endangered everywhere in the world. "Emerson, Hawthorne, Thoreau, Whitman and Melville all wrote literature for democracy," Matthiessen wrote. He added that "their tones were sometimes optimistic, sometimes blatantly, even dangerously expansive, sometimes disillusioned, even despairing but what emerges from the total pattern of their achievement...is literature of our democracy."

Sedgwick could be as optimistic as they were, especially in *Hope Leslie*, which ends on a note of joy and rejoicing, She could also be despairing, though not as dark as Melville in *Moby-Dick*. In *Hope Leslie*, she explains that her heroine has "to learn from that stern teacher experience" that "events and circumstances cannot be molded to individual wishes." She would write in her own journal, "I am more and more a fatalist. Events control us — not we events." Like many of her New England contemporaries, including Hawthorne and Child, she never entirely escaped from the Puritanism that she wanted to leave behind. "Religion has not overcome the evil in me...the fear and dread," she wrote near the end of her life.

Neither Sedgwick nor Child ached to live in Paris or London. Neither sought or held political office, as did Irving and Cooper, and neither aimed to affiliate themselves with presidents and millionaires such as Martin Van Buren and John Jacob Astor. Life in the United States suited them, though they criticized the get-rich quick, spend-it quickly spirit that took over the country in the 1820s and that soared in the decades before the Civil War, as Henry James and others noted. Sedgwick and Child found inspiration in the manners and the morals of their own day.

Heftier and more complex than Child's ethereal frontier romance, Sedgwick's sprawling narrative corrals a large cast of characters, including Cavaliers, Puritans and Indians, most of them clustered under a matriarchal umbrella. Nearly everyone in the novel conspires to ensnare and imprison, or alternatively to liberate someone else. Set in both Puritan America and in monarchial England, the narrative hints at the international theme that Henry James and Edith Wharton would both invigorate, though its strength lies in its sense of New England places and in the convincing group of Indian characters who feel real kinship with forests, woods and wild animals. Sedgwick and Child both had a sharp eye for trees and both used the tree as a metaphor. "Husbands don't grow on trees in these deserts," a character in *Hobomok* explains. In *Hope Leslie*, an Indian says that the "strokes of the English axes" have decimated "the trees that defended us."

Perhaps, as Henry James observed grimly in 1879 when he looked back at the early years of the American republic, there was "no great literature." But to say, as he did, that there were "no novels" in those days did an injustice to Child, Sedgwick and their work. Perhaps he thought of their books as romances and not as novels and wouldn't acknowledge the romance as a genuine contribution to great literature. Still, their narratives were "thoroughly American," to borrow a phrase that James used to describe Hawthorne; they also "came out of the very heart of New England" to borrow yet another phrase that James used to praise *The Scarlet Letter.*

In their own age, *Hobomok* and *Hope Leslie* made genuine emotional claims on readers, especially women, while the authors themselves served as role models for wives, mothers and young girls, too. Sedgwick and Child were gentler with one another than Cooper and Irving. At times, the two women could be sisterly. Irving and Cooper were never brotherly, though Irving tried to be. Child wrote glowingly about Sedgwick's work in a review in *Ladies Magazine.* She used Sedgwick's first novel, *A New-England Tale,* as a text for students in her own classroom. "I am but one among a large number whose minds you are enlarging, and whose hearts you are purifying," she wrote Sedgwick in the breathless tone she often adopted when writing to those she idolized.

Sedgwick instilled a sense of wildness in *Hope Leslie,* but she also created characters that abhor wildness and the woods. Mrs. Grafton, a member of the Church of England, argues that her sister's "resolution...to go into the wilderness, has no parallel in the history of human folly and madness." She looks at the Indians and insists that, "our civilized life is far easier — far better and happier than your wild wandering way." As in *The Pioneers,* nearly everyone in *Hope Leslie* has a different wilderness tale to tell.

Like Cooper and Sedgwick, Lydia Maria Child carved out

her own version of the wild. Born in 1802, she grew up resisting all attemps to civilize her; with woods just beyond her own
backyard, it was difficult for her parents to keep her from exploration. A kind of innate feminist, Child complained at the age
of 15, after reading *Paradise Lost*, that John Milton asserted the
"superiority of his own sex in rather too lordly a manner." At the
same time, she found inspiration in the "wild dignity" exhibited
by Sir Walter Scott's young heroines. Near the end of her life, she
looked back at the journey she had taken and noted that, "There
have been many attempts to saddle and bridle me, and teach me
to keep step in respectable processions; but they have never got
the lasso over my neck yet."

Wild at heart, she wielded wildness as a sword that cut both
ways; for her, the wild could be abhorrent as when she denounced
the pro-slavery forces in Kansas in 1859, just before the out-
break of the Civil War as "more ferocious" than "wild Indians."
Child also denounced the evils of civilization, though she clearly
wanted the blessings of civilization to triumph over the callous-
ness of barbarism. "War is a horrid barbarism," she observed. A
lover of woods, trees and wild animals, she described nature as
"the literature of God" and in the battle to end slavery, she envisioned "the sword of God's mighty angel flashing like sunbeams
over the field." A dreamer, a utopian and a passionate abolitionist
who admired John Brown, she defended the underdog, the freedom fighter and the persecuted until she died in 1880. At her
funeral, the abolitionist William Phillips noted that, "she was the
outgrowth of New England theology, tradition, and habits…she
could have been born and bred nowhere but in New England."

She married the lawyer and fellow abolitionist David Child,
but she didn't always live with him nor did she ever give birth to a
child, become a mother and accept the role of motherhood. Near
the end of her life, she noted, "masculine and feminine should

everywhere cooperate together." Though not as famous or infamous as Harriet Beecher Stowe — whose electrifying work she greatly admired — she denounced slavery in fiction and nonfiction with both passion and reason. Slavery, she argued, was an "outlaw" that had to be hunted down and brought to justice.

Child had at least two sides if not more: one overtly political and polemical; the other intensely personal and domestic. But she managed to bridge the personal and the political. "Are not we becoming luxurious and idle?" she asked rhetorically in *The American Frugal Housewife*. "Look at our steamboats, and stages, and taverns!" she exclaimed. "There you will find mechanics, who have left debts and employment to take care of themselves." She disdained selfishness and personal indulgence and at the same time urged self-reliance and individuality. "He alone is wise who forms his habits according to his own wants, his own prospects, and his own principles," she wrote.

Perhaps no popular nineteenth-century American woman writer — except Helen Hunt Jackson — felt as passionately and as steadfastly as Child did about Indians. In a letter of 1838, she wrote, "We certainly have done all we could to secure the deadly hostility of the red man." In 1873, she looked back at U.S. history and criticized President Andrew Jackson for "making nominal treaties" and then stealing land from Native Americans. She noted, too, that "White men have so perpetually lied to them that they don't know whom, or what, to believe." Child added that white men "again and again killed Indians who were decoyed into our power by a flag of truce." In addition to John Brown, her heroes were Indian warriors — Captain Jack of the Modoc and Osceola of the Seminole — and, while she opposed the use of violence to achieve political ends, she loved and blessed warriors who took up arms in the struggle for freedom.

Hobomok, the Indian protagonist in Child's novel of the

same name, is no fierce warrior of the sort one encounters in *The Last of the Mohicans*. More peaceful than the most peaceful of Cooper's Indians, he kills no one, and, when he hunts an eagle with a bow and arrow Child shakes her head in disapproval. Hunting eagles is un-American behavior. Handsome, moody and lithe, Hobomok seduces and is seduced by Mary Conant, a young Puritan who comes of age as the Pequod stage armed resistance to European colonization. Child didn't like the Pequod. In *Hobomok*, she depicts them as empire builders who "looked with hatred upon the English, as an obstacle to their plan of universal domination." But she admires the gentle Hobomok; he's the exception to the rule. Devoted to Mary — the "sylph-like" English woman abandoned by her English lover — Hobomok marries her and fathers her son.

Child depicts the Puritans as brave New World pioneers who push forward in the grand human quest for liberation. "We've come over into this wilderness to find elbow room for our consciences," one of her characters explains. In the woods of America, her Puritans find the space they need to express their own religious beliefs and to recreate civilization. A precocious twenty-one-year old when she wrote *Hobomok*, she was well aware of the fact that by casting the Puritans in a positive light she went against the Unitarian grain that had gained ground in her own lifetime. As she also knew, a generation of New Englanders — including women from elite families, such as the Sedgwick's — abandoned the Calvinism of their parents and grandparents and adopted religious practises that seemed more humane. By the 1820s, many Americans felt that the Puritans were extremists and ought to be shunned and ignored. By the 1840s, writers and intellectuals scoffed at them; then the backlash mounted, though there was certainly backsliding. Melville called the Puritans bigoted. Bronson Alcott — Louisa May Alcott's bookish father and a naturalist friend of Thoreau and Emerson

— called the Puritans "severe and staid." Still, Puritanism proved to be a hardy plant to eradicate from the soil.

Indeed, the Puritan determination to battle evil by any means necessary made them appealing to Child, and, shortly before the start of the Civil War, she lamented the passing of "the spirit of the Puritans." To abolish slavery, she felt that it was necessary to revive the passions of her ancestors. Unafraid to belong to a minority of one, she took unpopular positions and jeopardized her own literary career. The founder and the editor of the *Juvenile Miscellany*, the first children's magazine in the U.S., she published her own anti-slavery views in the pages of her publication and watched as subscriptions promptly plummeted, forcing her to close shop.

Defending the Puritans did not win her friends and supporters, though she aimed not to offend or alienate. "In this enlightened and liberal age, it is perhaps too fashionable to look back upon those early sufferers in the cause of the Reformation, as a band of dark, discontented bigots," Child wrote in *Hobomok*. She added, "Whatever might have been their defects, they certainly possessed excellencies, which particularly fitted them for a vanguard in the proud and rapid march of freedom."

Phrases like "vanguard" and "rapid march of freedom" sound as though borrowed from Cooper's *The Pioneers*, though even at 21, Child understood the dangers inherent in following a vanguard and marching behind moral crusaders. She also recognized the toll that oppression took on those who resisted it. That was the noxious nature of oppression; it tainted everyone. Wisely, she noted of the Puritans, "it is no wonder that men who fled from oppression in their own country...should have exhibited a deep mixture of exclusive, bitter, and morose passions."

Child fills the pages of *Hobomok* with Puritan rebels and Puritan conformists. She doesn't call her narrative a romance, but a "tale" and a "fable," by which she means that she doesn't have to abide by the rules of the English novel. A fable, she argued, could legitimately cast a "wild, fantastic light" on settings and characters. Eschewing realism, she explores the emotional attractions and attachments between Mary, the misguided English woman, and Hobomok, her "elastic" and "savage" lover, against the backdrop of wilderness warfare that snares Indians and settlers.

Sedgwick thought more deliberately about form and style than Child, though she came to more or less the same conclusions. Like Child, she didn't want to be bound by literary rules. Like Child, she was familiar with the notion of the "fable" as a genre which she linked to the wild as a place. At the start of *Hope Leslie* she warns readers about the narrative they are about to read. "We are confined not to the actual, but the possible," she wrote. A writer of romances by Simms's definition, Sedgwick recognized that a woman could liberate herself and her friends as effectively as any man. She also sensed that she could go too far beyond the possible and thereby lose readers. Worried that her audience would not find Hope a convincing character in a novel set in the seventeenth century, she explains her status as an outlier in the "strictest sect of the Puritans."

Drawing on her memories of childhood, Sedgwick writes that Hope was raised in "an atmosphere of love" that shielded her from Puritan coldness and enabled her to blossom like "the richest of flowers in a tropical climate."

At times, Sedgwick insists on historical veracity. She gives over a section of her novel to Magawisca, an Indian girl with "an air of wild and fantastic grace" who tells the novel's leading white boy, Everell, what she (and the author herself) regard as the true account of the atrocities perpetuated by the whites against the Pequod at Mystic. Magawisca's narrative refutes Cooper's idea that Indians simply disappeared "before the superior moral and physical influence of the whites." By giving voice to her Indian character and allowing her to speak about atrocities, Sedgwick puts "the truth" into Indian "hands."

The Pequod, Magawasca explains, were "courageous"; their bravery misrepresented as "ferocity." She adds that they were "exterminated…not by superior natural force, but by the adventitious circumstances of arms, skill, and knowledge." Sedgwick adopts an Indian view, or at least a point of view that she imagines as Indian. "The savage was rather the vassal than the master of nature," she wrote. "He did not presume to hew down her trees."

With Magawasca's narrative as the historical bedrock and the moral framework for her romance, Sedgwick offers a series of clashes between Indians and settlers. The novel culminates with Hope Leslie's daring rescue of her friend, Magawisca, from a dungeon where the colonial authorities hold her "like an imprisoned bird." Sedgwick uses the devices of the romance — disguises, secrets and conspiracies — so that her heroine can affect Magawisca's liberation. She reinvents the captivity narrative.

Not every thread in her romance is connected, and not every story in the narrative has an ending, in part because she knew that life itself didn't provide tidy endings. Near the conclusion of her romance, Sedgwick mentions the Pequod's "pilgrimage to the far western forests." Their story, she adds, "is lost in the deep, voiceless obscurity of those unknown regions." Sedgwick didn't want a tidy ending. Indeed, she offers a plea for "disorder," which she insists is but "the natural and beautiful order of nature." No American writer had ever expressed that notion so clearly.

Cooper influenced Child and Sedgwick and they in turn also influenced him. In his oddly entitled novel, *The Wept of Wish-ton-Wish* (1829), which he wrote in Paris, he offers versions of the kinds of characters that they had already created — as though eager to steal some of the thunder they'd stolen from him. In *The Wept of Wish-ton-Wish*, Cooper turned his attention to the pages

of seventeenth-century colonial history that he had avoided in
the Bumppo books. In *The Wept,* he describes conflicts between
Puritans and Indians in Connecticut and follows the fortunes of
two unusual palefaces of the sort he had not previously developed.
Whittal Ring, a young man, denounces whites, renounces his
own identity and reinvents himself as a redskin. Ruth Heathcote,
a young white girl, lives with Indians, becomes Narra-Mattah and
marries an Indian named Conanchet.

Still, Cooper couldn't do justice to the kinds of women characters that Sedgwick and Child created. In his view, America was
the "true Paradise" for women, a perspective that didn't make it
any easier to create complex characters such as Mary Conant, the
Puritan girl who finds true happiness with an English minister
and who adopts her redskin/paleface son, Charles Hobomok
Conant. The Conant family — mother, father and son — represents Child's hope for a nation that would bind together whites,
Indians, English, Americans, Puritans and non-Puritans alike.

DOUBLE CONSCIOUSNESS

Sedgwick enjoyed what every major American writer of her
time enjoyed: a sense of duality. When she looked back at her life,
she noticed her ingrained habit of looking at people, events, ideas
and movements from opposing points of view. "I have a double
consciousness," she wrote. Her "double consciousness" kept her
from joining the kinds of causes that demand true believers not
wayward members who doubt and question. Even Child, the consummate crusader, recognized the imperfections of crusaders and
reformers who could also be, she noted, "self-seeking" individuals.

In political life, Child was far more outspoken and defiant
than Sedgwick, though *Hope Leslie* is far more feminist than any

novel Child wrote. No writer in the early nineteenth century created a cast of women characters to match hers and no one defended
women's freedom as unequovically. "Marriage is not *essential* to the
contentment, the dignity, or the happiness of woman," Sedgwick
wrote in *Hope Leslie*. Those words served as her credo.

Child shared Sedgwick's sentiments about matrimony, though
in *Hobomok*, she presents a heroine who marries twice. Cooper
would probably have found Child's main character, Mary Conant,
an immoral woman because she has sex with an Indian; he might
have wanted to ban the book. Hawthorne also would have disapproved of Mary's behavior. His seventeenth-century relatives would
have put Mary in the stocks and made her wear a sign in which she
acknowledged her "whorish carriage" and acts of "fornication."

Cooper's Indians would probably kidnap Mary and hold
her captive. In the Bumppo books, redskin warriors gaze lecher-
ously, as well as reverentially, at paleface women. In *Hope Leslie*
and *Hobomok* more than lecherous gazing and reckless eyeballing
take place. Far less repressed than Cooper, Sedgwick and Child
both noticed and described the charms and sexual allures of the
American Indian male. In her autobiography, Sedgwick wrote
that Indians possessed a "masculine savage quality" and a "wild
flavor," though she also noted that by the late eighteenth century
they had already "imbibed the dreg-vices of civilization" and lost
the sense of manhood that made them attractive. By setting *Hope
Leslie* in a distant past before arms, alcohol and other civilized
vices destroyed "savages" and decimated forests, she was able to
make innate Indian wildness believable.

One wonders what Leslie Fiedler would have made of
Sedgwick's and Child's female protagonists as they walk into the
wilderness, fall in love, marry, have sex, give birth to children
and accept responsibility, too. To remind readers, Fiedler wrote
in *Love and Death in the American Novel*, that "The typical male

protagonist of our fiction has been a man on the run, harried into the forest and out to sea, down the river or into combat – anywhere to avoid 'civilization,' which is to say, the confrontation of a man and woman which leads to the fall, to sex, marriage and responsibility." In Child's and Sedgwick's romances, the heroines don't fit Fiedler's description; they don't flee from civilization, men, child rearing, parenting and the family. They aren't harried or on the run either; when Hope and Faith go into the wilderness they choose to go there.

In Child's and Sedgwick's narratives, the wilderness is a meeting place and mating ground for interracial couples. Hope doesn't applaud her sister's marriage to an Indian, but she doesn't aim to destroy it, either. Moreover, while Sedgwick allows Faith and her husband to elope and settle down, she doesn't envision or invite a mass mingling of whites and Indians. Magawisca seems to speak for Sedgwick herself when she says, "The Indian and the white man cannot more mingle, and become one, than night and day." In *Hope Leslie*, two women stand face-to-face as equals. The wild woman tells the tame woman what she doesn't want to hear: that they must go their separate ways.

*

American culture lost much more than the work of individual women when it lost sight of Sedgwick and Child. It lost much of its own identity. It forgot, buried and neglected the hope for human liberation that Sedgwick, Child and their literary sisters expressed. The feminist critics who unearthed their work and who publicized their contributions helped to make American culture far more whole and healthy than it had been for decades. And yet in the wake of feminist criticism, mass-produced popular culture continued to manufacture narratives that celebrated violence and revenge, and elevated the lone white male with a sixgun or a rifle into a national hero.

The comments that D. H. Lawrence made about Cooper's protagonist Bumppo as hard, isolate, stoic and a killer might well be applied to several generations of cinematic killers. The American infatuation with "Dirty Harry," "Rambo," "The Stone Killer," "The Terminator," "The Avengers" and much more add up to a curious cultural addiction to masochism, sadism and bloodshed. Cooper gave birth to the gestalt when he created Bumppo. He probably didn't set out to create an archetypal killer. But he did anyway. His imagination took him to places he had not wanted to go and enabled him to write prophetic works of fiction that inspired Balzac and George Sand, irritated Mark Twain, evoked admiration from Gorky and pushed Lawrence to come to grips with the realities of America itself. No matter how awkwardly he wrote, he managed to leave an indelible mark on national and international consciousness.

CHAPTER 7

RADICALS

Margret Fuller & Henry David Thoreau

EMANCIPATED WOMAN

In the run-up to the Civil War, the United States boasted dozens of female authors — the "damned tribe of scribbling women," Hawthorne called them during an outburst of misogyny. Still, there was no one single, dominant female literary voice heard across the nation. There was no female Emerson. In the 1820s, 1830s and 1840s, the American literary scene was too provincial, patriarchal and paternalistic to accept a presiding female genius who would share the stage with a presiding male genius. If it did have such a woman that person might have been Margaret Fuller, a friend of Emerson's and Thoreau's, and the editor from 1840 to 1842 of *The Dial*, the organ of the transcendentalist movement. Had she lived beyond 1850, she might have gone on to rival Emerson as a literary critic, public speaker and nature writer.

Many lively and informative books about Fuller have appeared in print since Vernon Lewis Parrington wrote glowingly about her in 1927 in *Main Currents in American Thought*. Still, it's worth repeating his comments because his language is vivid and memorable and because Lionel Trilling did a hatchet job on him in *The Liberal Imagination* (1950). Parrington deserved better treatment. He admired liberals and radicals while Trilling mostly disdained them, and he wrote with passion while Trilling too often held back his feelings and appealed to the intellect. Of Fuller, Parrington wrote that "she was the completest embodiment of the inchoate rebellions and grandiose aspirations of the age of transcendental ferment" and that her mind was "an electric current that stimulated other minds to activity." Parrington admired her love of luxury, children and love itself. He noted that she was the first woman after Mary Wollstonecraft to argue for the emancipation of woman from the world according to man and men.

It was a tribute to the Transcendentalists that they made room for Fuller as the editor of *The Dial* and an acknowledgement of her credentials, too. No one was better suited than she to hold the reigns of the publication and no one held them as vigorously as she. "We would have every path laid open to Woman as freely as to Man," she exclaimed, and lived by those sentiments, too. If a path didn't exist she created it. One might call Fuller a female version of Emerson, though she never ingratiated herself with audiences as he did and never wrote anything with as much punch and popular appeal as his essays, "Nature," "The American Scholar" and "Self-Reliance."

She apparently said, "I now know all the people worth knowing in America and I find no intellect comparable to my own." That might have been true, but it didn't endear her to readers of *The Dial*. Her closest friends forgave her her vanities. When she died in 1850, 32 years before Emerson, he noted in his journal, "I have lost in her my audience." The intellectual father of American literature mourned the passing of his own wayward daughter who had escaped to Italy, where she felt more at home than in Boston.

"Italy receives me as a long-lost child," she wrote. "How true was the lure that always drew me toward Europe."

Fuller lived a legendary life, as though she might have been a character in an American romance. At times, she spoke and acted as though she wanted to shape her life into an artistic whole. "What concerns me now is that my life be a beautiful, powerful, in a word, a complete life of its kind," she wrote. In *The Blithedale Romance*, which followed hard on the heels of *The Scarlet Letter* and *The House of the Seven Gables*, Nathaniel Hawthorne used Fuller as the inspiration for the character of Zenobia, a female firebrand and actress who has "the wildest energy" and whose mind is "full of weeds." For Hawthorne a mind ought to be as tidy as a well-tended garden. In *The Blithedale Romance*, the narrator, Miles Coverdale — a neo-Puritan poet trying to pass as a utopian — joins Zenobia's rural community, Brook Farm, only to reject it. "No sagacious man will long retain his sagacity, if he live exclusively among reformers and progressive people, without periodically returning into the settled system of things," Coverdale says and speaks for Hawthorne, too.

Orderly, settled systems didn't appeal to Fuller as they did to Hawthorne. Unsettling the conventional suited her. In the 1840s — the decade in which she came into her own — no woman was more iconoclastic than she and no one was more defiant in an intensely disciplined way. The words "civilized" and "urbane" define her sensibility far more than the words "wild" and "untamed." A social misfit, she didn't have as keen a sense of place as did Thoreau and Hawthorne, nor did she find a place in America where she could feel deeply connected, except perhaps between the covers of a book. Her inability to put down roots in the "right soil" convinced her that she had wasted her strengths on abstractions.

In the one Daguerreotype of her from 1846, she peers down at the open pages of a hefty tome, as though the words she sees

are the only things that matter to her. No one was more bookish than Fuller, not even Emerson and Thoreau. She ravenously
read ancient and modern literature: Virgil, Cicero, Shakespeare,
Goethe, Maria Edgeworth (the mother of the historical novel in
English), Madame de Staël, Adam Mickiewicz (the Polish poet),
Bryant and Cooper, who she rebuked for "shallowness of thought"
and praised for "the noble romance of the hunter-pioneer's life."
Fuller aimed for balance and for measured observations, though
she couldn't help but be outspoken as when she observed, "While
any one is base, none can be entirely free and noble." No wonder she inspired a generation of feminists, including Susan B.
Anthony and Elizabeth Cady Stanton, and no wonder she was
rediscovered by women's liberationists in the 1970s.

As new American writers emerged, Fuller swallowed them
whole and spat them out in one critical review after another. Indeed,
she wrote about Poe, Hawthorne, Melville, Longfellow, Frederick
Douglass (whom she rebuked for his "torrid energy and saccharine
fullness"), Lydia Maria Child and Catharine Sedgwick, who she
praised for her "scenes and personages from the revolutionary time."

Born in 1810 in the shadow of Harvard to an influential
Massachusetts family — her father was a four-term U.S. congressman — Fuller broke nearly all the rules that the patriarchy
imposed on her and on her nineteenth-century sisters. When she
died in 1850 — two years after the Seneca Falls Convention that
raised the banner of women's suffrage — she had served as literary editor and the European correspondent for Horace Greeley's
New-York Tribune. No woman wielded more influence over the
reading public and few if any scolded readers and editors as
harshly. "Authors are afraid," she wrote. "Publishers are afraid." It
took courage to rebuke publishers and authors alike and to keep
the book industry honest.

A teacher at Bronson Alcott's experimental school and an

intellectual mentor to Boston's bluestockings, Fuller traveled to Europe without a chaperone, rendezvoused with George Sand and embraced the cause of Italian Republicanism led by Giuseppe Garibaldi and Giuseppe Mazzini. In 1848, on the barricades in Italy and in the thick of the revolution there, she achieved a kind of apotheosis. Fuller may or may not have married her lover, Giovanni Angelo Ossoli, an Italian aristocrat eleven years younger than she. The evidence is ambiguous. She definitely give birth to their son, Angelo. Hawthorne assumed Fuller had not married and scolded her for bringing a child into the world out of wedlock.

When invading French troops crushed the Italian revolution and restored the dislodged pope, Fuller fled for safety with Giovanni and Angelo. She drowned, along with her son and his father, when a storm off the coast of Long Island battered their ship. No nineteenth-century American writer had a more dramatic death. Thoreau rushed to Long Island to search for Fuller's remains and to retrieve the book she was writing about Rome. Though he was unsuccessful in both endeavors, he helped to preserve her reputation. All through the 1850s, her name remained in the public eye thanks to the publication of two collections of her writings and an edited version of her memoir that sanitized her unconventional life.

Unafraid to take on big, controversial subjects, or to tackle the biggest names in American literature, Fuller aimed to change popular misconceptions about the American woman in *The Great Lawsuit: Man versus Men, Woman versus Women* that she reworked and republished as *Woman in the Nineteenth Century* (1845). Thoreau praised it as "rich extempore writing, talking with pen in hand." Lawrence might have pointed to it as an example of American "art-speech." The previous year, she published *A Summer on the Lakes*, a first-person narrative in which she describes her own adventures in New York, Illinois and along the Great Lakes. Published four years before Thoreau's *A Week on the Concord and Merrimack Rivers*, *A Summer* contains some of Fuller's most romantic writing. "As I rode up to the neighborhood of the falls, a solemn awe imperceptibly stole over me, and the deep sound of the ever-hurrying rapids prepared my mind for the lofty emotions to be experienced," she wrote of Niagara Falls, an iconic American landscape that had been desecrated and commercialized and that was a great shame, at least to Europeans.

Woman in the Nineteenth Century reveals Fuller's critical intelligence and her own personality, too. "I had put a good deal of my true self in it, as if, I suppose I went away now, the measure of my footprint would be left on earth," she wrote. Fuller grasped the importance of roles, role-playing and the power of the patriarchy. "The man furnishes the house; the woman regulates it," she observed of white middle-class society. Nearly everywhere she looked she saw inequalities between the sexes.

"There exists in the minds of men a tone of feeling toward women as toward slaves," she wrote. But she also argued that in the United States "women were better situated than men." They had more time to read, she pointed out, and they were not "so early forced into the bustle of life, not so weighed down by demands for outward success." From her point of view, the rat race, as it would come to be known, extracted a far heavier toll on men than women. The male rags-to-riches narrative might be reversed and end in rags again, though the bestselling novels by Horatio Alger, Jr. (1832-1899), another descendant of Puritans, made success seem within everyone's reach.

Fuller's strengths lay in her gumption and her ability to see the big picture — "woman in the nineteenth century" — though the century wasn't yet half over. She also recognized contradictions and synthesized seeming opposites. "Male and female represent the two sides of the great radical dualism," she observed. "But in fact they are perpetually passing into one another. There is no wholly masculine man, no purely feminine woman." That insight made Fuller a radical feminist in her own day and age, whether among Boston's bluestockings, Concord's Transcendentalists or Italian revolutionaries.

Her forays into the field of literary criticism, as in the 1846 essay, "American Literature," illustrate her bravado. She criticized her friend and mentor, Emerson, because his poems were "mostly philosophical, which is not the truest kind of poetry." Over and over again, she noted that American writers imitated European writers. William H. Prescott's history, she noted, was "wonderfully tame." Longfellow's poems "were derived from the works of others." Even Hawthorne, whom she described as "the best writer of the day," failed to attain greatness because, she wrote, he "intimates and suggests, but he does not lay bare the mysteries of our being." For Fuller, the bottom line was that, while books were "written by persons born in America," there was not yet an American literature.

Her memoir, *A Summer on the Lakes* reads like a brave attempt to forge an original American work that eschews "cant, compromise, servile imitation and complaisance." Fuller succeeds when she paints dramatic landscapes with "wild sky," "changing light" and "a kaleidoscopic variety of hues," but she also fails, as when she regards a group of Indians and exclaims, "Continually I wanted Sir Walter Scott to have been there." She faulted Americans for "the fatal spirit of imitation" and at the same she turned to European standards and imitated European writers.

When she looks at a Winnebago woman, she explains that her "position...reminded me forcibly of Queen Victoria's." Fuller apparently felt that her own writing would not be servile if she repeated the word "wild," as though repetition itself would persuade readers of her own unconventionality. So, for example, she writes about "wild beauty," the "wild road," the "Western wilds" and the "wild" dignity of the Indians that strikes her as antithetical to "the rudeness of the white settler."

In *A Summer*, Fuller offers vivid portraits of Western women, both Indian and white. Give her credit: she went into cabins and wigwams with real curiosity and observed the relationships between the sexes. She had to overcome her own blinders, as she herself knew. When she set off on her expedition to the West, she was haunted, she writes, by "unwelcome images...of naked savages stealing behind me with uplifted tomahawks." She had read too much Fenimore Cooper. But before long she went bravely into Indian villages where she was won over by Indian manners and morals. New England families, she felt, might learn from Indian tribes. "I have witnessed scenes of conjugal and parental love," she wrote. "In the evening, the Indian wigwam is the scene of the purest domestic pleasures." Here the reader might be in the midst of an English novel, say, *David Copperfield* (1850), by Charles Dickens.

No doubt, poetic license operates freely in *A Summer*. "The Indian cannot be looked at truly except by a poetic eye," Fuller writes. She adds, "I enjoyed a sort of fairy-land exultation never felt before." She might have been better served by Thoreau's plain style. Still, she offers unsentimental views of pioneer women: "The great drawback upon the lives of these settlers at present is the unfitness of the women for their new lot." Wives of settlers "become slatterns," she observed, while women from the eastern seaboard struggled continuously to uphold "refined neatness."

Frontier men enjoyed real advantages over frontier women, she insisted. They could always find fieldwork and "recreation with the gun and fishing-rod." Mothers and daughters, especially of the "poorer settlers," could "rarely find any aid in domestic labor." Fuller's heart went out to them, though she also rebuked them. "They can dance but not draw," she exclaimed. "Accustomed to the pavement of Broadway, they dare not tread the wildpaths for fear of rattlesnakes!"

About sex and sexuality on the frontier Fuller remained silent. Roger Williams provided more information in the 1640s than she did in the 1840s. He had advantages, including an ability to speak and understand Narragansett. Moreover, he lived with Indians for months and observed their customs over extended periods of time. When women menstruated they lived apart from men "in a little house alone by themselves," he observed, and when they gave birth they did so "more speedy and easie[sic]...than the women of Europe."

Nakedness didn't offend him, and at times, he transcended the Christian morality he brought with him. He noted, without scolding, that unmarried women and men were not required to be monogamous. "Fornication" wasn't a sin in the Indian world, he explained, if the man and woman were single individuals.

By the mid-seventeenth century, adultery and fornication had found a home among New England Puritans. In 1668, Hawthorne's ancestor, William Hathorne, a Puritan magistrate, sentenced a young, pregnant woman named Hester Craford (remarkably similar to Hester Prynne) to be "severely whipped" after she confessed to fornication. Moreover, in 1681, two female ancestors of Hawthorne's — on his mother's side of the family — were convicted of the crime of incest with their brother, Nicholas Manning. The sisters were sentenced to prison, public flogging and wearing signs that said, "This is for whorish carriage with my naturall [sic] brother."

Fuller was reticent about sex and sexuality. Perhaps because she was liberated, she drew a curtain around her private life, especially her romance in Italy with her Italian lover that would have made for lively reading and sensational headlines. After Fuller's death in 1850, Fanny Fern (1811-1872) — the pen name for Sara Payson Willis — took the lead as a literary critic and expanded the role of the woman writer in America. More at home in popular culture than Fuller, Fern wrote articles on subjects such as "The Model Husband" and "Hints to Young Wives." Helen Gurley Brown and *Cosmopolitan* weren't far away. Fern didn't promote herself as wild. She just was wild. Her pen name spoke volumes. "The woman writes as if the devil was in her," Hawthorne wrote. Uncowed and unwilling to compromise, she wrote in a conversational style as though talking to young women who were, she wrote, "bright-eyed, full-chested, broad-shouldered, large-souled, intellectual." You can hear her sassy, spunky voice in "Independence," an essay published on the Fourth of July 1859, in which she asks, "Can I...be 'President?' Bah — you know I can't. '*Free!*' Humph!"

RIVER WILD

By the 1840s the literature of the wild had come a long way since 1820. Indeed, it culminated in 1849, with Thoreau's deceptively simple autobiographical narrative, *A Week on the Concord and Merrimack Rivers*, which the critic Joseph Wood Krutch aptly described as a "mild adventure." Fuller's *A Summer on the Lakes* might have inspired Thoreau's *A Week on the Concord and Merrimack Rivers*. Of the 1,000 copies that Thoreau paid to have printed, only 218 sold between 1849 and 1853; the printer returned to the author all the remaining copies. "I now have a library of nearly nine hundred volumes, over seven hundred of which I wrote myself," he noted in his journal.

In the 1850s, no one seemed to notice Thoreau's remarkable book or gauge his rare genius, though that didn't cool his creativity. He went on writing as though success and fame didn't matter. They didn't. The "wild conceit" — to borrow Melville's phrase

— for *A Week* was so new and different that readers didn't grasp it. Instead of following the route of the pioneers and heading to the West, Thoreau set out from home to explore the territory that existed in his extended backyard. Traveling not by road but by river, which he described as "by far the most attractive highway," he and his brother John saw the backside of New England villages and the resurgence of New England forests.

"There is something indescribably inspiriting and beautiful in the aspect of the forest skirting and occasionally jutting into the midst of new towns," he wrote. He added, "Sometime this forenoon the country appeared in its primitive state, and as if the Indian still inhabited it." The return of the wilderness was perhaps wishful thinking, though de Tocqueville observed much the same phenomenon in *Democracy in America*.

In *A Week*, Thoreau aimed to write as simply and as cleanly as possible. "Plain speech," he insisted, was the most beautiful mode of expression, though he also wanted his own speech to go beyond the mere surface of things and to capture his own slippery thoughts and elusive consciousness and unconsciousness, too. "Our truest life is when we are in dreams awake," he wrote. To write *A Week*, Thoreau drew upon his memories of the two weeks in 1839, at the age of 22, that he spent floating and sailing on the Concord and the Merrimack. The book that he would draft and craft while he lived at Walden Pond in 1845 was no mere travelogue. Alchemy turned autobiography into art, mythology and philosophical reverie. Part naturalist and part archeologist, Thoreau slowed down on the river, let the current take him where it would, and wasn't sorry that he had left behind "the amusements of the drawing room and the library."

He might have called his book *The Drunken Boat*, and anticipated Arthur Rimbaud (1854-1891), the insurrectionary French symbolist poet. Like Rimbaud, Thoreau could write intoxicating prose. "I can fancy that it would be a luxury to stand up to one's chin in some retired swamp a whole summer day, scenting the wild honeysuckle," he wrote ecstatically.

Listening to his Indian muse, he traveled back to the past, revived Indian names and reminded readers that before white men named the river "Concord" the Indians called it the "Musketaquid" — the "Grass-ground River." If he could have, he would have erased the many European names that littered the landscape. He also would have tried to undo the industrialization of New England. "Pawtucket and Wamesit, where the Indians resorted in the fishing season, are now Lowell, the city of spindles and the Manchester of America, which sends its cotton cloth round the globe," he complained.

Nearly everywhere that he floated in his boat, he felt the presence of the Indian past just beneath the surface of the waters. An Indian way of life lay buried under the Merrimack River itself, he insisted. Antiquities cried out to him and he concluded that civilization offered no advantages over "savageness." He added that "The frontiers are not east or west, north or south, but wherever a man *fronts* a fact." The existential frontier lurked all around him.

Henry David and his brother, John, roughed it in the woods, though they also stayed at an inn where wayfarers from distant cities enjoyed room and board after a day's fishing. The Concord and the Merrimack were tourist attractions, the woods safe enough for men armed with little more than fish hooks. Thoreau refused to be a tourist, a cowed citizen or a coward in Concord. The same year that he published *A Week*, he also published the essay, "Resistance to Civil Government," in which he articulated the overtly political nature of his philosophy of wildness.

In 1846, to protest the Mexican War, westward expansion and slavery, Thoreau refused to pay his poll tax and spent one night in jail. Prison and the woods both provided him with an education into the ways of man, society and nature. "It was a closer view of my native town," he explained of his prison experience. "I had never seen its institutions before." "Resistance to Civil Government" grew from Thoreau's night behind bars. It went on to influence Tolstoy, Gandhi, Dr. Martin Luther King, Jr. and generations of nonviolent protesters the world over who harnessed their political passions to civil disobedience. "The mass of men serve the state," Thoreau wrote as though reporting a fact to a local newspaper. He added that they served "not as men mainly, but as machines, with their bodies" and that, "it is not too soon for honest men to rebel and revolutionize." Those incendiary words were not often heard in Concord.

In nearly everything he wrote and in nearly every gesture he made, Thoreau aimed to reverse the process of civilization. Even the act of changing his given name, David Henry to Henry David seems emblematic of his lifelong project of reversal and rebirth that his followers adopted and carried forward into the twentieth and the twenty-first century. In *American Renaissance*, Matthiessen could not have been more wrong about Thoreau when he noted, "it is doubtful whether most readers now sense in Thoreau more than a whiff of wildness."

There's more than a whiff of wildness in *Walden*, though the narrator and main character, one of Thoreau's personae, lives in a cabin, works with tools and wears clothes. He's not as liberated as he'd like to be, but he doesn't have a wife or children and he doesn't work nine to five in an office or on a farm. He boasts that he's freer than the bulk of Americans who are slaves to their jobs and the marketplace, and indeed, in the eyes of his contemporaries, he seemed to be freer than almost anyone in the State of Massachusetts. Turning to the Bible, Confucius and the Buddha, Thoreau called for readers to take voluntary vows of poverty and embark on journeys of spiritual revolution. Angry, sad and funny, he made war on imitation and imitators and praised the lives of Indians in their wigwam. Not merchants and bankers, but New England craftsmen were among his most beloved comrades, though he was alarmed — as was Karl Marx — that workers were alienated from their own labor and were "the tools of their tools."

Thoreau reached out with one hand to the fugitive slave and with another to the birds from whom he learned a great deal "not by having imprisoned one, but having caged myself near then." There was freedom in the captivity that was consciously chosen and freedom in the woods, too, where he went to "live deep and suck out all the marrow of life." Thoreau makes that assertion in the *Walden* chapter entitled, "Where I Lived, And What I Lived for." It took him a few chapters to find his gait, but once he found it, there was no stopping him. "Time is but the stream I go a-fishing in," he wrote wistfully. Angrily, he complained that Concord had no culture, "no taste for the best or for very good books even in English literature." Thoreau, the wild man, wanted good books to read and the time to read them. Unafraid to be alone, he observes that, "we are for the most part more lonely when we go abroad among men, than when we stay in our chambers."

Like Whitman, he contained contradictions and embraced the civilized and the savage, the wild and the tame. He realized that if he were actually to "live in a wilderness" he would be "tempted to become a fisher and a hunter in earnest." What he had done so far was mostly play. The pond and the woods didn't offer a real wilderness experience, he allowed, though they put him in touch with the animal in himself and with the wild animals that thrived around the pond itself that mirrored his own soul and took him into the soul of the Earth itself. "We need the tonic of wildness," he insisted, as though prescribing a remedy for a nation hurtling towards Civil War. He added wisely, prophetically: "Our village life would stagnate if it were not for the unexplored forests and meadows which surround it." For Thoreau, the life devoted to the critical exploration and investigation of the world appealed far more than the trappings of success. "Rather than love, than money, than fame, give me truth," he exclaims in the spirited conclusion to *Walden*. "There is more day to dawn," he writes. "The sun is but a morning star."

Thoreau's Concord contemporaries admired him because he went barefoot in summer, befriended Indians and didn't care for money or fame. They admired him, too, because he wasn't Emerson. Bronson Alcott (1799-1888), one of Thoreau's most ardent fans, as well as one of his closest friends, enjoyed his walks and talks with Emerson, but he could never spend too much time with Thoreau, whom he called "a walking Muse." In his journal, Alcott drew a sharp contrast between Thoreau who "took his position in Nature," and Emerson who "took refuge in the intellect."

Alcott's observations of Emerson and Thoreau, though offered in the 1840s and 1850s, seem to stand up today. "Take the forest and skies from their pages," he observed of his two friends, and they "have faded and fallen clean out of their pictures." Alcott predicted that "Emerson will go down as a solitary person" and that Thoreau was assured of "certain fame." For much of the twentieth century, critics elevated Emerson to the status of secular saint and demoted Thoreau to the sidelines as a delinquent New England boy. Matthiessen begins *American Renaissance* with Emerson and devotes far more pages to him than to Thoreau.

In the twentieth century, anthologists went overboard in their enthusiasm for Emerson. In the Penguin anthology of American Literature, for example, William E. Cain wrote, "Emerson is the essential American writer," as though only one writer fit the description. For backpackers, hikers and environmentalist, Thoreau's writings provided inspiration and instilled a dedication to the cause of conservation. The counterculture of the

1960s and 1970s rediscovered his anarchist philosophy and his back-to-the-land practices. For every professor who raved about Emerson and his essay, "Nature," there were dozens of naturalists who carried in their backpacks *Walden; or, Life in the Woods*. Still, building a cabin on the edge of a forest or in the woods wasn't a viable solution to the ills of civilization, as generations of Thoreauvian cabin-builders liked to believe. Soon enough the woods were dotted with cabins and crowded with urban refugees, and those cabins sometimes spelled the end of the woods.

CHAPTER 8

ALLEGORICAL

Poe, Hawthorne, Thoreau (Again), Muir & Melville

FALSE DOCUMENTS

By 1843, when Edgar Allan Poe noted that the wilderness was a theme of "universal interest," the wilderness and the wild appealed to him as the author of narratives that were, paradoxically, both "wild" and "homely" (to borrow his own words from the short story, "The Black Cat," in which a deranged husband murders his wife, then conceals her body and thinks he's committed the perfect crime). The ironical ending in which the cat gives him away and the police arrest him is pure Alfred Hitchcock.

By the late 1830s and the early 1840s, when Poe wrote his best short stories, the wild American narrative, which provided an escape from the mundane and the ordinary, had become a staple of the literature of the United States, along with the romance and the tall tale. In *The Narrative of Arthur Gordon Pym of Nantucket* (1838), Poe's protagonist and narrator, Mr. Pym, pursues "wild adventures" at sea and on land with a dog named "Tiger." On his voyage, he encounters "savages" and sees strange "white animals" that drive the natives "wild." Finally, anticlimactically, he reaches Antarctica.

In a preface, Poe frames Pym's story as a true-to-life account of a voyage, though he purloined much of the material for his tale from Benjamin Morell's *Narrative of Four Voyages to the South Seas and the Pacific* (1832). Poe never traveled to the South Seas or anywhere near the Pacific. Born in Boston in 1809, twenty years after Cooper and five years after Hawthorne, he attended school in England from 1815-1820, and then stayed close to home, closer than Cooper and Hawthorne, who both explored Europe. When he returned to the United States, Poe divided his time between New York, Baltimore, Richmond and Philadelphia. He never knew France, Germany or Italy from first-hand experience, though he set his stories all across Europe and purloined ideas and images from European writers, including Coleridge. "Talent borrows, genius steals," as the English literary genius Oscar Wilde observed.

In the Daguerreotype of Poe from 1848 he looks like the quintessential romantic artist: dark hair, thick eyebrows, a scarf tied tightly around his neck and eyes that struck observers as "strange" and "weird." It's no wonder that he lasted only a brief time at West Point. Military life didn't suit him, though he could be diligent and disciplined as a poet, essayist, short story writer, editor, and a reviewer known as the "Tomahawk Man." Like Cooper, Sedgwick and Hawthorne, he propounded the myth of a wild childhood. Nineteenth-century America practically required it.

An alcoholic for much of his adult life, Poe never escaped from stormy relationships with women, newspaper and magazine editors, fellow writers, and his own haunted self. Unlike Cooper, who inherited wealth and property, married well and settled down, Poe didn't overcome the real and the psychic dislocations of his own youth: his father, David Poe, abandoned the family soon after he was born; his mother died when he was an infant. His emotional wounds provided the sources for his art. Like Jack London, he was a feral artist who burned himself up in a blaze of creativity. Like London, he died at 40 after a brilliant literary career in which he plagiarized and tried to cover his tracks. He had plenty of company.

The twentieth-century poet, critic and exemplary California wilderness writer, Kenneth Rexroth, coined the phrase "false document" to describe works of fiction that disguise themselves as true and represent the make-believe as fact. E. L. Doctorow borrowed Rexroth's term for an essay that he called "False Documents" in which he explains that novelists couched fictions as true stories to give them "additional authority." Nineteenth-century American writers, including Poe, Hawthorne and James made the "false document" into an art form. They did so in part because the reading public was suspicious of literature. As Natty Bumppo says, "What have such a man as I, who am [sic] a warrior of the wilderness, though a man without a cross, to do with books!" A romance or a wild tale that looked, smelled and read like a real document might persuade skeptical audiences to suspend disbelief and to trust the teller of the tale to tell the truth.

In his introduction to *The Scarlet Letter*, Hawthorne mentions actual events from contemporary history, such as the California Gold Rush, as though to bolster his credibility. He drops the names of real men such as Emerson and Thoreau, includes names of real places such as Brook Farm, and even claims to have in hand a "rag of scarlet cloth" in the shape of "the capital letter A." The scarlet letter isn't a figment of the imagination, he insists, but rather an actual relic from seventeenth-century New England.

Like Hawthorne, Poe went to unusual lengths to persuade readers to willingly suspend their disbelief. In *The Narrative of Arthur Gordon Pym*, he provides specific dates and precise latitudes and longitudes on his surreal journey. Behind the mask of

Pym's false document, Poe created an imaginary space he wanted readers to accept as real. Like Hawthorne, he explored intricate psychological landscapes, weird states of mind and "the blackness of darkness" to borrow the telling phrase that appears in "The Pit and the Pendulum," his short story of madness, terror and torture.

As Lawrence noted, Poe was "an adventurer into vaults and cellars and horrible underground passages of the human soul." His obsession with colors — especially whiteness and blackness — along with his preoccupation with liberty, on the one hand, and bondage on the other, might be written off as the expression of a romantic artist torn between agony and ecstasy, except that American society couldn't take its mind away from black and white, slave and free.

The collective American unconscious found expression in Poe's tales. To his admirer and patron, John Pendleton Kennedy (1795-1870) — a novelist and Secretary of the Navy — Poe explained that he never "fully acknowledged" the aim or intention of his stories "even to myself." Melville used Poe's wonderful phrase, "the blackness of darkness," in a review/essay he wrote about Hawthorne's "wild, witch voice" and his "Calvinistic sense of Innate Depravity and Original Sin." After reading and rereading Hawthorne's short stories collected in *Mosses from an Old Manse*, Melville advised readers not to be "witched by his sunlight" but rather to take note of the "blackness of darkness" at the heart of his imagination.

BEAST & DETECTIVE

Poe adeptly explores the "blackness of darkness" not only in "The Pit and the Pendulum," but also in "The Murders in the Rue Morgue" in which he follows the urban Odyssey of the detective,

August Dupin, who is gifted with a "diseased imagination" and yet who solves the mystery of two gruesome murders that baffle the police. The corpse of the daughter, Mademoiselle L'Espanaye, is found in the chimney of her Paris apartment; the corpse of her mother, Madame L'Espanaye, Dupin surmises, was hurled head-first through a window before it crashed to the ground. Almost everyone in the story, including the police, assume the killer must be a European, though what nationality no one can say for sure.

Poe profiles a modern Babel inhabited by citizens from all across the continent who speak a variety of tongues and who exist in an environment of violence, disorder and death. Paris itself is a wild beast and white women are as endangered in the city as the paleface females in Cooper's frontier novels. As readers of "The Murders in the Rue Morgue" surely remember, the cold killer is a tawny Ourang-Outang captured in Borneo, then transported to Europe and prized for its "wild ferocity." The Borneo beast represents everything the civilized world believes it must capture and contain: the fugitive slave, the barbarian at the gates and the naked savage. Hollywood reincarnated Poe's jungle creature as King Kong, the cinematic beast at war with civilization and in love with beauty.

Poe reads like a forerunner of the noir novelist Raymond Chandler and the director Alfred Hitchcock, whose films *North By Northwest* and *Rear Window* captured 1950s anxiety and paranoia. Poe's characters commit grisly crimes and are haunted by them. They're drug-crazed, trapped and doomed, and they reflect an abiding American — perhaps a human — fear of losing control, losing one's own freedom, and dying a horrible death at the hands of one's archenemies.

From Cooper's novels, Poe learned about the perils of the American forest. The newspapers of the day provided him with stories about Ourang-Outang captured in Borneo and Sumatra, then brought to the United States, where they were an instant

sensation. They were also housed at the London Zoo, where
Charles Darwin studied them. In "Murders," Poe created a
Darwinian detective eager to locate the origins and the evolution
of a mystery that baffles the police. The trail of clues leads him
through the wilderness of Paris to the instinctive jungle killer.
Dupin solves the crime because he knows that it's essential to take
a "side-long" glance and not gaze directly at the crime. "Tell all
the truth but tell it slant," Dickinson advises in poem #1263.
(I'm indebted to those two majestic Dickinson scholars, Thomas
H. Johnson and R. W. Franklin. I use here and in the chapter
on Dickinson, Franklin's system of numbers.) Poe's mantra was
much the same as Dickinson's. He understood that "Success in
Circuit Lies." Dupin observes that, "truth is not always in a well."
The Paris inspector can't solve the crime because he holds "the
object too close."

Dupin is a street-savvy version of Bumppo: an outcast from
society with a loyal male companion who accompanies him on
his voyages into the forest of the city. In the eyes of the average
Parisians, Dupin and his nameless friend are both "madmen."
Indeed, they do their best thinking when the city sleeps and sleep
when the city goes to work. "We existed within ourselves alone,"
the narrator says of himself and the detective. What Cooper's hero
accomplishes outdoors, often in "impenetrable darkness," the
detective accomplishes indoors and in the midst of "true Darkness."

At the scene of the crime, Dupin immediately notices the tell-
tale signs — the blood, razor, nail and damaged windows — and
the fact that the room is "in the wildest disorder." Dupin knows
disorder from the inside out. A Parisian with set routines, he also
abandons the habitual and dives into the disorder in his own head.
So did Poe, though from about 1827, when he published his first
verses, to 1849, the year he died, he managed to carve out a sem-
blance of order in his personal life that provided a sense of security.

In his essay, "Philosophy of Composition," Poe explains that an author has to think first and foremost, not about the message or the meaning of a tale, but about the effect that he wants it to have on readers. Authors had to delay for as long as reasonably possible the reader's desire for solutions and closure. The savvy author, Poe suggests, had to play on the reader's longing for "self-torture" — or to put it another way, to enjoy anxiety for the sake of anxiety itself. Moreover, Poe argued, the author had to allow the audience to grasp the meaning of the story independently of anything explicit that the author himself says. That's what Cooper failed to do, Poe observed in his review of *Wyandotte*. He didn't *show*; instead, he *told* readers what they were meant to see and explained the conclusions they were to draw. "The characters of the drama would have been better made out by action," Poe wrote of *Wyandotte*. "The motives to action…might have been made to proceed more satisfactorily from their own mouths."

"Murders in the Rue Morgue" presents humans who act as animals and animals who act as humans. The Ourang-Outang behaves like an urban terrorist, while the detective, Dupin, thinks like an ape with an intellect. He solves the crime by entering the mind of the beast, and also because he's a scholar trained in an "obscure library." Like "William Wilson," "Murders" is yet another Poe tale about Doubles. The beast from Borneo is the twin and polar opposite of the detective who tracks him down and returns him to Paris's Jardin des Plantes — the nearest approximation to the wilds from which he comes.

The narrator of the story — a forerunner of Doctor Watson — sees his detective friend — a forerunner of Sherlock Holmes — as a double of himself. A deconstructionist, Dupin breaks things down into their component parts and rebuilds them into new wholes. Both "creative" and "analytic," he has "wild whims" and a wild imagination. Paris — "the populous city" of "wild lights and shadows" — offers a reflection of his own mind.

The English artist and illustrator Aubrey Beardsley thought of Poe as a kind of fin-de-siècle decadent. For "The Black Cat," he made a black-and-white drawing — a visual pun — in which a large black cat perches on the immense head of a woman with white hair. For "Murders," Beardsley created an Ourang-Outang who wears a ferocious expression on his face and walks on two legs — like a human being. He wears an earring, has a long tail, feet with delicate claws, and carries one of his victims in his bare hands. Behind the beast and his victim there's an immense white bed. Men are sexual predators, Beardsley seems to say, just as ready to kill women as to make love to them. He translated Poe's misogyny into a powerful image.

The death of a beautiful woman, Poe famously explained, was "unquestionably the most poetic topic in the world." The beautiful woman who doubles as the femme fatale has little choice but to be murdered by a man, beast or beastly man; her deadly seductive beauty is tantamount to a crime against society in a world of the ugly and the ordinary. "Each man kills the thing he loves," Oscar Wilde noted. In "Murders," the detective story in which beauty and the beast are linked, the French mother and daughter are dead when the narrator begins to tell his tale. They're beautiful because they're dead — for Poe death makes them beautiful — much as they're dead because they're too beautiful for the world of the living.

Hawthorne rarely, if ever, conjured anything as violent as the murder of the French daughter and mother in "Murders," but he shared with Poe a preoccupation with murder and death, both literal and spiritual, and with extreme states of consciousness, too. Not surprisingly, Poe recognized him as a kindred artist. In a review of *Twice-Told Tales*, published in 1842, he noted that Hawthorne was "a man of truest genius."

HATHORNE INTO HAWTHORNE

In *In the American Grain* — his meditation on the literature of the United States — William Carlos Williams described
Poe and Hawthorne as artists from opposite ends of the spectrum.
Poe flew to "the ends of the earth for 'original' material," Williams
observed, while Hawthorne stayed close to "the life of his locality"
and absorbed "New England melancholy." As Henry James put it,
"poor Hawthorne" was "exquisitely and consistently provincial." In
James's view, he relied far too heavily on allegory and on symbolism, though he allowed that he created a minor masterpiece in *The
Scarlet Letter*. Hawthorne's romance about sin, paranoia and perse-
cution was published in 1850, when he was forty years old and at
the peak of his creativity. Yes, wilderness is at the heart of *The Scarlet
Letter*, but it's a wilderness of Hawthorne's own making and a trope
to explore the nature of human society, not the Nature of Emerson.

Born on July 4, 1804 in Salem, Massachusetts, the site of the
witch trials of the 1690s, Hawthorne was haunted by Puritan history and by his own zealous ancestors, including John Hathorne,
who interrogated men and women accused of witchcraft, and by
Judge William Hathorne, known for inflicting harsh sentences on
fellow citizens. Gifted with a Double Consciousness all his own,
Hawthorne simultaneously recoiled from, and recognized the necessity of, the harsh punishments the Puritan fathers handed down.

Every colony had to have its prisons, governors and hang-
men, he believed, though he insisted that it also had to have an
appreciation for wild beauty and heartfelt compassion for outcasts. Inside and yet simultaneously outside Puritan cosmology,
Hawthorne execrated his ancestors in one breath and extoled
them in the next. Near the start of *The Scarlet Letter*, he expresses
disdain for the "dismal severity of the Puritanical code." By the
end of the tale he praises Puritan statesmen for their "fortitude

and self-reliance" and for standing "up for the welfare of the state like a line of cliffs against a tempestuous tide."

Too close to the wilderness for comfort, and yet too far from English law and security, the early New England governors had no other choice, Hawthorne argued, except to be autocratic. A curious conservative, he probably would have endorsed the Patriot Act that followed the attacks of 9/11 had he been alive in 2001. Yet he would also have felt compassion for those rounded up and persecuted by the state, some only because they were Moslems or Arabs.

Early in his career, Hawthorne changed the spelling of his family name from Hathorne to Hawthorne. The alteration of the spelling — along with his intellectual rejection of the extremism of his ancestors — created the wedge he needed to write about the past with a sense of distance and critical detachment. Still, he didn't sever all ties. He didn't become a Smith or a Jones or steer clear of Puritan history. Indeed, he wallowed in it. To truly liberate himself from the past, he would have had to do far more than insert the letter "w" in the name Hathorne. He might have moved into Thoreau's cabin and accepted Thoreau's notion that "if a man does not keep pace with his companions, perhaps it is because he hears a different drummer." Indeed, Thoreau might have been describing Hawthorne the misfit, oddball and outsider when he wrote that sentence.

The skeletons in Hawthorne's attic provided him with the bare bones that he needed to write short stories and longer fictions about the Puritans and their descendants, and, while he didn't come out of the closet about his Hathorne past, he didn't deliberately conceal it, either. Moreover, as a friend of Thoreau's, a reluctant utopian, and a Democrat loyal to his college friend Franklin Pierce — whose biography he wrote to bolster the campaign for the White House — Hawthorne was also firmly rooted in nineteenth-century America. A graduate of Bowdoin College

— a "civilizing influence," Henry James thought — he worked at the Custom House in Boston and Salem, lived at Brook Farm, married Sophia Peabody, an upstanding young lady from a good family and a transcendentalist, too, and knew the joys of parenting. On the outside he looked the picture of mid-nineteenth century New England normalcy.

When he wanted to, however, he could revert, with the flourish of his pen, to the haunted past and inhabit the consciousness of his ancestors in black hats. Hawthorne couldn't think or write for long without thinking about sin, the Devil, darkness and the sinister paths of the American wilderness. For a time, he couldn't go into a library and not pick up a book about Anne Hutchinson, witchcraft and the witch trials. From his forays into the past, he emerged sounding like a Hathorne.

Like his ancestors, he read the landscape as a map of the invisible spiritual world, though he surely didn't mean to be taken literally, as when he explained that a location in the Berkshires looked "as if the Devil had torn his way through a rock and left it all jagged behind him." At 16, he observed that "Authors are always poor devils, and therefore Satan may take them." To his college friend, Henry Wadsworth Longfellow, he noted, "By some witchcraft...I have been carried apart from the main current of life, and find it impossible to get back again."

While he wasn't a radical in the vein of Fuller and Thoreau, he was irked by the American worship of the dollar and by the spread of technology. He returned to the past, not to escape from the present, but rather to understand it and not have to repeat it. As he observes at the end of *The Scarlet Letter*, "We have yet to learn again the forgotten art of gayety." The Puritan past was probably the best teacher that he knew.

Hundreds of years after the Puritans first arrived in the New World, Puritanism continued to muffle and stifle — and

inspire — American writers and artists. Hawthorne looked back
at them with fear and loathing and admiration. The English in
England, unlike the English in New England, he observed, were
"stately, magnificent, and joyous." They enjoyed a "sunny richness." Hawthorne never joined the radicals and revolutionaries
of his time, at least not for long, but a part of him joined with
the Thoreau who exclaimed that "in wildness is the preservation
of the world." He might have said that, "in joy is the preservation of the world." Jugglers, actors and minstrels were just what
Hawthorne's healthy society needed.

The change in the spelling of his name coincided with his
emergence as a writer and the anonymous publication — in 1830
when he was 26 — of his first stories: "The Hollow of Three Hills,"
which makes skillful use of the eerie New England landscape, and
"Sir William Phips," which reflects the author's fascination with
American dualities.

Hawthorne portays Sir William as an authoritarian figure
who began life in the New World as a "rude man of the sea and
wilderness." A curious frontiersman hovers at his side, his garments
"intertwined" with "the leaves and twigs of the tangled wilderness."
In another early story, "Endicott and the Red Cross," Hawthorne
resurrects Roger Williams, though he doesn't idealize him.

In "Mrs. Hutchinson" he revives Anne Hutchinson, who he
describes as "a woman of extraordinary talent and strong imagination." Hawthorne's Hutchinson informs her congregation that
it has followed "unregenerated" priests "into the wilderness for
naught." The author insists that the early Puritans were defined
by "uncompromising narrowness," though he also argues that
"religious freedom" of the sort that Hutchinson advocated "was
wholly inconsistent with public safety." By today's standards, he
might support surveillance in the name of national security and
at the same time advocate for privacy.

From the moment that Hawthorne began his career as a writer, he wrestled with the darkness of the wilderness as though wrestling with his own soul and for his own salvation. He wrestled with it ferociously when he created his Puritan Everyman in "Young Goodman Brown," the 1835 story in which he revealed himself as a master of ambiguity. In that tale, Hawthorne/Hathorne walks a fine line between the factual and the fantastic. The author might have written the beginning of the story with a clear head and a sound mind. But the long middle section reads as though it might have been written under the influence of a powerful hallucinatory plant of the sort that the characters find in the forest.

In his paranoid, schizophrenic antihero, Hawthorne offers a surreal portrait of a good man so bewildered that he sees everyone in the village, including his wife, Faith, caught in the evil grip of a diabolical forest rite. Is Goodman Brown crazed, clairvoyant or both? Hawthorne doesn't say. When the Puritans of old saw the Devil in the wilderness, were they crazed? Hawthorne refuses to answer that question, too. Time and again, he adheres to Poe's rules of composition and allows readers to make up their own minds about the Puritans. As Henry James's pointed out in his essay on Hawthorne, he was both objectively and subjectively inside the Puritan state of mind. No one but a Puritan or a direct descendant of Puritans steeped in history and legend could have written "Young Goodman Brown," and yet no one could have written it if he was *only* a Puritan or a descendant of them.

OUTCASTS OF THE UNIVERSE

In the introductory chapter to *The Scarlet Letter*, Hawthorne alludes to "the divided segment" of his own nature as though to alert the audience to the dualities in his story. Indeed, for a

Hawthorne story to succeed it has to be steeped in ambiguity and it has to frustrate the reader's attempt to fix the author to a single point of view and one lesson. If they're to work, his "twice told tales," as he ingeniously called them, have to exist in a kind of twilight zone, as Rod Serling would call it for his long-running TV show in which the real and the surreal are intertwined. Indeed, Hawthorne's characters oscillate between dreaming and conscious thinking as in "The Haunted Mind" (1835), a tale that reads like the memoir of a man who has his clearest insights at the edge of sleep, which he calls a "passport" to another country. Eventually, the narrator in "The Haunted Mind" loses consciousness and plunges "into the wilderness of sleep" which he calls "the knell of a temporary death."

No one incorporated the wilderness into more different kinds of metaphors than Hawthorne and no one in nineteenth-century America, except perhaps Emily Dickinson, made the political more psychological than he. "In the depths of every heart there is a tomb and a dungeon," he observes in "The Haunted Mind." Psychological prisons preoccupied him as much if not more than prison made of stone. To reformers who would cry, "Free the prisoners," Hawthorne would say, "free the mind from its own fetters."

A man of two minds who lived in parallel universes, Hawthorne himself might have been the model for the alienated urbanite in the 1835 story "Wakefield" who leaves his wife and home, settles in the very next street, never sees wife or house again and is in danger of becoming "the Outcast of the Universe." Hawthorne stayed at home with wife and family, but in his imagination, he traveled to the edge of the universe. In "Wakefield" he dramatized the idea that one might be "carried apart from the main current of life" and find oneself unable to return to it, the very same situation he described as his own fate.

In *The Scarlet Letter*, Hawthorne offers the romance of a

beautiful woman who insists on absolute freedom, including the freedom to have sex with her minister, though she's a married woman. The author would have us believe that Hester's wildness jeopardizes her well-being and the welfare of the community, and that the community has no choice but to send her to prison. In the settlement again, she wears the sign of her sin, and through her penance emerges from her ordeal as a secular saint. Indeed, in *The Scarlet Letter*, Hawthorne resurrected Bunyan's Pilgrim as a Puritan mother who has "in her nature a rich, voluptuous Oriental characteristic — a taste for the gorgeously beautiful." In that regard she's a copy of Margaret Fuller. Seduced by Hester, Hawthorne pulls her toward him and simultaneously pushes her away, much as he hugs the wilderness and rejects it.

His characters are spooked by woods and forests, though Hawthorne himself apparently wasn't afraid to plunge into the woods and the fields of Massachusetts, either alone or with Thoreau, who he described as "a singular character – a young man with much wild original nature still remaining in him." Henry David ate dinner with Nathaniel and Sophia and shared the bounty of their garden. The two men swam at Walden Pond and walked together from Concord to Harvard. They also journeyed in Thoreau's canoe, *Musketaquid*, an Indian word meaning "the river of meadows." According to Henry James, Thoreau was "as expert in the use of the paddle as the Red Men."

They must have seemed like an odd couple when they traveled together by canoe on the Assabeth River that, James explained, had the power to "lave the interior regions of a poet's imagination." That was high praise indeed for a river from a writer who was inspired by English country homes and gardens far more than he was by scenes of American nature. Moreover, James noted without rebuke that Thoreau and his friend, the transendentalist poet Ellery Channing, (1818-1901) liked "to live like Indians."

The son of a Christian socialist and a Unitarian minister who left
Harvard before he graduated, Ellery married Margaret Fuller's sister, Ellen, and in 1873 published the first biography of Thoreau.
He also belonged to the radical circle that wrote, protested war
and helped fugitive slaves.

Hawthorne's notebooks from 1835-1841 show that he was a
naturalist in the vein of Channing and Thoreau, and that he paid
close attention to trees, birds and flowers, including the "wild rose
bushes devoid of leaves, with their deep bright-red seed-vessels." A
romantic, too, he thought of nature's workmanship as perfect and
man's workmanship as imperfect. He might have been a mainstay
of the Transcendentalist movement, except that he didn't care for
movements and isms, though he flirted with them. No Hathorne
could be a thoroughgoing Transcendentalist, a utopian, or a Marxist
— like Karl Marx himself, who worked as the London correspondent for Horace Greeley's *New-York Tribune* and who followed the
American Civil War as closely as any American journalist.

THE MAINE WOODS

A solitary forager in fields and woods, Hawthorne describes
himself, in his notebooks, as he gathers herbs, eats tasty weeds, dines
on nourishing wild grasses, and swims in "a cove overhung with
maples and walnuts — the water cool and thrilling." And then,
suddenly, he gazes at a "Distant clumps of trees" and notices their
"apparition-like appearance." He adds, "It would not be strange to
see phantoms peeping forth from their recesses." Whimsical and yet
more than a tad fanatical, he couldn't help but adopt the Puritan
mental habit of looking for apparitions in the woods, though as a
boy he played in the woods of Massachusetts and Maine.

"I ran quite wild, and would, I doubt not, have willing run

wild till this time, fishing all day long, or shooting with an old fowling piece," Hawthorne wrote of his boyhood. The Maine woods delighted him, as they did Thoreau, though Thoreau had to overcome his own fears in the wilderness of Mount Katahdin.

What struck Thoreau most about the Maine wilderness was the assault on timber, and the factories in the forest that produced hundreds of millions of board feet a year and turned the environment into a "waste land." As he walked deeper and deeper into the woods, he met Indians, loggers, hunters and explorers. He felt as though he traveled back in time to a place that reminded him of Daniel Defoe's *Robinson Crusoe* and that felt more authentic to him than the present. "The deeper you penetrate into the woods, the more intelligent…you find the inhabitants," he observed. From the lips of the Indians, he learned that the rivers of Maine once "ran both ways, one half up and the other down, but that since the white man came, it all runs down." That kind of mythology he loved. He certainly didn't dismiss it as poppycock.

In Maine, Thoreau's destination was Katahdin, the state's highest mountain peak. On the way to the top, he got lost — "buried in the woods," as he put it — and had to scramble on all fours "through Chaos." Most of the time, he enjoyed the sense of the unknown, though the final stages of the climb across dangerous territory made him feel weak and vulnerable. "Vast, Titanic, inhuman Nature has got him at disadvantage," he wrote, "caught him alone, and pilfers him of his divine faculty." Briefly, he felt closer to the apes than to the angels and he's exhilarated by that feeling.

For a moment, one expects that Thoreau will arrive in an American "heart of darkness" and meet a civilized fellow who has reverted to savagery. Here, nature is, indeed, "savage and awful." Here, too, he thinks there's room "for heathenism and superstitious rites." We're almost with Mr. Kurtz in Conrad's Congo, or, alternatively, almost in the forest of Hawthorne's haunted soul,

Goodman Brown. Thoreau meets a group of Indians who are far from noble savages. "Sinister and slouching fellows" they remind him of the "lowest classes in a great city." Still, Thoreau stops himself from descending the ladder of evolution. He spies an Indian alone in a canoe — an "ancient and primitive man" emblematic of the "red face of man" — and concludes with a profound sense of optimism — or wishful thinking — that, "The aborigines have never been disposed, nor nature deforested."

Thoreau piles adjectives on top of one another, as though he needs a mountain of them to describe the Maine wilderness that's "beautiful," "fantastic" and even full of "tenderness." By the conclusion of the essay about his climb, he came to see America itself as a land "still unsettled and unexplored." Indeed, he enjoyed what Wallace Stegner would call "the geography of hope." By Thoreau's time, Yankee pioneers had reached California and the Pacific. The telegraph and the steamship connected the nation. But in-between East and West, Thoreau insisted, there was the vast "virgin forest of the New World." One could still see America as Sebastian Cabot and John Smith had seen it in the sixteenth and seventeenth centuries, he argued. In the "intricate wilderness," Thoreau insisted, "men would live forever, and laugh at death and the grave." They wouldn't even think about the village graveyard.

THE MORAL WILDERNESS

With his graveyard comment, Thoreau parted intellectual company from his canoeing and hiking companion, Nathaniel Hawthorne. For Hawthorne, there was no place anywhere in North America, not in Maine or in Massachusetts, where men might exist without thoughts of a graveyard — and especially not in the wilderness, a landscape of dying and death. Indeed in the story "Roger Malvin's Burial," first published in 1832 and later included in *Mosses from an Old Manse* (1846), Hawthorne writes about death in the wilderness and the misfortunes of one New England family: the elderly soldier, Roger Malvin; his young daughter Dorcas; her fiancé and later husband, Reuben Bourne; and their son Cyrus.

Though not as well-known or electrifying as "Young Goodman Brown" or as sobering as "Wakefield," it's a literary waystation between "Young Goodman Brown" and *The Scarlet Letter*. "Roger Malvin's Burial" begins in the aftermath of a bloody clash between settlers and Indians. A sense of doom hangs over the landscape and the characters, including Malvin, a survivor of "Indian captivity" who is "deserted in his extremity." No actual Indians appear in the story. Unlike Cooper, Hawthorne had no desire to map military clashes between redskins and palefaces.

Near the start of "Roger Malvin's Burial," Hawthorne introduces Malvin's comrade-in-arms, a young soldier named Bourne who leaves him to die not because he's innately evil but because of his own "selfish love of life." Malvin's daughter Dorcas takes Bourne as her husband, though his misdeeds in the wilderness haunt him and taint their marriage. "It was a ghastly fate to be left expiring in the wilderness," Hawthorne observes. He also explains that there is nothing worse than to "die solitary, and lie unburied in this howling wilderness." For Hawthorne, "to perish in the wilderness" without a proper burial is a violation of the rites and rights of the individual and the society.

Reuben's secret gnaws at his heart "like a serpent" and he's transformed into a morose fellow eager to expiate his sense of guilt. "An unburied corpse was calling him out of the wilderness," Hawthorne explains. Years later, he and his son wander through the forest as though in a kind of waking nightmare; Reuben almost imagines himself a murderer. Bewildered in the forest, Reuben kills Cyrus.

Hawthorne implies that the death of the son is the penalty the father must pay for allowing Malvin to die alone in the wilderness.

Eighteen years later, he returned to an even richer and more complex wilderness in his first full-length romance, *The Scarlet Letter*. In his notebook, Hawthorne observed that as he wrote the novel, he experienced "a great diversity of emotion." His wife Sophia noted that at the time he was "very all sided and can look serenely on opposing forces and do justice to each."

The wilderness appears in both the background and in the foreground of the novel, as the location for the drama and the setting for the action. From the start of his fable/romance/novel Hawthorne links his own personal history to the landscape of New England and to the "wild, free days" that he once enjoyed with Thoreau. Then, when the narrative gets going, it's clear that the wilderness is the omnipotent force that makes and breaks the characters, young and old, men and women, the heretics and the orthodox. It's a wilderness all its own.

No lumberjacks operate in the woods outside Hawthorne's Salem as they do outside Cooper's Templeton; no one taps trees for maple syrup and no one hunts and fishes in forest and lake. In fact, no character seems to eat or work, though they're all shaped by the ubiquitous moral wilderness in which they collude, engage in subterfuge, and are caught in the tangled web that they weave. At times, *The Scarlet Letter* reads like an American version of Pierre Choderlos de Laclos's (1741-1803) wickedly satirical French novel, *Les Liaisons dangereuses* (1782).

Hawthorne's characters are victims, persecutors and would-be rescuers. No one is innocent and everyone falls from grace. Like her husband and her lover, Hester dissembles when she ought to be transparent and truthful. Long after she sins, she goes on sinning. For Hawthorne, it's not the wild sex itself that taints her and the society in which she lives, but the secrecy and the lies that surround the act and that envelop her and all the other characters. The wilderness represents the dark, tangled world of collusion and conspiracy.

In *The Scarlet Letter*, Hawthorne is too much of a Victorian to say much if anything about sex. When Pearl, her mother Hester and her biological father, Arthur Dimmesdale, come together for the first time, Hawthorne describes the "electric chain" that binds them. He uses the word "sex," as in "her sex," when he describes Hester, although he never writes explicitly about sex or sexuality. He's also fearless enough to strip away the mask of Puritan society and reveal the hypocrisy at its heart. As Henry James pointed out, Hawthorne knew "the secret that we really are not by any means so good as a well-regulated society requires us to appear."

No one could or did explain to the young James what the scarlet letter stood for. Adultery was too heinous a crime to discuss in public. At his best, Hawthorne invites the reader to imagine the wildness and romance of the sexual act that brought his two outlawed lovers, Hester and Arthur, together. Poe might have created a dark, perverted seduction between Hester and the minister, perhaps in a cellar or a cemetery. For Hawthorne, Hester and her lover are adults who have consented to have sex; he means to respect their privacy and not pry. Not until the 1920s, when Lawrence published *Lady Chatterley's Lover*, would a novelist writing in English describe sex explicitly. Still, Lawrence didn't exist in a vacuum. *The Scarlet Letter* lies behind his own novel that also explores adultery, secrets and silences. Lady Chatterley is a liberated Hester Prynne, her lover a liberated Arthur Dimmesdale, the woods on the Chatterley estate the English equivalent of the American wilderness.

"Trees glistened naked and dark, as if they had unclothed themselves, and the green things of the earth seemed to burn with greenness," Lawrence wrote. In opposition to the trees there's the appalling "utter negation of natural beauty, the utter negation of the gladness of life, the utter absence of the instinct for shapely beauty which every bird and beast has."

In *The Scarlet Letter*, Hawthorne asks readers to imagine the Reverend Dimmesdale caught in an egregious immoral act. Indeed, Hester's clandestine lover longs to do some "strange, wild, wicked thing" so that his true self will emerge and he'll be apprehended and punished. The more he tries to control himself and to repress his urges, the more they rise to the surface. Near the end of the narrative, Hawthorne peels away his pious mask and reveals him as a minister whose sermons are fueled by a perverted sexuality. Dimmesdale can "blight all the field of innocence with but one wicked look."

In one of the key scenes in the novel, which takes place in Dimmesdale's Poe-like chamber, the minister loses his composure, makes a "frantic gesture" and rushes away in a snit. In a comment worthy of Poe's Parisian detective, Chillingsworth observes, "He hath done a wild thing ere-now, this pious Master Dimmesdale, in the hot pursuit of his heart." If he sounds Shakespearean that's probably not a coincidence. Like Hamlet, Chillingsworth stages a scene to capture the conscience of the man who has cuckolded him.

In a novel that explodes and implodes with allegory, emblems and symbols, Hester's daughter Pearl represents the unbridled impulses that brought her parents together and then pushed them apart. Pearl is, Hawthorne writes, "the unpremeditated offshoot of a passionate moment." She is probably the wildest character in the book; it's in her blood. Hawthorne harps on her wildness: her "wild eyes," similarity to a "wild tropical bird," "wild and capricious character," and ability to look directly into the eyes of the Indians, as though she's as wild as they. In the fairytale ending, Pearl becomes the "richest heiress of her day," moves to England and settles there. "She might have mingled her wild blood with the lineage of the devoutest Puritan among them all," Hawthorne observes. Oh, how Hawthorne longed for reconcilation, harmony and peace between the past and the present, the wild and the Puritan, the Old World and the New World.

With the exception of Pearl's escape to England, a kind of environmental determinism operates in the pages of Hawthorne's romance. The characters are prisoners at "the edge of the Western Wilderness." Hester finds a secure place for herself not by resisting but by radical acceptance. The wilderness, with its brooding, howling personality, is the principal emblem of the moral crisis that engulfs her, her husband Roger, her lover Arthur and her daughter Pearl. It's not the scarlet letter in the title and in the text that's the dominant trope, but rather the wilderness itself. Hawthorne uses half a dozen words and phrases — "forest," "forest-land," "primeval forest," "mother-forest," "great black forest" and "woods" — interchangeably with "wilderness," which can mean a forest with real trees, or else a maze of lies, deceits and silences. The metaphors are all tangled up in a thicket.

Hawthorne uses the words "symbol" and "emblem" interchangeably in *The Scarlet Letter*, as though allegory and symbolism were not two mutually exclusive kinds of metaphors, as Matthiessen argues they are in *American Renaissance*. "Symbolism...shapes new wholes," he explains. "Whereas allegory deals with fixities." Matthiessen argues that in *Moby-Dick*, Melville fused "idea and image," while in *The Scarlet Letter*, Hawthorne made the "abstract, the idea" more important than its "concrete expression."

Curiously, Matthiessen never recognized the wilderness and the wild as the twin tropes in both *The Scarlet Letter* and in *Moby-Dick*. He dismisses the wilderness as merely "the backdrop of scenery" in *The Scarlet Letter* and he insists that the "scenery" doesn't intrude on the "interactions between the characters." He ignores the crucial scenes that take place in the wilderness between Hester and Pearl and between Hester, Pearl and Dimmesdale. Matthiessen focuses instead on the three scenes that take place on the scaffolding in Salem and give the novel its "symmetrical design." The staged scenes on the scaffold provide the novel with a pattern — an English pattern — but they don't bring it into the American grain. The wilderness as a trope, along with the wild form of the book and the wildness of the characters themselves, all make *The Scarlet Letter* an American work of fiction.

Arthur Dimmesdale sees New England as "the wild outskirt of the earth." His opposite, twin and double, Roger Chillingsworth — the physically misshaped alchemist and herbalist — comes out of the "perilous wilderness" bearing "new secrets" and the "black art" he has learned from the Indians. When the characters want privacy they go into the wilderness, though Hawthorne explains that in America privacy is less pronounced than in "The Old World, with its crowds and cities."

Few characters in nineteenth-century American literature are as evil as Roger Chillingsworth. Moreover, his evil is linked in a mysterious way to forests, woods and wilderness. In the company of Indians, Hawthorne suggests, the doctor was initiated into a dark rite and became an outcast of the moral universe. Chillingsworth does nothing to redeem himself. Dimmesdale tries. He loves truth and loathes lies and comes to loathe his own "miserable self" because he's a liar.

The town minister is also the strange leader of a cult that includes the "virgins of his church" — a touch worthy of John Updike. Near the end of the narrative, he delivers an archetypal Puritan sermon in which he traces the "relation between the Deity" and the settlement that the colonists are "planting in the wilderness." In Hester, his most complex and endearing character, Hawthorne created an emblematic figure who "wandered… in a moral wilderness…as vast, as intricate and shadowy as the untamed forest." He added, "The scarlet letter was her passport into regions where other women dared not tread." At the end of the narrative, the characters gather for a festival with wild music. The Puritans are joined by Indians and by a group of sailors with the "wildest features" who are far more outlandish than the "painted barbarians."

As if the wild, the wilderness and the scarlet letter weren't rich enough tropes, Hawthorne added more, including the "black flower" and the "wild rose" which suggest the opposite ends of the moral spectrum. Both the black flower and the wild rose stand out at the start of the narrative and at the very moment when Hester leaves the prison where she has served a seven-year sentence for adultery. The institution of the prison, Hawthorne writes, is the "black flower of civilized society" – a flower of evil as Baudelaire might have called it. The wild rose, he adds, "may serve ... to symbolize some sweet moral blossom that may be found along the track, or relieve the darkening close of a tale of human frailty and sorrow." For Hawthorne, the wild rose is as necessary as the prison. Without the prison, wildness will destroy the community. Without the beauty of the rose, the whole colony will become a prison cell.

In a curious passage in which he gave free reign to his romantic imagination, Hawthorne wondered how the rose happened to grow from the ground outside the prison. Had it "survived out of the stern old wilderness…that originally over-shadowed it," he asks, or had it "sprung up under the footsteps of the sainted Anne Hutchinson as she entered the prison door." The wilderness gives birth to beauty; incarceration and suffering lead to freedom.

As he wrote *The Scarlet Letter*, Hawthorne came to see the prison as an emblem for society itself. When Dimmesdale meets Hester in the woods and persuades her to flee with him, he feels like "a prisoner just escaped from the dungeon of his own heart." Liberated for the first time, he breathes in "the wild, free atmosphere of an unredeemed, unchristianized, lawless region." It's only in the lawless wilderness, Hawthorne seems to say, that one can feel liberated from the straightjacket of Puritan society.

Where does Hawthorne stand, if indeed he stands at all? In *The Scarlet Letter*, he's ambiguous about the wild and the free, the prison and the wilderness. After he wrote *The Scarlet Letter* he backed away from the wilderness as setting and as trope. In *The House of the Seven Gables* he primarily used the metaphors of house and garden and aimed to balance the claims of property and justice, the dispossessed and the obsessed.

If Hawthorne is a social conservative in *The Scarlet Letter*, he's moderately radical in *The House of the Seven Gables,* which takes place in the nineteenth century and includes the railroad, the Daguerreotype, socialism, and a bold hero who starts as a "wild reformer" and becomes "a conservative." In *The House of the Seven Gables*, Hawthorne aims his barbs at an insolent, lying American capitalist named Pyncheon, who exudes a sense of "feigned benignity." He's yet another prisoner, not of space but of time: meetings, appointments and schedules. At the exact moment his watch stops ticking, his life comes to an abrupt end.

In *The House of the Seven Gables*, Hawthorne reconnected to the fierce forests of Maine that he knew first as a boy, and that Thoreau came to love as much as the woods outside Concord. The settlers in Maine, Hawthorne observes — as though he'd caught the pioneering spirit of Cooper — had won "the wild hand of nature by their own sturdy toil." Then, too, as though he'd caught Thoreau's wild tonic and his penchant for myth, he wrote that Waldo County, Maine was "still an unbroken wilderness." From the safety of Concord it probably looked that way. By 1851, when *The House of the Seven Gables* was published, Americans had already begun to feel that the nation had better begin to protect the environment against men and machines or there would be nothing left to protect. Thoreau invited citizens to "give a forest or a huckleberry field" to the town of Concord. He added that, "each town should have a park, or rather a primitive forest… where a stick should never be cut for fuel."

The 1850s, with its political strife, brought a new kind of "wild man" into public life never seen before, not even in Daniel Boone and Davy Crockett. No figure, not a president, a senator or a general, attracted more attention from writers than the militant foe of slavery, John Brown, and no one polarized the authors of the 1850s more than he. Of Brown, Hawthorne noted that he was a "blood-stained fanatic" and that, "Nobody was ever more justly hanged. He won his martyrdom fairly and took it firmly." Emerson saw Brown's "martyrdom" from a radical perspective. It would "make the gallows as glorious as the cross," he wrote. In his 1860 essay, "John Brown," Emerson described Brown as a true son of New England and as a descendant of "Orthodox Calvinists." His plan to spark a slave insurrection was not a "piece of spite or revenge," Emerson argued, "but the keeping of an oath to heaven and earth."

Thoreau's views matched Emerson's. He, too, noted that Brown was a true New Englander, though he also added in "A Plea for Captain John Brown" that he "was the most American of us all." The abolitionist publication, *The Liberator*, denounced Brown's raid on Harpers Ferry as "wild and apparently insane." Thoreau took exception to that description and insisted that it was "evidently far from being a wild and desperate act." Like Emerson, he saw the purity of Brown's spirit and asked his fellow citizens to see that, "No man in America has ever stood up so persistently and effectively for the dignity of human nature." In Thoreau's eyes, Brown was the quintessential Natural Man. He noted, in "The Last Days of John Brown," that Americans recognized that "what was called order was confusion, what was called justice, injustice, and that the best was deemed the worst."

Two years later, Thoreau died; Emerson delivered a eulogy at his funeral. No one knew Thoreau better than Emerson and no one defined his contradictory aspects more succinctly. Emerson noted in the essay, "Thoreau," that his old friend was a true American, that he loved the woods and the Indians, that he denounced the axe as the foe of the forest and that he had a "a habit of antagonism." Emerson recognized Thoreau's penchant for extremes and for paradoxes. "He praised wild mountains" for their "domestic air" and "commended the wilderness for resembling Rome and Paris," Emerson explained. That, too, was quintessential Thoreau, and so was his remark, "What we call wilderness is a civilization other than our own...Art is not tame and Nature is not wild."

CALIFORNIA WILD

Thoreau and Emerson both inspired John Muir (1838-1914), the Scots-born American naturalist and nature writer who helped turn Yosemite into a national park and who co-founded the Sierra Club, the granddaddy of American environmental organizations. Conservationists borrowed his name and paid homage to him when they created the John Muir Wilderness in California, the state he adopted as his own and where he lived from 1868 until his death in 1914, though he was also a tireless global traveler. Muir could sound like Thoreau, as when he noted, "When we try to pick out anything by itself we find it hitched to everything else in the universe. The whole wilderness in unity and interrelation is alive and familiar." He could sound like Emerson, too, the only naturalist and conservationist from the early nineteenth century who lived to witness the creation of Yellowstone as a national park in 1872.

When Emerson made his pilgrimage to see the wonders of Yosemite in California in 1871 at the age of sixty-seven — and met

Muir, who was half his age — he might have felt that Thoreau had come back to life. Muir probably felt that he had finally come face-to-face with the father of environmentalism. "You are yourself a sequoia," Muir told him, perhaps appealing to his vanity. Emerson recognized Muir's genius and urged his newfound friend to write. Muir had all the makings of a nature writer: a deep sense of spirituality; an eye for birds and bees; and an appreciation of the web of life. As Gretel Ehrlich — who has written eloquently about the American West in *The Solace of Open Spaces* (1985) and Greenland in *This Cold Heaven* (2001) — observed, Muir "danced between the tiniest detail and the most panoramic view." He had real whimsy of the sort that Thoreau expressed. When he encountered a Grizzly in the California wilderness he didn't run away. Instead, he raced directly at the beast to conduct an interview, or so he insisted. From that experience, he would say, he learned "the right manners of the wilderness."

In 1911, three years before his death, Muir described his initial California wilderness experiences in *My First Summer in the Sierra*. Working part time as a shepherd, he climbed trees, examined single raindrops up close and listened to the songs of the robin — the most American of birds, he insisted. In the mountains, he met Indians and complained about them because they demanded that he provide tobacco and whiskey. They didn't believe him when he insisted he hadn't any. But Indians also took him in hand and taught him to forage in nature's "wild garden."

He was a quick learner and liked the idea of living "like the wild animals," though he never wanted to live as the Indians lived. They led lives that he found "strangely dirty and irregular." He couldn't understand how they could be so soiled in so pristine a place as the wilderness. "Nothing truly wild is unclean," he insisted. Nothing went to waste in Muir's wilderness, either, and nothing was ever destroyed. "Everything in Nature called destruction must be creation," he explained. Not surprisingly, pure destruction also unfolded in the Sierra.

The Indians who had lived in Yosemite for eons were slaughtered or driven from their homes in 1851 by the Mariposa Battalion, a vigilante group paid by the the state of California. Sightseers and then tourists followed once the Indians were dispossessed. Muir wasn't outraged. His "wide sympathies," Gretel Ehrlich observed, did not include "aboriginal peoples," though he worked himself into a rage about dams, skyscrapers and "commercial interests." Muir realized that national parks weren't a panacea. Soon after Yosemite came under protection of the law, developers arrived. Hotels, roads and a railroad were built to lure and accomodate tourists. Farmers cultivated crops in Yosemite, though that was illegal — as was logging, which also went on. Muir didn't expect the strife between conservationists and developers to end. It would go on, he predicted, as "part of the universal battle between right and wrong."

In *My First Summer*, tourists from the East irk Muir far more than the Indians. They spend time and money to get to Yosemite, he complains, and endure "long rides to see the famous valley." But once they're in the valley itself they don't appreciate it. "They care but little for the glorious objects about them," he muttered. Meeting tourists face-to-face unsettled him. He wasn't sure if he had anything appropriate to wear, though he found a clean pair of overalls, a shirt and "a sort of jacket" and joined tourists in a hotel where he felt decidedly out of place.

In the mountains, where he enjoyed "God's sunshine" and basked in "God's beauty," he felt at home and as close to God as anyone might get on Earth. Yosemite was his "temple." His experiences there prompted him to note, at the end of *My First Summer in the Sierra*, that, "This I may say is the first time that I have been at church in California." His God Trip, as one might call it, didn't prevent him from doing political battle or alienate him from practical-minded environmentalists who adopted him as their patron saint. And yet a hundred years after it was first published, *My First Summer in the Sierra* feels like an artifact rather than a living work, in part because Muir describes nature as an emblem of the spiritual world. How many environmentalists today would say they see God in the wilderness? Probably not many backpackers now would say that they hike in Yosemite and feel that they are in the presence of the Old or New Testament God, though they might describe Yosemite as a sacred space and their experience there as spiritual. (I speak for myself and my fellow California hikers who feel the restorative force of forest and mountain but don't borrow the language of organized religion to express our feelings and don't evoke a specific deity.)

Muir feels closer to Emerson than to Edward Abbey (1927-1989), the author of the contemporary classic, *Desert Solitaire: A Season in the Wilderness*, which helped to inspire Earth First!, the radical organization that engaged in acts of sabotage to stop development and settlement in the West. Perhaps no twentieth-century writer thought more deliberately than Abbey did about the sound, the meaning of the word and the concept of wilderness. "What does it really mean?" he asked, and didn't give a clear and unambiguous answer, though he added that wilderness suggested the past, the unknown, the lost, the remote and the intimate, too.

Emerson's 1871 meeting with Muir completed a circle that he himself began with the essay, "Nature," which was written in an era that looked innocent nearly half a century later. The nineteenth century ended with a bang, bang, bang. As Peter Matthiessen points out in *Wildlife in America*, the 1880s and 1890s were "the bloodiest and most ruinous of all periods in the saga of American wildlife."

Concerned citizens protested the assault on nature and the decimation of forests, but on the whole Americans didn't appreciate the necessity of protecting nature, if only for their own self interest. Nearly 300 years after Henry Hudson and Robert Juet described the New World as a place of infinte plenty, Americans still believed that supply would always outdistance demand and that nothing, not earth, air, and water, would ever run out. Moreover, it didn't seem to help matters ecological that Americans read Cooper, looked at Audubon's prints, and admired Emerson's essay "Nature." Reading anti-war epics and novels and watching anti-war films didn't put an end to war, either. Even when Americans aimed to protect the environment it was often because protecting pockets of nature was good for business.

Teddy Roosevelt loved hunting and camping in the Great Outdoors and listening to the songs of the birds, but he also wanted to preserve Yosemite because Yosemite made the Golden State truly golden. "The prosperity of California," he noted, "depends on the preservation of her water supply; and the water supply cannot be preserved unless the forests are preserved." Conservationists learned to accept wilderness from almost any source and from a variety of motives. As my environmental friends in the Adirondacks often say about the battles they fight to preserve and restore the land they love, "We have to win over and over again. If we lose, we lose forever."

The year of Emerson's death, 1882, was the same year as the last bloody slaughter of the buffalo. Nearly extinct, the wild beast became an emblem in an American allegory about the apocalyptic destruction of the continent, its wildlife and its indigenous population. Once the wild was destroyed, it was safe to memorialize it. The buffalo appeared on one side of the nickel, the head of an Indian on the other side.

That was the American way: tame and destroy the wild and then recreate fake wild and wilderness theme parks. Call it a weird kind of transubstantiation whereby the sacred was profaned. "What a terrible destruction of life," Audubon observed early in the nineteenth century. He added that, "The prairies are literally *covered* with the skulls of the victims." He also noted that strange American habit: kill and eulogize. After the Indians were slaughtered, entrepreneurs named hotels after them. The luxurious "Indian Queen" stood where teepees once stood. After the rabbits and the quail were killed, tract housing developments were called "Rabbit Run" and "Quail Hollow."

Peter Matthiessen charts the wanton destruction in *Wild Life in America*, a classic about the annihilation of species. Unlike F. O. Matthiessen, Peter Matthiessen understood that the wilderness was a trope, though he also thought of it as a real place and an actual space on the American continent. "The true wilderness — the great woods and clear rivers, the wild swamps and grassy plains which once were the wonder of the world — has been largely despoiled," he wrote. "Today's voyager, approaching our shores through the oily waters of the coast, is greeted by smoke and the glint of industry on our fouled seaboard." Sounds like New Jersey or Texas.

Peter Matthiessen chronicled every twist and turn in the destruction of wild life in America, not for abstract philosophical or narrowly academic motives, but because he hoped that "North America may not become a wasteland of man's creation, in which no wild thing can live." As much as Thoreau and Muir, his was a voice calling out from the wilderness for wilderness. At a point in history when the annihilation of all living things seemed like a possibility, if not a probability, he affirmed the geography of hope. Moreover, even when it seemed that humanity was "lost in space," he reconnected humanity to Earth. Equipped with an "imagination of disaster," to borrow Susan Sontag's title for a 1965 essay, he harnessed his own thoughts of doom and gloom to generate creative work. Indeed, from his own fear of nuclear apocalypse, he made art and predicted that even if human beings as a species was destroyed, "a few creatures will survive in that ultimate wilderness we will leave behind."

THE WHITE WHALE

Hawthorne's friend and kindred spirit, Herman Melville, pondered the apocalypse and, in *Moby-Dick*, his one true work of genius — along with *Billy Budd* — he sailed into the Pacific on a floating inferno that served as an emblem of untrammeled nineteenth-century American capitalism. A monster so wrapped up in self that he's bent on destroying the world, the *Pequod's* captain warps and twists everyone and everything that he touches. In all the pages of mid-nineteenth-century literature in the English language, only Emily Bronte's Heathcliff — a savage in trousers and shoes — comes close to matching Ahab's blasphemous words that madden a crew of pagans and barbarians. Civilized insanity meets primitive awe and superstition in *Moby-Dick* and all hell breaks loose. Only Ishmael, an outcast of the universe, survives to tell the terrible and wonderful tale.

Ever since colonial times, the American self went about the business of magnifying itself, perhaps because no church, state, king or pope stood in its way and no force had the strength to knock it down to European size. And perhaps, too, the vastness of the unbroken continent demanded an unbridled self to battle Indians, mountains, rivers, deserts and inner demons, too, all the way to the Pacific and back, like Lewis and Clark or the hunters, trappers and soldiers who followed in their wake. By Melville's day the self had grown grotesque and hideous, though in the hands of Walt Whitman it became a benevolent force that reflected the essential goodness of the Cosmos.

Americans hailed "self-reliance" and the "self-made man." (The twenty-first century manufactured "selfies.") The American self wrapped itself in the Bible and in the flag, and proceeded to cannabilize anyone who didn't bow down and worship it as a second God.

Like Hawthorne, Melville dipped his pen in the ink of darkness and despair. Calvinism took root in his soul, though he also expressed optimism about America's future. "We are the pioneers of the world," he wrote of the United States in 1850. Americans were, he added, "the advance guard, sent on through the wilderness of untried things, to break a new path in the New World that is ours." Not surprisingly, in *Moby-Dick*, he wrote lyrically about nature, pioneers and the progenitor of American frontiersmen, Daniel Boone. In the chapter, "Schools and Schoolmasters," Melville depicts Boone as "venerable" and "moss-bearded." He explains that, like Boone, whales are solitary creatures and "will have no one near him but Nature herself, and her he takes to wife in the wilderness of waters." That image sexualizes the very nature that Emerson purged of sexuality. Into the ocean and all its creatures Melville infused both eros and death.

Years before he put his sailors aboard the *Pequod*, he had an affinity for the wild and the wilderness. He wrote about wilderness in *Typee* (1846), published five years before *Moby-Dick*, and that he subtitled "A Peep at Polynesian Life During a Four Months' Residence in a Valley of the Marquesas." On a remote island in the Pacific, Melville's American sailors trek through a "wilderness...untenanted since the morning of creation" until they reach an "enchanted garden" inhabited by beautiful women. *Typee* has moments of excitement; Melville works himself up into a white heat and condemns "the white civilized man" as the "most ferocious animal on the face of the earth." But his romance descends into a tropical stupor and the dreamy philosophizing prevents the book from soaring into unknown territory.

In *Moby-Dick*, Melville went wild about the wild, albeit in a deliberate way. In the first chapter, Ishmael provides a glimpse of the "wild distant seas" that will take him around the world and nearly cost him his life. The Pacific provides the backdrop for Melville's

Shakespearean drama; his Shakespearean language colors the seas and the sailors on the *Pequod*. If Roger Williams's *A Key* offers a litany on the words wild and wilderness, *Moby-Dick* offers an orgy on the same two words, as befitting the wildest American novel of the nineteenth century. Published in 1851 when Melville was 32, *Moby-Dick* belongs chronologically with *The Scarlet Letter, Leaves of Grass* and *Walden*, though it's close in spirit to the frontier that Boone explored half a century earlier and at the same time akin to the postmodern frontier that mimics itself and echoes itself. No nineteenth-century novel exemplies "wild form" more than *Moby-Dick* as Kerouac recognized. And no writer of the American Renaissance ignited Kerouac more than Melville. "I'm making *On the Road* a kind of Melvillean thing," he wrote in 1949.

No one ignited Melville's wildness more than Hawthorne. "In token of my admiration for his genius, this Book is Inscribed to Nathaniel Hawthorne," he wrote on the dedication page. In his brilliant review/essay, "Hawthorne and His Mosses" which was published in 1850, when he was in the midst of *Moby-Dick*, Melville explained that the best place to read Hawthorne and to write about him was "in a fine old farmhouse...surrounded by mountains, old woods, and Indian ponds." Proximity to the wilderness, he recognized, enhanced tales that were touched by "Puritanic gloom."

Melville knew plenty about gloom, doom and the Puritans and recognized instinctively Hawthorne's dark genius. "This great power of blackness in him derives its force from its appeal to the Calvinistic sense of Innate Depravity and Original Sin," Melville explained. He added that "no deeply thinking mind" was ever free of it. His own mind was also steeped in a sense of evil and depravity; *Moby-Dick* was ballasted with the "power of blackness."

Moby-Dick reads like a sport in the field of American literature, but it belongs to a distinctive New World linguistic tradition that goes back to Roger Williams and *A Key* — that strange and wonderful book that's a bit of everything: dictionary, auto-biography, travelogue and sheaf of poems. A reliable observer of New World cultures, Williams knew Indian myths and legends. He heard Indian storytellers, and, like a good Christian, introduced to the Indians, albeit with variations of his own, the Biblical story of Genesis, in which Adam is the Earth itself and Eve is his double and opposite. Melville's curiosity about Indians, Africans and South Sea islanders knew no bounds and he, too, found myths and legends fascinating — the more obscure the better.

Creating art out of chaos and the irrational was his genius. Annexing Shakespeare and Americanizing him was a sign of his intellectual audacity. In chapter 36 "The Quarter-Deck," and chapter 37 "Sunset," Melville sets the stage for a Shakespearean drama, though no Shakespearean drama unfolds as *Moby-Dick* unfolds. "Death to Moby-Dick!" Ahab cries out to the polygot crew that he unites with all the subtle and the sly mass psychology of a dictator. "God hunt us all, if we do not hunt Moby Dick to his death!" he exclaims. In the very next scene, Ahab sits alone and offers a mad soliloquy that rivals the madness of Shakespeare's King Lear. "I am madness maddened!" he exclaims. "That wild madness that's only calm to comprehend itself!" To create Ahab, Melville drew upon his own unmapped inner labyrinths. While Thoreau inisted that "in wildness is the preservation of the world," Melville might have insisted that in "wildness is the utter destruction of the world." Indeed, he witnessed in his own lifetime the annihilation of much of the continent of North America and the madness of the men who slaughtered the buffalo, massacred the Indians, annihilated the forests and raped the earth. No wonder he saw the world darkly.

As he wrote *Moby-Dick*, Melville pondered the vast untamed territory of the West, the prairies and the pioneers. "We seemed to be sailing through boundless fields of ripe and golden wheat,"

Ishmael observes in the chapter entitled "Brit." In "The Advocate," he notes that, "the whale-ship has been the pioneer in ferreting out the remotest and least known arts of the earth." The history of the American frontier and the archetype of the voyage to the ends of the earth inform *Moby-Dick*.

In his epic, Melville offers wild men — Queequeg, Ahab and the crew — wild seas, a wild whale and wild whale hunts. The true wildness of the book resides in the language itself. Melville's description of the brutal assault on nature, and nature's refusal to lie down and die peacefully, demanded a sinewy and yet lyrical prose. Linguistic exuberances rise on nearly every page of *Moby-Dick*. Ishmael talks about "wild conceits" in the first chapter. He goes on to describe Queequeg's "wild pipe," the "wild-ocean born" sailors, the "wild vagueness of painfulness" associated with Ahab and Ahab's own "wild approval." There are also "wild exclamations upon the whale" and "wild longings," plus comments from Ishmael in which he reflects on his own true nature and that of his fellows.

"Your true whale-hunter is as much a savage as an Iroquois," he exclaims in the chapter in which he explores the representations of whales in paint, wood and stone. In true American fashion, Ishmael declares his independence from his fellow citizens, insists on his disloyalty to civilization and defies all authority figures. "I myself am a savage, owning no allegiance but to the King of the Cannibals; and ready at any moment to rebel against him," he cries.

In the chapter entitled, "The Honor and Glory of Whaling," he reveals the workings of his own mind and explains, "There are some enterprises in which a careful disorderliness is the true method." Indeed, deliberate disorderliness is Melville's method in *Moby-Dick*. Critics who fault the novel for its shapelessness, moodiness and bleakness miss the point. F. O. Matthiessen criticized Melville because he "did not achieve in *Moby-Dick* a *Paradise Lost* or a *Faust*." That's using a European stick to beat an American leviathan and not fair to Melville, Milton or Goethe, all of them literary rebels in their own way and in their own day.

Matthiessen's criticism of *Moby-Dick* is echoed in other books about the literature of the United States. In *The American Novel and Its Tradition*, Richard Chase scolds Melville for the "awkward philosophizing that encumbers portions of the book." Chase also faults Melville for writing chapters such as the "Whiteness of the Whale" because they don't advance the plot. Melville's conception of the novel was much bigger than Matthiessen and Chase allowed.

Newton Arvin — one of the foremost critics of nineteenth- century American literature — lauded Melville's unparalleled achievement in *Moby-Dick*. Ahab, he explains, is "what our wildest, most egotistic, most purely malevolence would wish to be." He suggests that, "the Whale embodies nothing so much as the normally innocent forces of wild nature." That seems obvious. What might not be as obvious is the wildness of the book itself, its form and its voice, as well as the underlying force of Melville's creativity that tracks and charts self-destruction, annihilation and apocalypse in the Pacific.

Melville had to have known that he was creating a wild book. He had to have known that in the process of writing *Moby-Dick* he broke with Milton and the giants of English literature. American independence and freedom cry out in the chapters set in Manhattan and New Bedford and those set on distance seas. As George Orwell noted, "Melville owed much to American liberty" and to "the American wildness of spirit."

The words wild and wilderness ripple across Melville's epic, except in the wildest chapters of all, 133, 134 and 135, which describe "The Chase" for Moby-Dick. It would have been superfluous to roll out those words for the final assault on the white whale. At the end of the book, fate asserts itself. Chance and free will fall into place and help to shape a kind of fearful symmetry as Blake would call it.

In his letters, Melville describes his ideas about uninhib-
ited expression, the reading public and publication. His goal, he
explained, was to unmuzzle himself. To do that, he knew, required
courage. In 1849, on the cusp of writing *Moby-Dick*, he explained
to his friend and editor Evert A. Duyckinck "that an author can
never — under no conceivable circumstances — be at all frank
with his readers." He wasn't generalizing about the circumstances
that all writers faced. He was talking about himself and about the
reading public in America in 1849.

"Could I, for one, be frank with them – how would they
cease their railing," he insisted. Readers of the worst kind —
barely literate and largely uncultured — exercised a kind of tyranny over the writer, he complained. "This country & nearly all
its affairs are governed by sturdy backwoodsmen — noble fellows enough, but not at all literary & who care not a fig for any
authors except those who write those most saleable of all books
nowadays," Melville wrote. The pioneers and frontiersmen that
he dearly loved also inhibited the development of a real American
culture. They weren't the only problem. In one of his best-known
letters, Melville rebuked himself for his own failure to be frank.
"Dollars damn me," he exclaimed. "What I feel most moved to
write, that is banned — it will not pay. Yet, altogether write the
other way I cannot."

Caught between popular fiction and the marketplace on
the one hand, and genuine literature for the ages on the other,
he worked himself deeper and deeper into an artistic dilemma
before he worked himself out of it. After he finished *Moby-Dick*,
he acknowledged its secret sources and called it "a romance of
adventure, founded upon certain wild legends in the Southern
Sperm Whale Fisheries." Borrowing another metaphor, Melville
explained that his romance of adventure was written from hemp
and not from silk. He never suggests that Ishmael and Queequeg

smoke cannabis or any mind-altering substance in the cannibal's "wild pipe," but that possibility has occured to readers. Something intoxicates Ishmael, perhaps language itself that might be called the last wild frontier. In 1849, 1850 and 1851, the language of Melville's letters became increasingly unrestrained.

Casting himself as a literary chef, he noted of *Moby-Dick* that he had "to cook the thing up" and " throw in a little fancy." Divided in his feelings for nature, romanticism and the outdoors, he explored them to the edge, egged on by his determination to show optimistic writers such as Emerson just how destructive and ornery nature could be. Indeed, he ridiculed the romantic idea of going to the woods, which he connected to Goethe, the chief culprit, in his eyes, of the whole school of romanticism. At the same time, Melville noted the joys of "lying on the grass on a warm summer's day." In the mode of the pantheists, he exclaimed, "Your legs seem to send out shoots into the earth. Your hair feels like leaves upon your head. That is the all feeling." He could be as romantic as Goethe, Emerson and Thoreau.

The quintessential man in the open air, Melville boasted that like the French romantics he went "Jacquesizing in the woods" and that "the heavens themselves looking so ripe and ruddy, that it must be harvest-time with angels." Had it been merely infused with Calvinism, *Moby-Dick* would probably have sunk beneath the waves. Fortunately, it moves back and forth from a Calvinistic view of human nature to a pantheistic view. It moves, too, from the seas of adventure fiction into uncharted philosophical depths. In *Moby-Dick*, Melville broke free from the demands of the dollar, and, as he realized, wrote a "wicked book" though he also felt "spotless as a lamb." It felt better to write a wicked book than a goody-goody tale that would be appealing even to uneducated backwoodsmen. "Woe to the writer who seeks to please rather than to appall," he wrote.

Wickedness and wildness both inhabit Melville's earliest
books, though he toned them down to please the public and perhaps to satisfy his own censorious self. Not so in *Moby-Dick*, in
which his hero and narrator not only lives with and among barbarians, but also empathizes with them. In *Moby-Dick*, Melville
allowed the primitive to express itself through him. Indeed, he
felt that he looked out at the wilderness of the sea and saw it
through the eyes of barbarians from the far corners of the world.
As Melville's biographer Newton Arvin pointed out, "only a
man who had himself been a hunter of wild beasts...could have
re-entered so far into the intense and complex feelings with which
the primitive hunter regards the animals about him and especially
his chief prey." It helped him, too, that he'd lived among South
Sea islanders and witnessed the spread of the toxicity of European
and American civilization.

With *Moby-Dick* and with the volumes that followed it
— *Pierre* (1852), *Israel Potter* (1855) and *The Confidence-Man*
(1857) — Melville cut himself off from the reading public and
the success and fame that he briefly enjoyed with his South Sea
romances, *Typee* and *Omoo*. Like Hawthorne — like almost all
great American novelists, one might say — he wrote himself into
the wilderness and died largely unknown and forgotten. The
twentieth century rediscovered him and his classic; the reading,
the teaching and the writing of American literature haven't been
the same since.

*

I read *Moby-Dick* when I was a teenager and have never
stopped rereading it over the past sixty years. The opening line,
"Call me Ishmael" still excites my imagination, the quest for the
white whale carries me along at breakneck speed and the chapters

about whaling and whales continue to intrigue me. *Moby-Dick* has been my Harvard and my Yale. I'm sure that my character and my personality — my own wildness and wickedness, too – have been shaped by my experiences with Washington Irving, Poe, Melville, Hawthorne, Whitman, Thoreau, and Dickinson. Their work has probably made me as disloyal to civilization as any overtly political tome or pamphlet. I'm revived and restored by their work in much the same way that I'm revived and restored when I go into woods, forests, mountains and deserts. Moreover, when I've read to children and to adults, too, I've chosen to read the classics of American literature.

CHAPTER 9

COQUETTE

Emily Dickinson

WHITMAN & MATTHIESSEN

In an essay about Walt Whitman and *Leaves of Grass*, the Argentinian author Jorge Luis Borges notes that Whitman "carried out the most wide-ranging and audacious experiment that the history of literature records" and that "he came up with a strange creature we have not yet fully understood, and he gave this creature the name Walt Whitman." In *Song of Myself*, the poet names himself, advertizes himself, puffs himself up and provides his local and galactic coordinates. "Walt Whitman, a kosmos, of Manhattan the son," he explains. "I give the sign of democracy." A citizen of America, the world and the universe itself, Whitman defies almost all boundaries, moves back and forth to the city, to the North and the South, among the free and the slave, with men and women, immigrants and natives, Indians and settlers in the vast rambunctuous territory of North America. "Not a bit tamed," he proclaims, he's also more than a bit tame as befits a poet who is "large" and contains "multitudes." In the line in which he sees himself accurately, he writes, "I contradict myself."

Emily Dickinson claimed ignorance of *Leaves of Grass*, though she admitted that she'd heard of it. "I never read his Book — but was told that he was disgraceful," she explained in 1862. Like Whitman, Dickinson sang a song of herself and like him she contradicted herself. A localist and a globalist, she wrote as boy and girl, Pagan and Christian, meek and defiant, ecstatic and gloomy, a Calvinist and a Romantic, pansexual and asexual.

In her writing and in her life, which she crafted into a work of art, she showed that the wild and the wilderness are available to anyone with an imagination, a hunger for adventure, and no attachments whatsoever to a particular destination at the end of the road or the end of a poem. Emily Dickinson's wilderness lives in the commons, belongs to writers and readers, outcasts and outsiders, to everybody and nobody. Order and disorder provide bookends for work that broke down barriers and found its own shape. She lived and wrote as wildly as Whitman.

"Mad" in the sense that Kerouac and the Beats used the word, she recognized as they did that "Much Madness is Divinest sense." At the start of *On the Road*, Kerouac explains that the only people who appeal to him are "the mad ones, the ones who are mad to live, mad to talk, mad to be saved, desirous of everything at the same time, the ones who never yawn or say a commonplace thing." Dickinson must have occasionally yawned, but life didn't bore her; she could be entertained by the kinds of common ordinary occurrences that seemed sacred to Kerouac and who found beatitude among the beaten down. Like the Beats, she empathized with men and women deemed dangerous and placed in prisons and asylums. Jerome Charyn captures Dickinson's intensity in his novel about her in which she loves wildness and lives as though she's mad to live and to talk, though perhaps not mad to be saved. She was in no rush for Christian salvation.

Fictions about Dickinson — Charyn's *The Secret Life of Emily Dickinson*, Barbara Dana's *A Voice of Her Own*, Daniela Gioseffi's

Wild Nights, Wild Nights and Joyce Carol Oates's short story about her in the short story collection *Wild Nights!* — offer complex portraits. Indeed they trace ambiguities, nuances and contradictions often missing from biographies. There's a certain fugitive quality about her that has attracted the attention of poets, as well as novelists and literary theorists who have found in her life and work keys to unlock the mysteries of art, creativity and genius.

Dickinson was patronized by the patriarchy in her own day, touted as a modernist by the modernists and turned into a radical feminist by radical feminists near the end of the twentieth century. Largely unknown to the literati of her own day, she was consecrated a supernova in the twentieth century by poets and critics such as Amy Lowell, Allen Tate and Conrad Aiken, a Pulitzer Prize–winner and the author of more than thirty books, who noted that, "she came to full 'consciousness' at the very moment when American literature came to flower." Indeed, she's as much a part of the American Renaissance as Whitman or Emerson.

Academics were slow to appreciate her genius and to accord her her rightful place in the flowering of our national letters, perhaps because she didn't belong to a movement or even a ladies' luncheon club. She didn't set herself up in a literary capital such as Boston or New York and didn't have influential friends in the White House, as Hawthorne did.

Every writer needs something or someone to act as buffer, someone to be a mentor or a coach. Dickinson had help all along the way from friends and family, though she never married, never had a husband, a fiancé, a literary agent or a secretary. She never went West like her long time friend and booster, Helen Hunt Jackson, the author of *Ramona*, who became a popular writer in her own day. With support from her intimate circle, Dickinson wrote complex lyrics that sometimes seem to come apart at the seams. In poem #867 from about 1864, she wrote, "I felt a

Cleaving in my Mind —/As if my Brain had split."

F. O. Matthiessen mentions Dickinson briefly in *American Renaissance*, though he also wrote about her in an essay, "The Problem of the Private Poet," published in 1945 in *The Kenyon Review*. When readers turn to *American Renaissance* to look for Dickinson they're usually disappointed. Still, even Matthiessen's brief comments about Dickinson say a lot about her. In the section of *American Renaissance* in which he discusses the language of the Transcendentalists, he observed that, "Emily Dickinson's poems, because they have such tension, are much more authentically in the metaphysical tradition than Emerson's are." In a seminal passage a few hundred pages further on, he wrote that, "Emily Dickinson's comprehension of Shakespeare's treatment of good and evil was as undoubtedly as keen as Melville's." He added a caveat, however: "her own drama, however intense, remained personal and lyric."

Another critic might have used the phrase, "personal and lyric," in a wholly positive sense. There's nothing innately wrong with the personal and the lyric. Every writer doesn't have to write epics and tragedies and create mad, sad, bad characters like Lear, Macbeth, Roger Chillingsworth and Captain Ahab. Dickinson knew Shakespeare's benchmark tragedies, but she also enjoyed *Antony and Cleopatra* and *As You Like It*.

Matthiessen gravitated toward artists such as Herman Melville, who knew the darkest of Shakespeare's dramas and grappled with the theme of the individual at war with society and with nature. He was also deeply attracted to those two Anglo-American artists, Henry James and T. S. Eliot, who were tightly wound. In his 1918 essay on James, Eliot noted that he "had a mind so fine that no idea could violate it" and in his 1919 essay "Tradition and the Individual Talent," he explained that, "Poetry is not a turning loose of emotion, but an escape from emotion; it is not the expression of personality, but an escape from personality." Dickinson liberated her emotions in poetry and poured out her own personalities.

Her bookishness took her into the nineteenth-century English novels of George Eliot — "she is the Lane to the Indies," she exclaimed — and into the pages of the "gigantic Emily Bronte," as she called her. She curled up with the Brontes, whom she described whimsically as "the Yorkshire girls." Dickinson preferred female writers, including Sappho, to male writers, though how much she knew of Sappho isn't clear. From fragments she formed whole worlds.

By Matthiessen's standards, Dickinson was poorly educated; she didn't have a college degree and could hardly have been called an academician. She might have responded to Matthiessen as she responded to Thomas Wentworth Higginson, another Harvard graduate as well as a minister, writer and soldier during the Civil War, who cultivated an intense curiosity about Dickinson. She amused him, flirted with him in the manner of a coquette and kept him at a distance, too. "I went to school — but in your manner of the phrase — had no education," she told him in one of the many letters in which she both informed him and teased him.

Dickinson knew Harvard men; Matthiessen wouldn't have fazed her. Moreover, she was soundly educated at school and self-taught at home. Her favorite authors, she explained to Higginson, included Ruskin, Keats, Sir Thomas Browne, and Robert and Elizabeth Barrett Browning. She weighted the list she sent him in favor of men perhaps because she felt that he would disapprove of her preference for women writers.

An outlier without direct connections to faculty members at major universities and editorial committees at publishing houses, she nonetheless understood the male world of professors, students and editors. She came close to the male academic world through the experiences of her brother, Austin, who surrendered to his sister the field of poetry, his first love, then attended Harvard and followed his father into the legal profession. As the first-born child and only son in a prosperous bourgeois family, Austin was obliged to graduate from college, put on a collar and work in an office. Emily, as the older of two daughters, was expected to stay at home and attend to the household, to her demanding father and invalid mother. College was out of the question. Radcliffe, Harvard's all-female counterpart, didn't exist until 1879, seven years before her death. She could not have attended even if she had wanted to. Forty-nine years old when Radcliffe opened its doors, she would have been told she was too old to apply.

She did, however, attend Mt. Holyoke Female Seminary — the first college for women in the United States — for one brief but incisive academic year. Her education ought to have impressed Matthiessen. At Mt. Holyoke, she studied history, chemistry and physiology, read poetry, the Bible, Shakespeare and more. She also learned not to fear science and technology, realized that religion was a kind of fiction made up by humans, and that God was no more real than those two fictitious gentlemen Jack Frost and Santa Claus.

On several occasions, Dickinson came physically close to Harvard. Long before Matthiessen arrived on the campus, she visited Boston — in 1844, 1846, 1851 and 1864 — wandered about the city and along the Charles River. With her eyesight failing, she consulted a doctor in 1864. Even with diminished eyesight, she knew how to navigate urban as well as rural settings. Ten years earlier, in 1854, she visited Philadelphia and Washington, D.C. with her father and her sister, Lavinia, sailed down the Potomac River, visited George Washington's tomb and attended church.

In an 1864 letter that she wrote to Lavinia, she referred to Cambridgeport and its adjacent neighborhoods, as "Strange Towns." But even there, "in the wilderness" of those unfamiliar territories, she was happy to report that she made friends. That she found the wilderness in the East, not the West, amused her.

Like Thoreau, she found frontiers wherever she fronted a fact. Like Emily Bronte, she often felt alone and lonely, a solitary creature in a world from which there was no escape, save through the imagination and in the richness of the natural world that always awaited her.

Matthiessen might have been as lonely and as tense as Dickinson, though like her he surrounded himself with friends, except on the day he committed suicide. Had he wanted to find his own distressed state of mind reflected in poetry, he could not have found many poems more prescient than hers. She wrote about suicide in poem # 994, in which she describes a man who caresses a trigger and then wanders out of life.

WOMAN IN THE OPEN AIR

Matthiessen allowed himself to be moved by a few of Dickinson's poems, especially #124. The first draft was written in 1859 and describes a death in life and a life in death for "the meek members of the Resurrection." In his essay on her work, Matthiessen described # 124 as a perfect "union between metrical delicacy and philosophical discovery." You wish he had been able to relate to more of her poems. But there was no way that he could revere Dickinson and her verse with the same intensity that he revered Melville and his fiction, and no way he could bring himself to say anything about her as praiseworthy as his words about the author of *Moby-Dick*. He didn't see that if Melville was Man in the Open Air, Dickinson was Woman in the Open Air, and that she spoke with a public as well as a private voice. Like Whitman, she could speak for the nation and the cosmos, as well as for the local and the microscopic.

Matthiessen didn't see that, like Melville — who celebrated

"the great God absolute, the center and circumference of all democracy" — she, too, revered the great God absolute and American democracy, too. Her democratic way wasn't Melville's manly democracy, but it was no less deep and genuine. Her patriotism and nationalism were no less pronounced, either. "I am more and more convinced that this is a great country," she wrote at 22. At 55, she wrote, "I saw the American flag last night in the shutting West, and felt for every Exile."

"My Business is Circumference," she told Higginson, though she would also say, "My business is to love" — and love she did, with an undiluted passion. Moreover, like Melville and Whitman she sang of the common man — beggars, blacksmiths, auctioneers and miners — who were as splendid specimens of humanity as Melville's sailors. Dickinson didn't cross the Pacific or embrace it in her work as Melville did, but she traveled there and back in her imagination.

Despite his criticism of her, Matthiessen recognized that she and Emerson marked "the beginning and the end of the New England renaissance." He knew that while she didn't write a major work in the 1850s — the decade of *The Scarlet Letter*, *Moby-Dick*, *Leaves of Grass* and *Walden* — she shared the ethos of the era. Emerson and Dickinson serve as the book ends for a literary movement that was linked to the very soil and spirit of New England.

Matthiessen recognized that her "great gift was for poetic thought" and that she "possessed the dramatic, indeed, the tragic sense lacking from Emerson's radiant eloquence." Perhaps if he hadn't committed suicide — he hurled himself from a hotel window in 1950 — and had revised *American Renaissance,* he would have understood that no one single author can write the enduring signature of an age — except perhaps a William Shakespeare or a "Judith Shakespeare," to borrow the name of the imaginary sister of the Bard that Virginia Woolf decribes in *A Room of Her Own*. Had Matthiessen lived into the 1960s, witnessed the new generation of American women writers, he might have allowed that Dickinson offers one of the most enduring signatures of mid-nineteenth-century America. Indeed, we might call it the Age of Whitman and Dickinson. As the post-modern poet Brenda Hillman notes in a preface to *The Pocket Emily Dickinson* (1995), Dickinson and Whitman are "the spiritual mother and father of American poetry."

Despite his flaws, Matthiessen offered a method that might be useful to interpret and understand women writers as well as men. I've used his approach all through this book, even while I've taken issue with him. An astute student of diction and rhetoric, Matthiessen noted that, "an artist's use of language is the most sensitive index to cultural history, since a man can articulate only what he is, and what he has been made by the society of which he is a willing or unwilling part." Had he applied his own method to Dickinson, he would have made startling discoveries.

Take, for example, the key words that run through this book — "wilderness" and "wild" — as pivotal in a frontier society such as the United States as the word "democracy." Dickinson wrote intensely about wilds and the wildernesses of her own making. She didn't use the words to mean the wide-open spaces of the American west with its vast forests, mountains, deserts and prairies, but as metaphors, tropes and symbols. Cooper would probably have been perturbed by her use of the words, but Hawthorne and Melville would have been pleasantly surprised and even excited. She could write conceits as wild as Melville's and she explored the psychological wilderness as extensively as Hawthorne in poems that test the limits of truth, hope and despair.

Explore Thyself

A geographer of the soul, Dickinson mapped the wilderness inside, as might be expected from a poet who wrote in poem # 814: "Soto! Explore thyself!" Hernando De Soto (1496/1497-1542) led the first European expedition into the heart of North America and died on the banks of the Mississippi River. Dickinson knew his story and saw him as an apt illustration of the outward-bound European who looked everywhere but into his own undiscovered self.

All her life, she explored her inner continent of fears, fantasies and hopes — and urged her friends and family members to explore themselves. "Travel why to Nature, when she dwells with us," she observed in a letter to Elizabeth Holland (1823-1896), the wife of Dr. Josiah Holland (1819-1881), with whom she shared a great many poems. The Hollands were practically her own family. On the subject of nature, Dickinson added, "Those who lift their hats shall see her, as devout do God."

In her cosmology, nature and the wilderness were two separate entities, much as woods and wilderness were also separate. Dickinson's Nature, with a capital N, might be a she or a he, feminine or masculine. Her nature included the rat and the snake as well the robin and the rose. It was "red in tooth and claw," to borrow a phrase used by Tennyson, the Victorian poet whose work she knew. Her nature came with sharp thorns as well as with lush flowers.

"Nature begins to work and I am assisting her a little," she wrote in May 1874 as spring unfolded in her garden. Nature welcomed her and she welcomed it with an open heart and not just in spring but also in winter, summer and fall. Not so the wilderness. She often envisioned it as a force antithetical to life and saw it as sexless, timeless, borderless, and not unlike Infinity and Eternity, those two twin territories she dreaded and yet explored bravely in her poetry.

In a wonderful letter that she wrote at sixteen, she asked her friend, Abiah Root, "Does Eternity appear dreadful to you?" and answered it herself. "It seems so dark to me that I almost wish there was no Eternity," she explained. Subversive at sixteen, she carried on her subversive ways and dared to ask probing questions all her life. In 1850 — on the verge of beginning to write poetry — she asked her friend, Jane Humphrey, whether her life had been "filled with hope and the future or waste and a weary wilderness and no one knew the end?" Webster's dictionary, her near constant companion, listed the word "waste" as a synonym for wilderness. For settlers, the point was to use it, exploit it and extract wealth from it through labor. Otherwise it had no commercial value.

As a young woman, Dickinson interrogated language intensely. Like the village blacksmith whom she read about in Longfellow's poetry, she hammered away — with force and with delicacy, too — at words. In the smithy of her soul, she made metaphors into precise tools. Her image of the blacksmith might seem odd given her own gender and social class. But she identified with the village blacksmith as a craftsman in poem #401, probably from 1862, that Higginson referred to as "The White Heat."

Like Emerson, she used organic metaphors for her art. "Is not a bulb the most captivating floral form," she wrote to Maria Whitney. The bulb seems an especially apt metaphor for her own poems that came from deep inside her, went through a process of maturation and reached an apex or flowering. "Split the lark — and you'll find the Music," she wrote in poem #905 from about 1865. Her own song, the song of her self, came from deep within and was inseparable from her very being.

All her life, she pushed back the edges of the frontier in her own consciousness, where she lived more fully than anywhere else, except in poetry. At times, she dreaded the future, but mostly she looked forward to it with a sense of anticipation. Life was a kind of ecstasy. Nature offered hope; spring always arrived, though not always on time, and brought with it a pagan resurrection of all living things. For Dickinson, the outside reflected the inside and the inside reflected the outside; up and down, near and far, big and little, high and low fit together in a picture puzzle.

From Dickinson's perspective, a traveler could set foot in nature and plunge in the woods, as she herself did, to take in the open air spectacle of trees, flowers, birds and the elemental drama of sunrise and sunset, the rising and the setting of the moon, and the movement of the stars in the sky.

As the author of nearly 1800 poems written over the course of more than thirty years, she experimented with form and content, revised and reversed direction. To use words like "always" and "never" to define her oeuvre would be misleading. Still, it's fair to say that she wasn't a nature poet in the conventional sense of the phrase. She didn't write, as Joyce Kilmer did, "I think that I shall never see / A poem lovely as a tree," though she might have endorsed the sentiment.

In Dickinson's world, one couldn't literally step into a wilderness, though the wilderness could and did invade human space, take one hostage, and hold the psyche prisoner. Dickinson's wilderness often accompanies death and despair; it requires all one's inner resources to resist its onslaughts.

Sometimes she used the word "wild" interchangeably with "wilderness," as when she wrote to her cousin, Perez Cowan, in 1869 to say, "Dying is a wild night and a new road!" Death wasn't the end of the road. It opened another door, though she didn't believe in the conventional notion of Heaven. As inevitable and as inescapable as death, wild days and wild nights arrive in her world whether she wanted them or not. "Life is so rotary that the wilderness falls to each, sometime," she told her cousins, Louise and Frances Norcross who, like Dr. and Mrs. Holland, were among her soul mates.

In her view, it was necessary to remember that the wilderness and the wild were a kind of negation. Even as a young woman, she conjured up a vision of "primeval nothingness." The wild, the wilderness, and nothingness were the antithesis of joy, ecstasy and home. "Within," she wrote, "is so wild a place we are soon dismayed." But the wild world within, the primeval nothingness, had to be endured. There was no way around it, no way to skirt it. One had to go through it. The inner wild offered wonders.

Intensely self-conscious, she recognized that she bridled when she was told, "No" and "don't" and "that's forbidden." In a letter of 1861, she observed, "Odd, that I, who say 'No' so much, cannot bear it from others." As a mature woman, she realized that "No" was as much a part of life as "Yes." "No" was the tip of nothingness. "Dont you know that 'No' is the wildest word we consign to Language?" she asked Judge Otis Lord who had a crush on her, and she a crush on him. She loved him and yet she kept him at bay. She cracked the word "No" in his face knowing its power, knowing, too, that when she told him "No" he wouldn't hear it or accept it. "No" was the wildest word in the language because it sparked its opposite. To Otis, she explained, "Dont you know you are happiest while I withhold and not confer."

Camille Paglia, the author of *Sexual Personae*, describes Dickinson as a decadent artist and as a "sadomasochist imagist." A provocative idea, it's over the top, like a great many of the author's remarks in *Sexual Personae*. Dickinson saw nature as pure and simple, albeit all powerful. A naturalist and an optimist, she was too much of a millenarian and a utopian to be a decadent poet, and, if she toyed with images of whips and chains, it was not to inflict pain and suffering, but to express the wildness of her own heretical imagination. No thought, image or sentiment was off limits. "Title divine – is mine!" she wrote in poem # 194 initially drafted in 1861, in which she scoffed at the notion of divinity and matrimony, and mocked the narrow roles that husbands and wives played with one another.

Wild at heart, she realized that human beings as a species were uncivilized once you removed the outer layer. Crack the whip in their faces and try to tame them, and they would resist, rebel and revert to their innate wildness. Repeatedly, she came back to the vital wildness that stirred from within. Repeatedly she came back to the barren wilderness of dying and death. Matthiessen might have argued that her wilderness was private and that her idiosyncratic use of the word presents a hurdle for readers. He'd have a point.

Readers coming upon the word "wilderness" in her poetry — especially if they're familiar with Puritan texts — might be puzzled. Dickinson worked with definitions all her own, along with a personal Weltanschauung of the wilderness. Still, patient readers can decipher meanings by zooming in and zooming out. It helps to pay close attention to the particular text at hand, relate the word "wilderness" to the words around it, and gage the relationship of individual wilderness poems to her entire body of work. Readers who expect the unexpected and who anticipate the paradoxical and the contradictory will be prepared to grapple with her lyrics.

Dickinson's most intimate dance with the wilderness coincided with her most productive period as a poet from 1861 to 1865, a five-year period in which she wrote 937 poems. To borrow an image from the American wilderness experience, one might say that she cleared 937 separate tracts in the wilderness of words. In poem #230, from about 1861, she exclaims, "No Wilderness – can be/Where *this* attendeth me." As long as she chooses to breathe in and out she knows that she'll not experience the death and decay that accompanies the wilderness.

In poem #400, from 1862, she explores the idea of the survival of the fittest and expresses a kind of Darwinian perspective on plants, animals and humans. She read Darwin — or at least heard her contemporaries discuss him — and concluded that Darwinian science and Christianity were incompatible. In #400, inhospitable nature brings out the essential identity in all living things. "The Hemlock's nature thrives – on cold," she wrote as though identifying with the hardy hemlock.

What's notable about poem #400 is that the wilderness includes human beings. With a sense of awe, Dickinson writes that, "men, must slake in Wilderness — / And in the Desert — cloy." Dickinson came back to wilderness in poem #421, also from 1862. Once again, she grasps at something she can't see, something from the past that's painful. All that she knows for certain, she suggests in the poem, is that for a very long, indeterminate period of time, she lived with hurt. Now, as she looks back, she can't say for certain when or why it ended, only that she had become accustomed to it. The "Wilderness" — she capitalizes the word — appears in the next-to-the-last line in contrast to the domestic world of her childhood. Ironically, only in the vast, unmapped "Wilderness" can she locate the site of her own localized ache.

The contrast between wilderness and domesticity informs poems #421 and #512, from about 1863. "It may be Wilderness — without," she writes. "But Holiday — excludes the night — / — And it is Bells — within." Books create a buffer against the wilderness; the "Kinsmen of the Shelf" stand against the "failing men" outdoors. The books in her "small Library" provide food for body and soul. Dickinson eroticizes the act of reading through the words "Enamor," "obtained" and "satisfy." Moreover, she suggests that the reader of books enjoys spices and flavors in the library more than in the dining room.

In poem #770 from about 1863, Dickinson weighs society and the intellect against a wilderness where the mind, like "Wine," must be "sealed." When the speaker finds her mind refreshed by the transcendental "Hermetic Mind," she knows she can bear the "Desert or the Wilderness" and "go elastic — Or as One." There's a sense of "Mystery" in Poem #794, from about 1864, that tells the story of an unnamed woman not seen for a year, though whether dead in the "Wilderness" — again capitalized — or alive in "that Etherial Zone" no one knows, or can know, for certain.

Dickinson's letters parallel her wild/wilderness poems. When her mother died in 1882 after a prolonged illness, Dickinson relayed the news to Maria Whitney, a modern-language teacher at Smith College who ought to have appreciated her shrewd use of language. "We bear her dear form through the Wilderness," she wrote. A literal-minded reader might imagine the members of the Dickinson clan carrying a weighty coffin toward the town cemetery. More metaphorically inclined readers might derive a mood, a feeling and a state of mind.

Implicit in Dickinson's use of the word wilderness was a rejection of the Puritan view of North America as a place of the devil and his disciples, and as a territory of witches practicing witchcraft. Dickinson's wilderness harbors no evil witches, no sinister trees and no diabolical Indians. It led to no Promised Land and to no Heaven.

Unlike the Puritans, she liked witches, witchcraft and necromancy, or so her poems suggest. Indians rarely appear in her world but when they do they're not terrifying. She didn't want to drive them out, but invite them in. When an Indian appeared at the kitchen door of the Dickinson home with wild berries to sell or to barter with her sister, Emily used the colloquial phrase "tawny" to mean Indian and wrote, "Vinnie trades Blackberries with a Tawny Girl." On another occasion, an Indian woman with a "dazzling baby" and "gay baskets" came to the door. Dickinson invited the woman inside. They talked across cultures and generations about life and death, birds, buttercups, and the Indian baby who had recently learned to walk.

If Puritans hated it — whatever it might be — Dickinson was sure to love it. If they revered it, she was likely to unmask it and deconstruct it. The family Bible, she knew, was "sacred" to her father. Not to her. "The Bible dealt with the Centre, not with the Circumference," she complained. In poem #1577 from about 1882 she looked back at The "Good Book," as orthodox Christians called it, and offered heretical thoughts: "The Bible is an antique Volume — /Written by faded Men." (She revised #1577 several times. Here I quote from the last version she wrote.)

Stripping aside its sacred halo and taking on a jocular tone, she described "Eden" as "the ancient Homestead." She preferred, she said, Orpheus's "Sermon" to any sermons drawn from "the Antique Christian Volume."

When she was informed that Theodore Parker — the abolitionist, transcendentalist and Unitarian minister — was "poison," she replied, "Then I like poison very well." Parker's books, including *The Two Christian Celebrations,* which she read and enjoyed, undermined Puritan orthodoxy, helped to build the transcendental movement, and fueled her own version of transcendentalism. Dickinson read the literature of the transcendental movement, including Emerson's poems. She shared Emerson's notion that "Ours is the Revolutionary age when man is coming back to Consciousness," though when Emerson came to Amherst to speak and visited her brother and sister-in-law, she didn't make a fuss about the event. The idea that readers would lionize an author unnerved her.

Even a naïve reader notices that Dickinson turned Puritanism inside out and upside down. After all, she enshrined the erotic and pursued the sexual, reinvented the Garden of Eden and resurrected Adam and Eve as young lovers. Like William Blake, who recognized paradise in England, she saw paradise in New England. In a letter that she wrote to her brother Austin in 1851, she broke from prose into poetry, and addressed him directly. "Never mind silent forests, Austin," she exclaimed. "Never mind silent fields." In their place, she offered a "*brighter* garden" with magically "unfading flowers." The poem ends with a seductive invitation, "Prithee, my Brother, into my garden come!" She was Eve herself and the goddess of nature in a world in which she declared God the father dead.

Still, the Puritans might have enjoyed her dark, gloomy poems including #407 from about 1862 that begins, "One need not be a Chamber – to be Haunted" and #340, also from 1862, that begins "I felt a Funeral, in my Brain." Dickinson explored morbidity with a passion.

Her inner self burrowed deep down into the nineteenth-century zeitgeist and took up its concerns with success and failure, victory and defeat. In poem #383, from about 1862, she wrote a paean to the railroad. Her father, who brought the iron horse to Amherst, would have approved of her cheerful advertisement for travel by that miracle of modern transportation.

On the whole, however, she didn't believe in technological progress. The soul that she explored could be as dark, deceptive and terrified as any Puritan self, especially in the image, "Ourself — behind ourself — Concealed" which appears in poem #407. In Dickinson's world, one has to navigate one's way through corridors and cut one's way through thickets in order to surprise the authentic self behind the concealed self. The primitive, with its totems and taboos, exists beneath the veneer of the rational and the respectable.

Despite Dickinson's affinities with modernism and postmodernism, she would have been surprised and perhaps even shocked by the modern environmental movement. Surely she would have been dubious about the efficacy of the 1964 Wilderness Act and amused by the idea that one could camp, hike and backpack in a national park. She would chortle at government regulations and wonder about fences, signs and uniformed rangers, though she understood conservation and preservation. An anarchist, or perhaps a libertarian at heart, she bridled at restrictions. "Don't fence me in" would have been her theme song — at least one of them. "Over the fence —/... I could climb," she wrote in #271 from about 1861 and went on to trespass and transgress further than real and imaginary fields.

Dickinson's elaborate dance with Puritanism concludes an American dance that began with Anne Hutchinson and Roger Williams, resurfaced with Hawthorne and Melville. It reemerged again on the West coast in the wild poetry of Robinson Jeffers. She also began a new chapter in which she reframed the history of European settlement of the New World as the unsettling of America. The Civil War, the single most unsettling force in her life, required the settling power of poetry.

TOMAHAWK IN MY SIDE

Subversive in a playful way, the speaker in an early poem speaks coquettishly. "Put down the apple Adam/And come away with me," she exclaimed, then mailed the poem to William Howland, an Amherst College graduate, who studied law with her father and who promptly sent it to the *Springfield Daily Republican* where it appeared as an anonymous Valentine verse on February 20, 1852. Six years later, in 1858 another Dickinson poem, #11, also appeared in the *Springfield Daily Republican*, with a title not her own, plus editorial changes she had not approved. Perhaps her seeming indifference to publication had something to do with the ease with which her early poems appeared in print, and the failure of her friends to ask permission before sending them into the world.

As she aged, Dickinson didn't cease to be playful and subversive, though as her art matured she created far more surrealistic and grotesque images, many of them linked to a fantastic frontier of her own making. In an 1862 letter to an unknown recipient, she wrote, "I've got a Tomahawk in my side but that dont hurt her much." Again, to an unknown recipient, she wrote of her own "Backwoodsman ways." To Higginson, she spoke of her own "Barefoot-Rank" as though she saw herself as a backwoodsman's wife or a simple, shoeless peasant girl. A romantic, she identified with gentle "Forest Folk" and with "the Druid."

The inner tensions that inform Dickinson's experimental poems from the 1860s first appeared in the letters she wrote in the 1840s and 1850s. Prose came first, poetry second, though in many of her early letters she was already poetic if not clearly a poet. To appreciate the shifts she made from prose to poetry and to understand her long self-imposed apprenticeship that preceded her emergence as an original American artist, it's helpful to remember two D. H. Lawrence comments. In the Preface to his *Collected Poems* (1928), he noted that his own poems constituted a biography that shed light on his "emotional and inner life." Lawrence also observed that, "even the best poetry when it is at all personal, needs the penumbra of its own time and circumstance to make it full and whole."

That holds true for Dickinson's best poetry. From the cauldron of her teens and twenties came compressed lyrics that shed light on her innermost heart and on the frontiers of her private life. Moreover, knowing the penumbra of the place and age in which she lived suggests that even when she was obscure she drew on a culture she shared with contemporaries. Dickinson's wildly disciplined imagination was shaped by the culture of her own home, the town of Amherst with its Puritans and its Irish immigrants, and the contours of Massachusetts and the United States in the years before, during and after the Civil War — the cataclysmic event that cut through her life in much the same way that World War I cut through the lives of D. H. Lawrence, Virginia Woolf and their generation.

The guns of the union and the confederate armies killed a great deal of the kind of romance that thrived in poetry in the 1850s, including Dickinson's. After 1861, she couldn't write the same way again, much as Lawrence couldn't write the same way after 1914. World War I, Virginia Woolf observed in *A Room of One's Own* (1929), destroyed the illusions that enabled Alfred Lord Tennyson and Christina Rossetti to "sing so passionately." The Civil War destroyed Dickinson's illusions and yet she went on writing with more passion and precision than ever before. For decades, she had prepared herself well for life in a small room in a nation at war and news of casualties from the battlefield.

Dickinson had everything that Virginia Woolf insisted a woman needed in order to write. She had a room of her own, not with one but two different views. While she had no bank account and no trust fund that might have provided fifty pounds a year — the minimal amount necessary for a woman writer, Woolf insisted — she could count on her father to pay for everything she needed. Father and daughter had an unwritten agreement.

She could be as wild as she wanted to be at night in her room, if she behaved like a proper member of the bourgeoisie downstairs during the day. She needed the discipline of the first floor so that she could flourish in the liberty of the second, and, while she didn't know Gustave Flaubert or his novels, she lived in accord with his formula for stimulating the creative juices: "Be regular and orderly in your life, so that you may be violent and original in your work."

Dickinson played by the rules of bourgeois society so that she could break them. At times, she felt trapped in her house and a prisoner of domesticity, but she learned to turn captivity into creative space. Unlike Walt Whitman, who broadcast "his barbaric yawp over the roofs of the world" and eagerly posed for photographers, Emily seems to have run from them. In the one authentic Daguerreotype of her from her teens — taken by an unknown, itinerant daguerreotypist in 1847 or 1848 — she sits upright in a chair and rests her right arm on a small table. A book nestles close to her. In her left hand, she holds a bouquet of flowers; her eyes stare straight ahead. In the Daguerreotype, she looks like an anxious teenager not "a creature of the stolid bourgeois world" as Brenda Wineapple insists in *White Heat,* her dual biography of Dickinson and Thomas Wentworth Higginson. She wears no jewelry, her black dress looks as plain as can be, and her hair, parted down the middle, isn't held in place by a showy clasp or tie.

As a gallivanting teenager, it wasn't easy for Emily, or Emilie as she also called herself, not to dart about. In the Daguerreotype she looks ill at ease in her own body; she weighed about 100 pounds and stood about five-feet tall. "I do not care for the body," she wrote soon after she sat for the Daguerreotype. The body, she noted, was "obtrusive." She added, "I love the timid soul."

In Dickinson's case, a Daguerreotype isn't worth a thousand words. Her letters from the 1840s and 1850s — when she was in her teens and her twenties — reveal a great deal about her as a girl who evolved into a woman and a student who morphed into a scholar. One can't help but observe the ongoing tension between the wild Emilie and the tame Emily, the conventional and unconventional daughter and sister, as well as the clash between the awkward social butterfly and the poised young woman.

From the start of her letter-writing days, she focused on the minutia of daily life — washing dishes and dusting furniture — as well as the larger drama of living, loving and dying. None of her schoolwork remains, but one insightful comment from a teacher at Amherst Academy has. Years after Emily graduated, Daniel

Fiske remembered that her "compositions were strikingly original; and in both thought and style seemed beyond her years and always attracted much attention in the school and, I am afraid, excited not a little envy."

Her letters reveal her struggles to find the precise word — *le mot juste* Flaubert would have said. By the age of 15, she consciously thought of herself, if not as a writer per se, than certainly as a person who wrote. "My writing apparatus is upon a stand before me, and all things are ready," she explained to her confidant Abiah Root in 1845. By 1853, she boasted to her brother, who had also put ink to paper, "I've been in the habit *myself* of writing."

At the same time, she complained, "I am lonely lately." While she liked to write, she didn't like to be alone and lonely and of necessity writing demanded that she sit solitary at her desk. Dickinson was twelve when she began to complain about loneliness; she went on complaining for years, though she also came to realize that she could be by herself and not feel lonely, as when she wrote serenely to her sister-in-law to be, Susan Gilbert: "I...walk the Streets alone — often at night." She took her dog, Carlo, and a lantern to light the way.

GIRLHOOD

The world was a siren that offered a series of temptations. The agitated girls at Amherst Academy and at Mr. Holyoke Female Seminary tugged at her heart and she spent nights romping with them. In a letter to Jane Humphrey, a doctor's daughter who would break with Puritan tradition and marry a businessman, not a minister, she remembered the "good times we used to have jumping into bed." Her imagination turned memories into poetic narrative. "Your image still haunts me and tantalizes me," she told Abiah.

In her haunted mind, she mythologized Abiah, turning her from plain teenager into flower goddess. Dickinson wrote that she would never forget the day when she "ascended the stairs, bedecked with dandelions." The passage of time both magnified and diminshed events; in hindsight, her prankishness looked sedate, though she observed, "I used, now and then, to cut a timid caper."

Nearly all the girls cut capers. Then, they graduated, found husbands and settled down. Emily seems to have remained wilder longer than others. She jumped, raced, "dashed down stairs" and made "flying retreats" to her own chamber where she gathered her wits and wrote in a furiously composed way. Slow she didn't understand; alacrity she did — and she welcomed the days to come when her heart would "gang wildly beating."

Ecstasy she craved, especially outdoors, where she roamed with "pleasure parties" made up of girls and boys, or went alone on "rambles" in the hills and the mountains to collect flowers: adder's tongue, yellow violets and blood-root. Foraging for flowers reduced the tensions she accumulated. "How it calms my mind… to walk out in the green fields & beside the pleasant streams," she explained. To prepare herself for her expeditions she read, perused and reread Edward Hitchcock's invaluable *Catalogue of Plants Growing Without Cultivation in the Vicinity of Amherst College* (1820). She and her classmates plunged into woods and fields, collected flowers for botany class and learned valuable lessons from their conservation-minded teacher.

Miss Lyon imposed strict rules for foraging. Indeed, the girls were restricted "in the plucking of wild flowers…lest many species which have been abundant in this vicinity should become extinct." The extinction of flowers would mean the end of botany class. Dickinson found the news sobering. By 1848, when she was 18, she observed, "There are not many wild flowers near, for the girls have driven them to a distance, and we are obliged to walk quite a distance."

The American ecologist, Garrett Hardin, the author of the seminal essay, "The Tragedy of the Commons" (1968), would probably have pointed to the actions of Dickinson and her fellow students as an example of the hurt that innocent individuals inflict on the environment. The girls surely caused less harm than the railroad and the turnpike, but picking flowers wasn't as idyllic a pursuit as it seemed.

Walking far afield, Dickinson gathered plants and flowers for her *Herbarium*, a hardbound album with a green cover, now housed at Harvard and published in a facsimile edition in 2006. The plants and flowers are native and invasive, cultivated and wild: dandelion, Indian pipe (said to look like an Indian pipe), tobacco, cannabis, poppy, ginseng, comfrey, hollyhock, lavender and hundreds more that added up to 424 species on 66 pages. She knew that flowers had the power to medicate and intoxicate; no wonder she wrote, "Inebriate of air am I" in poem #207 from 1861, in which bees are drunk on foxgloves and she is tipsy. She had only to breathe the country air around Amherst to feel transcendent in the manner of Emerson and Thoreau. Flowers in the woods appealed to her sensibility more than cultivated flowers, though she grew peonies, dahlias, lilies and lilacs. She plucked weeds because they were not meant for gardens, though they were appropriate for the woods. Flowers that exploded in bright color under dark canopies caught her eyes.

Dickinson arranged her prize specimens neatly on the pages of her *Herbarium* and identified them with the classification system devised by Carl Linnaeus, the eighteenth-century botanist and zoologist. But she did not place her flowers in a logical sequence, as though she meant to preserve the wildness of the outdoors. She didn't describe the provenance of the flowers, either. She might have picked them in a meadow, a backyard or from a windowsill. She didn't say. Moreover, she didn't give her *Herbarium* a title and didn't include her name on the cover or inside the book. Here, as in her poetry, she hid behind a mask of anonymity as though fame was foreign to her nature.

Her letters reveal her love for foraging as well as for flowery language. Not content to describe the specimens she collected on her woodland rambles as mere plants and flowers, she called them the "beautiful children of spring." Moreover, she quickly came to see language as a flower. In a densely packed letter from October 1848 she told Abiah that the thoughts she put down on paper were "fictions," "vain imaginations" and "flowers of speech."

Playing the role of temptress, Dickinson explained that her thoughts were not harmless products of her imagination, but explicitly dangerous, even poisonous. She advised Abiah to "avoid them as the snake." Not surprisingly, snakes didn't terrify Dickinson herself — no plant or animal did, not even the leopards she befriends in her poetry as though they were simply big beautiful cats. Dirt didn't make her anxious or frighten her, either.

As an adult she looked back at her years as a precocious teenager and explained that she resisted the fictions adults told her about woods, snakes and forest folk. Two hundred years after the original New England heretics — Anne Hutchinson and Roger Williams — were driven into the woods by the self-appointed guards of public morality, the elders of Amherst repeated the old Puritan bugaboos.

"When much in the Woods as a Little Girl," Emily wrote, "I was told that the Snake would bite me, that I might pick a poisonous flower, or Goblins kidnap me, but I went along and met no one but Angels, who were far shyer of me, than I could be of them." Here as elsewhere, she retold the story of Genesis; in her version the snake wasn't evil, Adam and Eve didn't fall forever and the Garden of Eden didn't vanish in a puff of smoke. At school when she felt homesick she described home as "a bit of Eden."

A child of Puritans and Puritanism, she gradually shed Puritan ideas about the perils of the imagination, the pitfalls of fiction and the snares of metaphor. In her teens, she toyed with metaphor and took tentative steps toward poetry as a lifelong passion and avocation. At 15, she observed that, "poetical…is what young ladies aim to be now-a-days." Young ladies in Amherst didn't aim as high as Elizabeth Barrett Browning but they could turn a poetical phrase in polite society and in a letter.

Pop poetry went hand in hand with mass culture in mid-nineteenth century New England. Dickinson noticed, read and commented on the poems that were published in the daily newspaper. Florence Vane's "Are We Almost There?" struck her as "beautiful." But she craved poetry of a higher sort and found it in the work of Emily Bronte. She also read, albeit with far less enthusiasm, Oliver Wendell Holmes's *Poems* and Emerson's *Poems*, too, and noted tepidly they "are very pleasant to me."

At Mt. Holyoke Seminary, girls were forbidden to write the "foolish notes called Valentines," but they found ways to write them and post them anyway. At first Emily disapproved. "I have not written one nor do I now intend to," she boasted. But she disobeyed the rules, wrote and posted her own Valentines. She enjoyed subterranean communication and the joys of the clandestine rendezvous; she aided and abetted her brother and her future sister-in-law, Sue, when they courted one another secretly.

School drilled discipline into Dickinson and encouraged a love of disobedience, too. As far as teachers were concerned, free time didn't exist. Nearly every minute had to be accounted for. The girls might have been back in the seventeenth century. At 9:45 p.m. the final bell of the day signaled bedtime. "We dont often obey the first warning to retire," Dickinson boasted. She belonged to the collective "We" and felt proud that neither she nor the other girls had become slaves to the clock. Even as a teenager she belonged to nighttime. In poem #61, written a decade after she left Mt. Holyoke, she acknowledged that affinity in the image, "My Wheel is in the dark."

At Mt. Holyoke, Dickinson complained about girls with "rough & uncultivated manners." On the whole, however, she appreciated their "grace" and applauded their "desire to make one another happy." She loved Jane Humphrey, Abiah Root, Emily Fowler and beautiful Sophia Holland, who died in 1844. Her instructors could also make her swoon. "I love all the teachers," she explained. In love with love itself, she gave herself up to romance and wrote what she called *billet doux* to her girlfriends. When she summoned the courage to write her first Valentine, which begins "Oh the Earth was made for lovers," she included the names of her friends — Sarah, Eliza, Emeline, and Harriet — and herself: "she with *curling hair.*"

She wrestled with teachers who told her that she would be an eternal "castaway" unless she committed herself to the church, Christianity and Christ. To complicate matters, the voices commanding her to convert were inside as well as outside. "I continually hear Christ saying to me Daughter give me thine heart," she wrote in 1846. She heard Christ's call in 1846, 1848 and again in 1850 when nearly all of Amherst's respectable citizens took Christ as their savior. Thrice she was tempted and thrice she turned away. "Many are flocking to the ark of safety," she wrote. "I have not yet given up to the claims of Christ."

Attracted to Christ and yet loath to accept him, she was buffeted across an existential void. "I am alone with God," she wrote. "I feel that I am sailing upon the brink of an awful precipice, from which I cannot escape & over which I fear my little boat will soon glide."

Emily didn't feel superior to the converts. "I am not happy… that I did not give up & become a Christian," she wrote at the end of a prolonged spiritual bout. She rejected Christ and yet the language and the imagery of Christianity stuck with her. She wrote about "Satan" as though he might be in the next room and described the world as "sinful" and "wicked," as though she inherited Cotton Mather's mission in the New World, though she also proclaimed, "I love to be surly – and muggy – and cross." She even seems to use the word "cross" subversively. Indeed, she thought of herself as "wicked" and wrote poetry that the poet and critic Allen Tate called "blasphemous" and "almost obscene." Tate suggested that, "Cotton Mather would have burnt her as a witch."

When her days at Mt. Holyoke came to an end, she went home to face her demanding family and the tasks of housekeeping. Nature beckoned and gentlemen called. "Some members of another sex come in to spend the hours," she wrote. On a day in May, a young man invited her to ride in "the woods, the sweet still woods." A day outdoors with a boy tempted her. She wanted to bolt from home and from responsibilities, but she knew that she could not go. "I wanted to exceedingly," she wrote. "And told him I could not."

"In the end," she allowed that she had won "a kind of helpless victory." Domesticity didn't suit her and she mocked herself. "I am yet Queen of the court, if regalia be dust and dirt," she wrote. Ennui took her hostage; one day seemed like the next and she thought she might be mad: "I do long for the time when I may count the hours without incurring the charge of *Femina insania*."

She railed against "ugly time — and space," wanted to "fly away," then took refuge in her "little chamber," which felt like a prison, and found refuge in the liberty of her own mind. Nathaniel Hawthorne's romance *The House of the Seven Gables* helped to calm her nerves; she identified with Hepzibah, the descendant of Puritans who becomes a fiery "dragon" and who is saved after she no longer wants to be saved or to go on living. Freud might have called Dickinson hysterical; pop psychologists would label her high strung. "When I am not happy there is a sting in every enjoyment," she wrote.

Indifferent to social movements and causes — she never mounted a barricade, didn't attend the 1848 Seneca Falls Convention that launched the feminist movement — she nonetheless imbibed the zeitgeist of revolution. She knew about Shelley's and Byron's days as rebels, read Dickens's *A Tale of Two Cities,* and noted that her sister-in-law looked like Madame Roland and played at revolution. Dickinson parodied and echoed radical rhetoric. "We'll pull society up to the roots, and plant it in a different place," she wrote ecstatically. "We'll build Alms-houses, and transcendental State prisons." Escalating her imagery, she added, "Alpha shall kiss Omega – we will ride up the hill of glory – Hallelujah."

WILD THINGS IN CAPTIVITY

In his poem, "Wild Things in Captivity" D. H. Lawrence wrote, "Wild things in captivity/While they keep their own wild purity/Won't breed, they mope, they die." Dickinson moped, didn't breed, and yet she didn't die either. She learned to keep her mind alive and to observe nature if only from behind kitchen windows. When she foraged she came home with an acorn, a few moss blossoms and "a little shell of a snail so whitened by the snow you would think 'twas a cunning artist had carved it from alabaster."

Her reverence for nature grew stronger as she aged and in nature she found models for poems that seemed to have been sculpted from alabaster. Dickinson wanted readers to regard her images as faithful reproductions. "Do I paint it natural...so you think how it looks?" she asked her sister-in-law. She aimed to depict New England landscapes realistically. "Tell all the truth but tell it slant," she wrote in poem #1263 from about 1872.

Readers usually remember the phrase "tell it slant" but not "Tell all the truth." It might be useful to remember that telling the truth mattered as much to her as telling it slant. The artist had to sneak up on the truth and present it at an angle or readers wouldn't see it at all. *She* might not see it all.

In 1861, a year before the start of the Civil War, she began to write letters to someone she addressed as "Master," a mysterious figure who might be a fiction or a "flower of speech" to borrow her own expression. Her master might even be the "*Femina insania*" to whom she uttered the wildest, craziest ideas and images that came to her. In the first letter to Master, she reverted to a narrative about childhood and confessed that she wanted to "play in the woods till Dark." She also took on the identity of a mother and wrote about the child in herself who "outgrew Me." She added that she "got tired holding him." In the second letter, she calls herself "Daisy" — she's the flower who bends to the needs of Master — and promises him, "I will be your best little girl." Soon other powerful figures made themselves available as correspondents: the newspaper editor, Samuel Bowles; her brother Austin; and Higginson, who was appointed colonel of a regiment of African American soldiers in 1862 and became a bright light in Dickinson's firmament.

In her second letter to Higginson she confessed, "I had a terror — since September — I could tell to none – and so I sing, as the Boy does by the Burying Ground — because I am afraid." What was she afraid of? What couldn't she confide to anyone? Though she was a night person, she was also afraid of the night, afraid of the wild and afraid of the force that might rise up in her like Vesuvius, the Italian volcano that fascinated her. The Civil War terrified Dickinson as she had never been terrified before and distant battles impinged on her consciousness. The social order she inhabited seemed to come undone.

In a letter to Samuel Bowles in the winter of 1862, she

conjured a vision of "Chaos," "Treason" and "Decay." To her cousin Louise, she asked, "When did the war really begin?" She asked a similar question fifteen years earlier about another military conflict: "Has the Mexican War terminated?" Scholars point to her question as evidence of her ignorance about war and peace, but it could just as well be interpreted as a sign of her genuine curiosity about the causes of the war as the nation was swept up in military fever.

The Civil War came home to her world in a terrifying way in the winter of 1862, when she learned that Frazer Stearns, the son of the president of Amherst College, died in the battle of New Bern, North Carolina. A telegram brought the news; then his body arrived along with a union officer. The funeral took place in the village church. "Crowds came to tell him good-night, choirs sang to him, pastors told how brave he was — early-soldier heart," Dickinson noted.

She continued to think and write about Stearns in part because his death "chilled" her brother, who told Emily that his "Brain keeps saying over 'Frazer is killed.'" Two years later, Austin himself was drafted; he paid $500 for a substitute. The word "killed" kept going around and around in Emily's head, as did news of the war and Higginson. With Stearns on her mind, she wrote to Higginson to tell him, "I trust you may pass the limit of War" and "Could you, with honor, avoid Death, I entreat you — Sir." She also offered her reflections on war itself that, she noted, "feels to me like an oblique place." To her Norcross cousins, she dispatched a letter about the emotional climate of the country in wartime. "Sorrow seems more general than it did, and not the estate of a few persons, since the war began," she wrote.

In her letters to Higginson she combined war talk with poetry talk; the two were inextricably connected. She explained to Higginson, who had to be told *how* to read her poems, "When I state myself, as the Representative of the Verse — it does not mean — me — but a supposed person." True enough the "I" who appears in Dickinson's poems isn't always Emily Dickinson, but the "I" often comes close to the author herself. In fact, she usually kept the Sabbath at home, while others kept it in church, as she confessed in a poem that ends "So instead of getting to Heaven, at last – / I'm going, all along."

Higginson cringed when he read her work. Without success, he tried "to lead her in the direction of rules and traditions." She tried to please him and to mend her unruliness. Along with the poems she mailed him, she included a letter in which she asked him if they were "more orderly?" In her own defense, she explained — using both military and political imagery — "I had no Monarch in my life, and cannot rule myself, and when I try to organize, my little Force explodes, and leaves me bare and charred." It was as though the Civil War raged inside.

Dickinson and Higginson spoke different literary languages and inhabited different cultures. He looked at her and saw "a coquette" and an "enigma." She described herself to him as "the only Kangaroo among the Beauty." Her poems struck him as "weird & strange." She deferred to his expertise as a critic and promised him, "I will be patient, constant, never reject your knife." But knives cut and could injure. When Higginson's wife Mary died in 1877, the dynamic between Emily and Thomas shifted. She presented herself as a guide and offered to go through the grieving process with him. "The Wilderness is new — to you," she wrote. "Master, let me lead you."

From 1862 when she first wrote to Higginson, until 1877, the year his wife died, she wrote more than 1,000 poems. Her body of work would have reinforced Hawthorne's notion, expressed in *The Scarlet Letter,* that, "It is remarkable that persons who speculate the most boldly often conform with the most perfect quietude to the external regulations of society." Dickinson adhered to Amherst's rules: didn't gamble, get drunk or beat servants as neighbors did. She cooked and cleaned house, attended to the needs of her mother, father, brother and sister. When a friend, a relative or acquaintance married, died or gave birth to a child, she sent a card, usually accompanied by flowers.

"Regular and orderly...like a bourgeois" in her public personae, she wrote like a libertine in poem #269 from about 1861 that begins "Wild nights – Wild nights!" and that offers erotic images of luxurious nights "Rowing in Eden." The "I" who imagines the wild occasions with an unnamed other wants to be "Done with the Compass —/ Done with the Chart!" At the end, the speaker dreams of calm: "Might I but moor — tonight —/ in thee!" When Higginson co-edited, with Mabel Loomis Todd, the first edition of Dickinson's verse he was afraid to include #269. "One poem only I dread a little to print — that wonderful 'Wild Nights,' lest the malignant read into it more than that virgin recluse ever dreamed of putting there," he wrote. But he and Mrs. Todd included it. It was too "wonderful" to omit.

In poem #276 from about 1862, there's no "I," but the narrator clearly affiliates herself with a tawny Leopard and reviles the civilization that means to stifle and suppress her. Shaped by nature and spurned by civilization, Dickinson's Leopard is pitiable, though unbowed. Removed from her native habitat and attended by a "keeper," she retains her "Memories – of Palm." Poem #764 from 1863 begins "My Life had stood – a Loaded Gun." Here, Dickinson draws upon memories of the woods and transforms them into a meditation on death, mastery and eternity. Few Dickinson poems are as violent or as original. The "Loaded Gun" — the narrator of the poem — roams the woods, hunts the doe and guards her master. Curiously, master can sleep and die peacefully. The Loaded Gun can kill but not die.

In a 1976 essay about Dickinson entitled "Vesuvius at Home," the poet and critic Adrienne Rich scrutinizes the "Loaded

Gun" metaphor, and while she admits that it eludes interpretation, she also says that, "it is a central poem in understanding
Emily Dickinson, and ourselves, and the condition of the woman
artist, particularly in the nineteenth century." For Rich, it's the
perfect Dickinson poem about "psychic extremity." In her view,
Dickinson lived a dangerous life that divided her. Split between
her "publicly acceptable persona" and an inner self that was "unacceptable," "creative" and "monstrous," Dickinson moved in opposing directions, and never as violently as in "Loaded Gun."

"More than any other poet," Rich wrote, "Emily Dickinson
seemed to tell me that the intense inner event, the personal and
psychological, was inseparable from the universal." There's a savvy
rejoinder to Matthiessen's complaint about her verse.

Until the end, Dickinson went on writing wildly. "The mob
within the heart / Police cannot suppress," she wrote in poem
#1763 as though prepared to storm the Bastille within. She also
wrote about the wilderness until the end, as in poem #1646 from
1884 that begins with an image of "The Auctioneer of Parting."
Composed not long before her death, the poem links the sacred
and the sacrilegious, money and faith. Dickinson drew on memories of New England auctions and auctioneering as well as on
her private reservoir of spirituality. Her auctioneer "Shouts even
from the Crucifix" and "brings his Hammer down." She adds,
as though mocking a property owner calculating expenses and
losses: "He only sells the Wilderness, / The prices of Despair."

*

In hindsight, Thomas Higginson looks like a bewildered
fellow who had little sense of the cultural innovations going on
all around him. In 1861, he published an article in the *Atlantic
Monthly* in which he noted of the United States, "There is as yet

no literature, but only glimpses and guideboards." Unappreciative of *Moby-Dick*, *The Scarlet Letter*, *Walden* or *Leaves of Grass*, he noted snidely in 1871, "It is no discredit to Walt Whitman that he wrote *Leaves of Grass*, only that he did not burn it afterwards." The American Renaissance went over and under Higginson, though it went over and under a great many other readers and critics, too.

It wasn't until the 1920s that the literary world recognized the magnitude of American art and expression in the decade that ran up to the Civil War. In the 1920s — as Americans experienced a Second Renaissance, brought on by Jean Toomer, Willa Cather, Eugene O'Neill, Gertrude Stein, William Faulkner, Ernest Hemingway and F. Scott Fitzgerald — literary and cultural critics finally paid homage to the groundbreaking work of Melville, Thoreau, Dickinson and their contemporaries.

In one masterful book after another — Lawrence's *Studies in Classic American Literature* (1923), Mary Austin's *The American Rhythm* (1923), William Carlos Williams's *In the American Grain* (1925) and Lewis Mumford's *The Golden Day* (1926) — the contours of American literature began to take shape. Lawrence and Mumford didn't write about Dickinson, but Williams did. In his view, she was the only "true woman in flower," and starved "of passion in her father's garden."

Lawrence, Williams and Mumford took different directions to get to the heart of American literature, but they recognized the same elements: the power of the Puritans; the force of the frontier and the wilderness; the proliferation of bloodshed and violence; and the ability of Americans to rise above their own provincialism and desolation. "Whitman, the great poet, has meant so much to me," Lawrence wrote in the last chapter of *Studies in Classic American Literature*. "Ahead of all poets, pioneering into the wilderness of unopened life." Lawrence caught the American sense of place and echoed the American idioms of the nineteenth century.

Higginson came through when Dickinson died. At her funeral, he read Emily Bronte's poem "No Coward's Soul is Mine," which she selected as the one verse she wanted to be recited after her death. Amherst's leading citizens, including the president of the college, aided by Irish workmen, lifted her "dainty white casket" and carried it out the rear door of the house and through a field of buttercups.

Emily scripted her funeral perfectly. Family members and friends followed the coffin "irregularly through ferny footpaths to the little cemetery." According to *The Springfield Daily Republican*, "The grave was lined with green boughs and all of the flowers of which there were a profusion were planted in the grave with her." To friends and neighbors who knew her and who had read her work, Dickinson was neither a myth nor a mystery. In an obituary, the newspaper noted that Dickinson was a "magician" who "caught the shadowy apparitions of her own brain." The author of the piece noted that she was driven by the "electric spark" of her "intuitions and analyses," and that she sifted through libraries, "seized the kernel" of truth and expressed it in "the fewest words." It would be decades before anyone wrote about her with that kind of verve and precision.

A spy in the house of the bourgeois, Emily mapped its spacious rooms, dark closets, haunted attics and subterranean passages. She also kept herself from going mad and ending up in a sanatorium or a prison. "Assent — and you are sane —/Demur — you're straightway dangerous — And handled with a Chain," she wrote. Armed with a compact lexicon that was as dangerous in her hands as a loaded gun, she disguised herself as dutiful daughter. Upstairs she "undressed," to borrow the word she used in a letter to Higginson when she described her authentic thoughts. Undressed thoughts, she explained, were discriminating and elevating.

Dressed thoughts all looked "alike and numb," she complained.

Dickinson inhabited a prison of her own making. Still, it was her prison and no one else's, and that's what mattered. In her chamber she had everything she needed. Downstairs during the day, she attended to housekeeping. Upstairs she threw herself into "Wild nights – Wild nights." Dickinson was a coquettishly innocent Eve, or perhaps simply an Eve conscious of her sex and her sexuality who wanted to go back to a Garden of Eden of her own making with birds, flowers and snakes. She liked to give herself a fright. She liked to write undressed and naked on the page.

CHAPTER 10

SATIRIST

Mark Twain

BARBARIAN

W hen Mark Twain arrived on the national literary scene with a folksy tale about a celebrated
jumping frog in a remote county in California, the United States boasted a genuine literature all its own. The frog from Calaveras joined a venerable
American bestiary that included Poe's raven and Melville's whale.
Faulkner's bear would come later. Seemingly out of nowhere,
Mark Twain carved out a place for himself as a humorist who
poked fun at sacred cows and at himself, too. Still, as late as the
1860s, British and American critics rarely recognized the innovative fiction and poetry born in the United States that set it apart
from the work of Shakespeare, Milton and Byron. There were exceptions to the cultural blindness. The unconventional Scotsman
Andrew Lang (1844-1912) dubbed Twain "one of the greatest
contemporary makers of fiction." He lauded *The Adventures of*

Huckleberry Finn as "the great American novel" and praised it as a work of "art," too, at a time when the Concord, Massachusetts public library — Emerson's library no less — banned it. Lang, the maverick Scotsman, anticipated Ernest Hemingway and F. Scott Fitzgerald, who both hailed *Huckleberry Finn* as the great American novel, though that was not until the 1930s. In time, even T. S. Eliot, a royalist, conservative and traditionalist, would join the fans of Twain, albeit with reservations.

"*Huckleberry Finn* is not the kind of story in which the author knows, from the beginning, what is going to happen," Eliot scolded. He also observed that Twain remained boyish for much of his life and "never became in all respects mature." American biographers such as Bernard DeVoto echoed Eliot and described Twain as immature. They psychoanalyzed him as a man-child suffocated by his mother and his wife. Poor Mark Twain. He brought much of the abuse down on his own head by erupting with pithy remarks that offended genteel New Englanders.

Born in Missouri in 1835 to a slave-owning family, he abhorred the system of slavery and loved individual slaves, including his "Mammy" who helped to raise him. Perhaps the quintessential peripatetic nineteenth-century American author, he brought literature into the wide-open spaces of the West and around the world. He skewered American presidents and plutocrats — "wild beasts," he called them — who turned the nation into an imperial monster. Near the end of his life, he denounced King Leopold's atrocities in the Belgian Congo, and, closer to home, exposed the sham philanthropy, as he called it, of Andrew Carnegie. Then, too, he denounced millionaires such as Jay Gould because they "taught the entire nation to make a god of money." The old South, even with its "puerile sentimentality" and "soft, sappy, melancholy" struck him as "preferable" to the "lust for money" ushered in by the California Gold Rush and the robber barons.

No one knew Twain better than his teenage protagonist Huck Finn, who explains in his playfully deferential voice, "Mr. Mark Twain…told the truth, mainly." Huck adds, "There was things he stretched, but mainly he told the truth." Sometimes, the only way for Twain to tell the truth was to tell a lie and sometimes a half-truth was all he managed to tell. "We keep half of what we think hidden away on our inside," he explained, "and only deliver ourselves of that remnant of it which is proper for general consumption." Like the doctor who sugarcoats the pill, Twain wrapped sermons as entertainments so they went down easier.

Andrew Lang's praise of Twain separated him from proper Victorians on both sides of the Atlantic. An anthropologist fascinated by myth, magic and ritual, Lang noted that "Persons of Culture" saw Twain as "a Barbarian," though he politely named no names in the crowd of the cultured. The author of *Huck Finn* associated with Negroes and worked alongside rough men and boys as a pilot on the Mississippi, where he leaned to navigate the shoals of metaphor as well as the currents of the river itself. Outlandish Mark Twain even posed shirtless for a photographer, and then allowed the picture to be circulated. Bare-chested with a bushy mustache, he looks positively Barbarian, though in photos in which he wears his trademark white suits he appears to be the epitome of the Southern gentleman.

Proper Victorians in Concord, Massachusetts and elsewhere looked askance at Twain's uncouth comedy, anarchic wildness and feral if not foul language. Then, too, neither the New England Victorian Thomas Wentworth Higginson — Emily's Dickinson reluctant patron — nor Matthew Arnold, the English poet and author of *Culture and Anarchy*, knew much about the Great American Novel or American literature, either, as an entity apart from English literature. In *Civilization in the United States* (1888), Arnold extended his long literary arm and insisted that Americans "were the English on the other side of the Atlantic." He added that American and English writers were "all contributors to one great literature — English Literature." Decades earlier, Thoreau insisted that American literature was an entirely different beast than English literature. "English literature," he wrote, "breathes no...wild strain." He added, "It is essentially a tame and civilized literature." For him American literary wildness was the distinguishing element. In the age of the genteel tradition, American Victorians didn't want to be independent of British culture or find space on the shelf for *Huck Finn*. Concord's prim, proper citizens called Huck's autobiography "more profitable for the slums than it is for respectable people." In those days slum inhabitants read books.

Twain often ignored the critical comments about himself and his work, but he was outraged by Matthew Arnold's comments about Ulysses S. Grant (1822-1885). He rushed to defend the Union general who defeated Lee and the Confederacy, and who served two terms as president of the United States. In Twain's view, Grant was one of the best American writers ever. Charles L. Webster, Twain's company, printed, distributed and sold hundreds of thousands of copies of Grant's memoirs. Defending Grant meant defending himself, his own financial interests and a fellow American citizen against an English prude.

The battle lines between Arnold, on one hand, and Twain on the other, were drawn not around overtly political topics such as culture and anarchy, but about "bad grammar and slovenly English," as Twain called them. Not surprisingly, Grant's grammar didn't meet Arnold's standards, and, as the keeper of the culture, as well as an inspector of schools in England, Arnold had to speak out. So did Twain. In an 1887 speech that was warmly received and widely distributed in a printed version, he pointed to grammatical errors and blemishes in the writing of Arnold himself and in the great English writers — Shakespeare, Milton, and Sir Walter Scott, whom he lambasted and found responsible in great measure for the Civil War.

For Twain, leaving out a comma or a semicolon wasn't a crime. It was criminal, however, he insisted, to write romances about the Middle Ages that bolstered Southern slavery. In his view, the civilization of the South was a "sham" because it revered religion and slavery, neither of which deserved reverence. Southern writers, Twain complained, "write for the past, not the present; they use obsolete forms and a dead language." As late as the 1880s, Twain was still complaining bitterly about Scott and the deleterious effects of his fiction.

On the subject of General Ulysses S. Grant and the rules of grammar, Twain stood worlds apart from Arnold, and yet ironically he agreed with Arnold on the subject of American literature. For Twain, as for Arnold, American writers were nearly identical to English writers, though for Twain the similarities were a sign of disgrace. In *Life on the Mississippi,* published five years before Arnold's *Civilization in the United States,* he noted sadly that American literature "was almost wholly English — stolen mainly." Twain looked at the literature and the civilization of the United States as a writer who aimed to Americanize the culture, speech and manners of his own country. His point of view came close to anarchy and even to nihilism, or at least to freewheeling American democracy. A fierce critic of the civilization to which Arnold belonged and defended, he wrote indignantly in 1888, "Yours is the civilization of slave-making ants."

SIVILIZED

Civilization was to Twain what Catholicism had been to Dante: a rich vein of ore that sustained his art and enabled him to develop his career as a writer who was praised by the rich and the powerful, though he condemned wealth and power. Mark Twain walked a fine line. In an essay entitled "Disloyal to Civilization," the poet and critic Adrienne Rich pays homage to black and white women who violated the moral and social codes of their day to create more humane cultures. "Disloyal to civilization" might also be applied in a complimentary way to Mark Twain.

In a working vocabulary that included eye-catching words and phrases such as "hive it," "lit out," "goody-goody," "jimcracks," and "nigger," "civilization" came to him almost automatically as a dirty word he couldn't resist. On the lips of the politicians and preachers that he reviled, it sounded high and mighty, but in his view it covered up foul deeds. Granted, Twain allowed that there was a "genuine and wholesome civilization of the nineteenth century." Somehow, however, the healthy and the genuine elements were corrupted. It might have been human nature itself that was to blame for the decline and fall of civilization, or it might have been the environment.

In *Pudd'nhead Wilson*, he meant to write a fable in which he illustrated the notion that, "environment shapes the man," to borrow a phrase that the African American author Langston Hughes uses in an essay about the novel. But the plot itself suggests the exact opposite. "Every human being carries with him from his cradle to his grave certain physical marks which do not change their character," Twain explained.

Unable to decide if nature or nurture defined human beings, he tilted at "civilization" and at slavery, too, the bugaboo he spied behind all civilizations, whether ancient or modern, and that undermined the wildness and essential goodness of humanity. Nothing sparked Twain's ire more than the civilization that had taken over the United States and that would soon capture the whole world, too. What's more, big cultural critics such as Matthew Arnold applauded it.

Not Twain, who lamented the victory of the civilized in *The Innocents Abroad* (1869), *The Adventures of Tom Sawyer* (1876), *The Adventures of Huckleberry Finn* (1885), *A Connecticut Yankee in King Arthur's Court* (1889) and *Following the Equator* (1897). Civilization with its discontents and malcontents was the monster with which he had to engage, much as Huck Finn must flee from it and return to it, then flee again in an unending pattern of avoidance and confrontation. Huck goes back and forth from the river to the parlor, eager to evade the Widow Douglas's attempts to civilize him and yet he's never entirely free, either. In his autobiography (another American false document), Huck spells the word "civilize" as "sivilize." He explains to readers that Tom Sawyer, his comrade and a thorn in his side, too, uses a word "becuz it tasted good in his mouth." For Huck, words also taste good; they make him feel good and give him a sense of empowerment.

Huck's "sivilize" is a form of verbal aikido more effective than the lances used by the medieval knights in *A Connecticut Yankee in King Arthur's Court*, the parable that begins as a satire on feudalism and ends by savaging modern civilization with its deadly technology and its murderous weapons. Like Hank, his fictional Connecticut Yankee, Twain wanted to blow up civilization — not always, but at his most ornery and persnickety. Slang, dialect and the colloquial were explosive devices he used to dynamite the pillars of respectability.

Twain also knew that he had to put away barbs, censor himself and allow friends and family members to gag him and cuff him. His friend, editor, fellow novelist and second self, William Dean Howells, edited his work. His beloved wife Livy, who called him "Youth" (a more civilized version of "Barbarian") crossed out hefty passages in his manuscripts and edited his person, too. Before their marriage, Sam Clemens told his beloved Livy, "you will break up all my irregularities when we are married and civilize me and make of me a model husband and an adornment to society."

A big part of him wanted to be married, civilized, a model husband and an adornment, too, if only so that he could rebel against roles and rules and write a book "without reserves" — "right out of my heart, taking into account no-one's feelings and no-one's prejudices." Back and forth he went, determined to express what he wanted to express, uncensored and yet eager not to offend. The Barbarian of American literature went to Oxford to accept an honorary Doctorate of Literature, and, shortly before his death in 1910, he played a round of golf with Woodrow Wilson, then the president of Princeton University and soon to inhabit the White House.

Then, too, shortly before his death, after using the word "civilization" for decades, he finally came up with a satisfying definition. "I was puzzling once more over how one might define the word civilization in a single phrase, unencumbered by confusing elaborations," he confided to the stenographer who took down his every word for the book that would become his autobiography and only begin to be published, uncensored, 100 years after his death. Twain had wrestled with a definition for years, he confessed, until, knowing that he was near the end of his life, he realized he had to nail the word down or die trying. Clarity was essential, provided it didn't minimize complexities. "Civilization is a condition wherein every man is of necessity both a master and a slave," he observed. "It means forced labor, compulsory labor —— every man working for somebody else while imagining that he is working for himself." He nailed it.

A Southerner, a Westerner, an Easterner, a comedian, a deadly serious writer, a patriotic American and a critic of almost all things American, he encountered complexities wherever he turned. Nearly everything he wrote and thought about, he realized, had at least two sides, often in opposition: public and private; lawful and lawless;

civilized and uncivilized. In the world according to Mark Twain, ironies abound, ambiguities proliferate and dualities multiply.

No wonder he often wrote about twins, doubles and mistaken identities that lead to mischief and mayhem. In *Huck Finn*, Huck becomes Tom Sawyer, takes his name and passes for him. "I was playing double," he says playfully.

Samuel Clemens and Mark Twain — twins and doubles — explored an America that wasn't one nation but two: "One that sets the captive free and one that takes a once captive's new freedom away from him and picks a quarrel with him with nothing to found it on; then kills him to get his land." In that sentence, Twain offers a twist on the American captivity narrative. In his version, the captive is freed, recaptured, bullied, provoked and then killed, his land expropriated. Wasn't that a hefty chapter of U.S. history in a nutshell?

With his double-edged, razor-sharp wit, he mocked civilized life or what passed for it. He ridiculed the hypocrisy of the aristocracy and skewered the idiotic customs and values of small town America with its lynching, alcoholism and prostitution, though he also looked back fondly to his own hometown, Hannibal, Missouri, as a democracy imbued with liberty, equality and the spirit of the Fourth of July. The older he became, the more sarcastic he sounded. In the last two decades of his life, the contradictions of civilization appeared increasingly absurd and increasingly impossible to reconcile, and so he resigned himself to gloom, doom and dark humor.

TWAIN & COOPER

In 1897, in an article about Queen Victoria's Jubilee that was commissioned by the publishing tycoon William Randolph Hearst and published in the *Examiner*, Twain noted that "Modern civilization" — as opposed to "ancient civilization" — was "easy

and difficult, convenient and awkward, happy and horrible, sooth-
ing and irritating, grand and trivial, an indispensable blessing and
an unimaginable curse." Talk about Double Consciousness! There
it was full blown.

In the *Leatherstocking Tales*, Cooper touts civilization,
though he also reveals its dark side and extolls the spiritual beauty
of the untamed American wilderness. For Cooper — whose novels Twain read and loved as a boy — the wilderness stood at the
opposite end of the spectrum from civilization. Cooper's forests
take his characters into the West; civilization nurtures them in settlements such as Templeton. For Cooper, the wilderness evoked
the past, sentimentality and romance; civilization called up the
future, fact and reality. In his own day, the wilderness seemed vast
and unending and also an underdog that needed defending.

Critics and teachers of American literature present Twain as
the anti-Cooper and point to his frequently anthologized 1895 essay
"Fenimore Cooper's Literary Offenses" in which he exaggerates the
flaws and remains silent about the strengths of the Bumppo novels.

By the time that he crafted "Fenimore Cooper's Literary
Offenses," Twain had been in the habit of aiming darts at Cooper
for nearly thirty years. His 1895 essay, which is a model of negative criticism, sums up a lifetime of grievances about Cooper
and his work. Twain doesn't offer a single laudatory comment or
acknowledge his own robust literary debts to the founding father
of American frontier fiction. Apparently, he'd forgotten or didn't
want to remember his affection for *The Last of the Mohicans*, *The
Pathfinder* and *The Deerslayer*. Apparently, too, he didn't want to
remember that he borrowed from Cooper, including his wilderness, his Indians and his white hunter.

Twain began as an apostle of Cooper. He provides a good
example of T. S. Eliot's observation that writers are often most
like their literary forefathers precisely when they're consciously

rebelling against them. In *Roughing It*, his non-fiction work about the West, its outlaws, fugitives and barren landscapes, Twain was honest enough to call himself "a disciple of Cooper." He might have been ironical, but if so his irony contained a kernel of truth. As a boy, he burrowed deeply into the *Leatherstocking Tales*, fascinated by Cooper's Indians and his hero, Natty Bumppo. By the time he indicted Cooper for transgressions against literature, he was no longer an apostle, but an apostate, though as writers they shared common ground. Like Cooper, Twain hated mobs and demagogues. Like Cooper, he could be patriarchal and a patrician and like Cooper, he looked to wilderness for inspiration.

To crown himself the reigning King of American literature, Twain had to topple Cooper from the throne and expose his nakedness. Cooper cluttered his work with unnecessary details, Twain observed, and undermined his narratives with bad grammar as well as with "devices, tricks, artifices" that he repeated over and over again until they were threadbare. In Twain's view, Cooper also harmed his tales because he viewed "nearly all things as through a glass eye, darkly." Samuel Clemens might have leveled much the same complaints at Mark Twain. He could have found examples of bad grammar in Twain's books, though bad grammar was, more often than not, intended. Huck's bad grammar is consistent with his shifty character and his consistently inconsistent personality. Grammatical rules, along with the rules of society, exist so that Huck can break them. "All human rules are more or less idiotic," Twain wrote in *Following the Equator*. Huck Finn shares that idea with his creator.

Like Cooper, Twain looked at nearly all things darkly, and not just at the end of a long literary career when he wrote "To the Person Sitting in Darkness" and "The Man That Corrupted Hadleyburg." In *Huck Finn*, Twain plumbs the depths of human depravity in the towns along the Mississippi that Huck invades with two veteran hucksters, the King and the Duke, who dabble in fake medicine, sham spirituality and bogus sentimentality, and exploit the gullibility of young girls.

"Human beings *can* be awfully cruel to one another," Huck observes. Twain had more reason than Cooper to filter life through a "glass eye, darkly." Idyllic villages that Cooper extolled in *The Pioneers* turned into monstrous cities. Modest manufacturing shops became bloated factories that chewed up workers. Bumppo's rifle "Killdeer" became the Gatling gun and Manifest Destiny became a mission to civilize colonial lands and annex them into a global American Empire. Twain brought wilderness writing into the age of imperialism, and, along with William Dean Howells, joined the Anti-Imperialist League that opposed the U.S. annexation of Hawaii and the Philippines.

Perhaps he envied Cooper's innocence and his literary triumphs. Cooper succeeded where Twain failed. He wrote sequels and prequels to *The Pioneers*. Twain tried again and again to extend the life and times of Huck, Jim and Tom in several books including *Huck Finn and Tom Sawyer Among the Indians* and *Tom Sawyer's Conspiracy*. He never completed those narratives of the frontier, perhaps because they felt like tired copies. Then, too, writing about Indians in the 1890s just wasn't the same as writing about them in the 1820s. If they weren't dead or on reservations they were, like Sitting Bull, performers in Buffalo Bill's Wild West Show that turned the frontier into an entertainment for the masses.

Huck Finn loves to perform and wants attention, but he seems to know that he's not meant to appear in yet another book. At the conclusion of the meandering narrative in which he describes his adventures on, off and around the Mississippi, he tells readers, "There ain't nothing more to write about it and I am rotten glad of it." He adds, "If I'd a knowed what a trouble it was to make a book I wouldn't a tackled it and ain't agoing to no more." Years later, in *Tom Sawyer's Conspiracy*, which Twain began to write in 1897 and never could flesh out, Huck wisely observes, "I knowed you can translate a book, but you can't translate a boy."

At the end of Twain's life, only his autobiography excited his imagination and enabled him to recast familiar characters in new roles and new voices. "Mr. Roosevelt is the Tom Sawyer of the political world of the twentieth century," he wrote in 1907, assuming that everyone who had read the books in which Sawyer appears as a character would understand his analogy between the all-controlling boy and the all-controlling president. Of Roosevelt, he added, "His judgment has been out of focus so long now that he imagines that everything he does, little or big, is colossal…He is still fourteen years old after living half a century." The mature Twain invited readers to laugh at Roosevelt, at Sawyer and at civilization, too. His satire lifted him above and beyond Cooper and brought him into the twentieth century. Scalding satire makes him seem almost as contemporary as Kurt Vonnegut, who extended Twain's brand of humor and revived his exhilarating version of pessimism in novels such as *Breakfast of Champions* and *Cat's Cradle*.

Irreverent, raucous comedy came naturally to Vonnegut and to Twain and so did irony. In his first book, *The Innocents Abroad*, or the *New Pilgrims Progress* (1869), Twain pokes fun at pilgrims, progress and the holy land. The author himself appears in *The Innocents Abroad* not as an innocent American but rather as a worldly-wise globetrotter who brings to Europe the moral and aesthetic standards he's learned in the American West. So, he compares Lake Como unfavorably with Lake Tahoe, measures "swarthy" Arabs against American Indians and lumps all of them together as "savages." Then, too, he looks at Palestine and describes it as yet another "deserted wilderness." In *The Innocents Abroad*, Mark Twain, the good-natured cynic, crucifies the Old World on the cross of the New.

A generation of European writers, among them Mrs.

Trollope, had traveled widely in the United States and exposed the bad manners, bad food and bad habits of Americans in best selling books that hurt the feelings of the English on the other side of the Atlantic. Unlike most of his countrymen, including Fenimore Cooper, Twain praised Mrs. Trollope's candor. In *Innocents*, he reversed the tables on her and on foreign travelers in the United States, and, as a writer from the wilds of America, took aim at European art, architecture and painting.

In the 1820s and 1830s, Cooper played a staring role in Paris as a writer from the backwoods. Fifty years later, Twain made much the same persona work for him, albeit with more bile in his pen than Cooper had in his. The Barbarian from the West dismissed Notre Dame as a "brown old Gothic pile," reviled the paintings of the old masters as "nauseous adulation of princely patrons" and rejected France as a staid land of "clockwork." Near the end of the book, he insists that his conscience is clean and his motives pure. He didn't mean to posit America's superiority over Europe, he said, but rather to show that all travel was "fatal to prejudice, bigotry and narrow-mindedness." Moreover, he softened his own satire by turning a critical eye on his own fickle self. "Things I did not like at all yesterday," he wrote, "I like very well today." Good natured and good hearted, he reserved the right to "poke fun… without ever saying a malicious word."

And yet he came close to maliciousness when he claimed that there was no American Indian poetry "except in Fenimore Cooper Indians." Twain claimed expertise in that matter. "I know the Noble Red Man," he claimed. He also boasted that he "scalped them, had them for breakfast" and that he "would gladly eat the whole race if I had a chance." He could joke about scalping and cannibalism, though Indians surely would not have appreciated his humor.

In his second book, *Roughing It* (1872), he presented himself as "a disciple of Cooper and a worshipper of the Red Man" and in that capacity he recounted his real-life adventures far from civilization in a territory ruled by violent gunmen who were also, he insisted, the territory's most valuable citizens. Only outlaws, Twain claimed, could bring peace and order to a society teetering on the brink of chaos.

Twain described the Goshute as "treacherous, filthy and repulsive." Along with the Bushmen of Africa, they were, he explained, "descended from the same gorilla, or kangaroo, or Norway rat." Still, in *Roughing It*, Twain honors the "wild spirit" of the Western mining camps, Nevada's "wild, free" horsemen, and a gunfighter named Slade who lives a "wild life" avoiding lawmen, battling Indians and bringing rough justice to the frontier.

Despite the jabs at Cooper, Twain borrowed from his verbal arsenal and described frontiersmen as "half-savage, half-civilized." Moreover, despite his mockery of romance, he wrote in the vein of romance about the "unvisited wildernesses" of the West and the Western tales that read "like a wild fancy sketch." *Roughing It* captures the romantic ethos of the American desert; one of the "waste places of the earth," Twain calls it, that's haunted by "solitude, silence and desolation." Brief yet vivid portraits conjure the mining camps of Nevada and California — "a wild, free, disorderly, grotesque society" — where there is "nothing juvenile, nothing feminine," and where money is as "plentiful as dust." Twain's frontier with its violence and civilized barbarism was no fit place for women and children. When he arrived in San Francisco — after crossing "a vast, waveless ocean stricken dead and turned to ashes" — Twain thought of it as "Paradise." Indeed, he would memorialize San Francisco's Occidental Hotel — where he lived briefly when he wrote for *The Californian, Golden Era* and *Enterprise* — as "Heaven on the half shell." That sort of civilization he enjoyed.

After roughing it in the American West, it's not surprising that Twain traveled widely in Europe, where he was wined and dined as a visiting dignitary; met Robert Browning, Charles

Darwin and Ivan Turgenev; and lectured to admiring crowds. For years, he lived a global literary life, even as he continued to write fiction for children and for adults, and nonfiction, too, including a series of articles about his pivotal experiences as a pilot on the Mississippi that Howells published in *The Atlantic*, the premiere American literary magazine of the day.

MRS. JANE CLEMENS

In 1876, the same year that *The Adventures of Tom Sawyer* appeared in print, first in England and then in the United States, Twain began to write *Huckleberry Finn*, though after sixteen chapters his creativity ran aground and he apparently put the manuscript aside. *The Gilded Age*, a novel he co-authored with Charles Warner, and that proved to be far less challenging to write, appeared in 1873, three years before *Tom Sawyer*. Though it didn't sell well, it established Twain's reputation as a caustic critic of American society. In 1882, a journey on the Mississippi rekindled his creativity and enabled him to expand his essays about the river and about his life as a pilot. *Life on the Mississippi* arrived in bookstores in 1883. His 1882 voyage on the river also reignited his imagination and enabled him to complete his narrative about Huck Finn. The three inextricably connected books — *The Adventures of Tom Sawyer*, *Life on the Mississippi* and *The Adventures of Huckleberry Finn* — brought Twain notoriety, critical acclaim and (briefly) financial stability. More than one hundred years later, they still feel as though they grew organically into and around one another, and adhered to the rules of "wild form," the American literary mode that Melville and Hawthorne exploited in their narratives.

Two essays that Twain drafted late in life suggest the rich

sources for his narratives about Tom Sawyer, Huck Finn and the
black slave, Jim. Both point to the roots of his art in the local and
the regional. Hannibal, Missouri was to Twain what Cooperstown
had been to Cooper: a frontier town with a cast of unusual characters. Twain's father John, a landowner, a judge and an entrepre-
neur, played a role in Tennessee and Missouri similar to the role
Cooper's father played as an early settler in New York.

Moreover, both Cooper and Twain appreciated matriarchal
as well as patriarchal power. Twain's 1890 essay, "Jane Lampton
Clemens," provides a sympathetic portrait of the woman who
gave birth to him. It also offers a series of grim vignettes of African
American slaves that he retrieved from his own "mental camera."
His 1897 essay, "Villagers of 1840-1843," provides illuminating
notes on Hannibal, Missouri's poor white citizens that were meant
to supply material for a novel with the working title, "New Huck
Finn." Both essays show that while Twain may not have always
known where his art was headed, as T. S. Eliot complained, he
usually knew where his art came from, and that its sources were
close to home, family and personal experience.

Twain depicts Jane Clemens as a white Southern woman
who was "not conscious that slavery was a bald, grotesque and
unwarranted usurpation," but who empathized with the plight of
the slaves in her home, and who had a remarkable though unconscious knack for the comic. She had the ability, Twain explained,
"to say a humorous thing with the perfect air of not knowing
it to be humorous." Not only did he inherit her wry sense of
humor, he also instilled it in Huck Finn, who like Jane Clemens
can be unconscious of the bitter/sweet, sad/funny comments that
he makes in his "autobiography."

Twain's memories of his mother and his childhood reveal
his complex feelings —— they range from muffled indignation to
half-hearted apology — about slavery. In one poignant memory,

he describes "a dozen black men and women chained to each other... awaiting shipment to the southern slave market." Twain also remembers that as a child he wanted "to kill" a "little slave boy...who sang the whole day long." His mother told him that the boy sang songs "to transcend his grief" and that it would break her heart if he "should stop singing."

In "Villagers of 1840-1843," Twain exhibits very little compassion for the inhabitants of Hannibal, many of whom he portrays as alcoholics, brutes and hellions who descend the ladder of civilization and disappear in the Wild West. Of Charley Meredith, he wrote, "went to California and thence to hell"; of Neil Moss, "the envied rich boy" who at thirty became a "graceless tramp in Nevada." A black man rapes and murders a thirteen-year-old white girl, then leaves her body in the woods. A young white boy chops off his left hand because he thinks it has sinned, and a young white woman marries a "showy stranger" who, she discovers, is "a thief and a swindler."

Then there's the impoverished Blankenship clan: the parents "drunkards," the children "never sent to school or church" and the daughters "charged with prostitution." Tom Blankenship apparently inspired Twain to create Huck Finn, who first shows up as a character in *The Adventures of Tom Sawyer*, the narrative in which Twain develops a contrast between the freedoms of the wild and the restraints of the civilized. He also traces the curious attraction/repulsion between the respectable and the disrespectable that's at the heart of *Huckleberry Finn*. Sounding like Rousseau, who noted that "man is born free, but he is everywhere in chains" and also like Marx who wrote, "workers of the world unite, you have nothing to lose but your chains," Twain noted of Huck, "the bars and shackles of civilization shut him in and bound him hand and foot." Unwilling to be captives of their society, Huck and Tom escape to "the virgin forest" and play outlaws, pirates and Indians. No political party or union is big enough for them.

TOM SAWYER & HUCK FINN

In *Tom Saywer*, Twain's descriptions of the wild sound as though they come out of the pages of *The Last of the Mohicans*. Then, too, Tom and Huck are adolescent versions of Bumppo. Children of the woods and incipient boy scouts, they enjoy the company of butterflies, foxes, catbirds and all "the wild things" that have "probably never seen a human being." Nature is capitalized and personified in the mode of nineteenth-century romantic writers and naturalists. Twain describes "Nature" as a "marvel" that wakes in the morning, shakes off sleep, goes to work and weaves a spell around the boys.

In *Tom Sawyer*, Twain doesn't idealize Huck. In fact, he describes him as "idle and lawless and vulgar and bad." Still, the boys in town imagine that he has "everything that goes to make life precious." Twain idealized Tom Blankenship, the model for the fictional Huck, as "the only really independent person...tranquilly and continually happy." Tom Sawyer envies Huck's independence and longs to be like him if only because the town mothers hate him, dread him and forbid their sons to associate with him.

The relationship between Tom and Huck illustrates a concept that Twain expresses at the start of the novel: "in order to make a man or a boy covet a thing it is only necessary to make the thing difficult to attain." If Tom is attracted to Huck's status as "romantic outcast," Huck, the illiterate son of the town alcoholic, is drawn to Tom, especially to his "facility in writing, and the sublimity of his language."

Admired by his peers precisely because he's unlike them, Huck becomes, by the end of the novel, like the other boys in town once he inherits money, which Twain characterizes as the root of evil. "Huck's wealth and the fact that he was now under the Widow Douglas's protection introduced him into society," he explains. "The widow's servants kept him neat and clean… He had to go to church; he had to talk so properly that speech was become insipid in his mouth." Huck and Twain abhor the language of respectable society, the language of widows, servants, the dinner table and the church. More than anything Twain loved the language of the outcast, the vulgar and the lawless.

In Twain's world, bad boys and wild men express themselves in language that's more vivid and colorful than the language employed by good boys and civilized men. In *Life on the Mississippi*, his hymn to the river and to the men who made their living on and around it before the Civil War, Twain honors the pilot as a "king without a keeper" and as a "wild creature" who "swears," "sings," "whistles" and "yells." The riverboat pilot is an adult version of the freedom-loving, unfettered Huck, though unlike Huck, the pilot works and loves to work. He's not a slave to his job.

The pilot shares the starring role with the river, and not surprisingly the river has a language all its own. The Mississippi is the wildest thing in the book, wilder than any man and wilder than anything on shore. *Life on the Mississippi* also describes the destruction of the wilderness, the industrialization of the natural world and the monstrous sugar plantations with "smoke like Satan's own kitchen." It's hell along the banks of the Mississippi.

Twain turns *Life* into a political springboard that enables him to denounce American swagger, praise the French Revolution that "broke the chains of the *ancien regime*" and complain about "quiet orderly men of a sedate business aspect." Once again, he attacks civilization, albeit with more fury than ever before, and explains that whiskey was always "the earliest pioneer of civilization" in the United States, not the newspaper, the Sunday school, the missionary, the farmer, the lawyer, the undertaker, the immigrant, or the trader, all of whom banded together, he explains, to "build a church and a jail — and behold civilization is established forever in the land."

Still, lyricism runs parallel to bitterness. The river evokes a range of moods and takes Twain on several journeys all at once: literally downstream; back into the pages of American history; and to the banks of his youth. In Hannibal, he feels "like a boy again." Along the wooded shores of the Mississippi, he enjoys the spectacular beauty, and at sunset he relishes the "eloquence of silence," the "haunting sense of loneliness," and the "remoteness from the worry and the bustle of the world."

One of the aspects of modern life he enjoyed most of all was the public park, specifically Forest Park in St. Louis, which was created in 1876, when Grant was president and General George Armstrong Custer and his troops clashed with Sitting Bull and the Sioux at Little Big Horn in Montana. Forest Park, Twain explains, has the merit of "having been made mainly by nature." The book ends as it begins with the American Indians who were, he writes, robbed, enslaved, converted and slaughtered, and who he describes, in the manner of Cooper, as "the simple children of the forest" who are eternally "noble" in their freedom.

MISSISSIPPI

In *The Adventures of Huckleberry Finn*, the "lawless" Mississippi River carries the novel's two main characters, Huck and Jim, downstream into an exhilarating realm of freedom, natural beauty and good fellowship. At the same time, paradoxically, it takes them deeper into the world of slavery, exposing them to the ugliness of human nature and to the vulgarities of life along the shore. The two opposing trajectories — away from civilization and into civilization — have prompted critics to view the novel as a flawed masterpiece that just doesn't adhere to basic rules of narrative logic.

Why would an African American fugitive and his poor white companion want to travel deeper and deeper into the South and the bastion of slavery when they ought to go North, critics have asked. It's a valid question that draws attention to a knotted text, though it's not the only valid question about a novel that poses as many, if not more, questions than it answers. A maverick work of fiction, *Huck Finn* tests the limits of literary criticism and the art of interpretation itself.

Huck's and Jim's journey downstream, rather than upstream or across the river to freedom in Illinois, allowed Twain to follow the crosscurrents of the American captivity narrative that hadn't lost its vitality, though the identities of the captives and their keepers had changed dramatically since the seventeenth century. The southern journey of his main characters inspired him to riff on the linguistic differences between the mighty river and the mercenary towns along its shores. It enabled him to showcase the holiness of the world aboard the raft and illuminate the profanity of the world inside the church.

The Adventures of Huckleberry Finn looks back at the past and reviews the bondage of chattel slavery that existed before the Civil War. It also looks squarely at the author's own day in the 1880s when white Christian folk sabotaged Reconstruction and recaptured free African Americans. In *The Adventures of Huckleberry Finn*, Twain suggests that the ongoing problem of the nineteenth century (to borrow W. E. B. DuBois's well-known phrase) "is the problem of the color-line." He knew that it wouldn't be solved any time soon and that his main characters would continue to haunt Americans. Jim is timeless and timely much as Huck is eternal and temporal. Together they work a kind of magical mumbo jumbo that runs counter to the pieties of the white Christian folk that the author satirizes in fiction and non-fiction.

Critics who have insisted that the novel has a single thread, a single climactic scene, and a single all-encompassing phrase ignore the novel's contrapuntal movements, climactic scenes (plural) and electrifying phases (also plural). Time and again, *Huck Finn* has slipped through the hands of critics who have tried to catch it once and for all. Time and again, Twain's multifaceted masterpiece has refused to be reduced to a one-dimensional work of fiction. Even the most astute critics have fumbled, sometimes magnificently.

In a 1950 essay about *Huck Finn*, T. S. Eliot argued that "the River makes the book a great book," not a surprising comment since Eliot was born in St. Louis and grew up around the Mississippi — and because rivers, from the Thames to the Ganges, and gods, both primitive and civilized, appear in *The Waste Land*, his mediation on the urban wilderness. The "monstrous big river" does propel Twain's novel, but the Mississippi can't rightly be considered apart from Huck and Jim or from the indelible characters they meet along its banks: killers, undertakers and pious citizens who, Twain explains, blow their noses irreverently in church and at funerals more than any other place.

In his seminal essay, Eliot offers a contrast between Conrad's *Heart of Darkness* and *Huck Finn* and argues that while Conrad is an outsider, "Mark Twain is a native and the River God is his God." His comment steers the narrative into the realm of myth, symbol and primitivism. Eliot also notes that *Huck Finn* "ends with the right words." To remind readers who might have forgotten, the novel concludes with a declaration of independence: "I reckon I got to light out for the Territory ahead of the rest, because Aunt Sally she's going to adopt me and sivilize me and I can't stand it. I been there before." Eliot rightly draws attention to this passage in which the key word "sivilize" appears, tying the ending to the beginning in which Huck explains, "the Widow Douglas, she took me for her son, and allowed she would sivilize me." Other critics have echoed Eliot's remark and used it as a key to explore *Huckleberry Finn* as a mantra about American independence and a chant for the freedom of the Wild West.

When he wrote his first draft of *Huck Finn*, Twain lost his bearings at the end of chapter sixteen in which a Mississippi steamboat — an obvious emblem for the destructive power of technology and civilization — smashes into the raft, and Jim and Huck dive into the river for safety. At that juncture, Twain put the novel aside. He didn't return to it until he figured out where he wanted to take his characters, and how the remainder of the novel would develop the themes he had already introduced. When he started anew, he knew that Huck and Jim would have to return to the raft, and that Huck would have to have a series of adventures on shore that would bring him into conflict with the monster of modern civilization.

Peter Coveney, an English academic and the author of *The Image of Childhood*, emphasizes the moral conflicts that divide Huck. In an essay about Twain's novel, Coveney insists that the key line in the book is Huck's defiant cry in chapter 31: "All right then, I'll go the hell!" Coveney would like to abolish the twelve chapters that follow chapter 31, including the madcap scenes that bring Huck and Tom Sawyer together again as adversaries and co-conspirators, and that return Jim to slavery.

Ironically, Huck thinks he's bad precisely when he aims to do good by and for Jim. He *is* bad, even evil, by the ethical standards of the slave masters on shore, though he's good and even virtuous by the moral values of the abolitionists who haunt the novel and that taunt his own conscience, though he never actually meets a single abolitionist face-to-face. Drawing attention to the line, "I'll go to hell," as Coveney does, underlines *Huck Finn* as a moral tale about Huck's dilemma as a Christian boy in a society that merely provides lip service to Christianity. Make no mistake about it, *Huck Finn* is a moral tale. "I have always preached," Twain explained near the end of his life. "That is the reason I have lasted thirty years." But preaching follows adventures.

On the raft, Huck's freedom-loving life with Jim clashes with the entreanched values of slave society. Once Huck's conscience is awakened, it refuses to go to sleep. Again and again, he's tormented, as Coveney suggests. But to stop reading the novel with Huck's vow, "all right, I'll go to hell," makes little sense. Indeed, it abolishes the necessary ordeals that Huck must undergo and that lead to the emotional crescendo in "Chapter The Last." In the final pages of the book, Jim writes his own slave narrative. He emerges "Out of Bondage." Twain hoped that phrase would echo *My Bondage and My Freedom*, the slave narrative by Frederick Douglass, whom Twain met not long after he met Harriet Beecher Stowe. *Huck Finn* builds on decades of American literature about slavery and its abolition and prompts readers to rethink racism.

The literary critic Van Wyck Brooks insisted in *The Ordeal of Mark Twain* (1920), published just a decade after Twain's death, that the author of *Huckleberry Finn* was a "case of arrested development" and that the conflict in the novel "is simply the conflict of Mark Twain's own childhood." Granted, Twain drew on memories of his white childhood in a world of black slaves, but he went beyond the personal and fused his own conflicts with the conflicts of American society. Huck's own private war tears him apart, much as the Civil War tore the United States apart and ended the life of freedom that Twain knew as a Mississippi riverboat pilot.

For African American novelist Ishmael Reed, the key line in the book is Huck's cry, "I want my nigger." For Reed, Huck is a progenitor for white boys in suburbia who identify with black boys but don't and won't trade places with them. Huck expresses the "bizarre hunger" and the "exotic yearning of those who despise blacks yet wish to imitate them," Reed insists. In Kerouac's *On the*

Road, Sal Paradise, the white hipster, says he wants to be a Negro, though he's not willing to suffer the indignities of American racism.

Long before Reed dissected the text, and long before Eliot waded into the waters of Twain criticism, Ernest Hemingway and F. Scott Fitzgerald tried to steer the novel into their own literary territories. "All modern American literature comes from one book by Mark Twain called *Huckleberry Finn,*" Hemingway insisted in 1936 in *Green Hills of Africa,* his paean to Africa and to America, which figures as a lost, dark continent that occasionally rises to the book's surface and that allows the author to complain about the desecration of the Earth itself by colonizers.

Hemingway offered strict guidelines to readers: "you must stop where the Nigger Jim is stolen from the boys. That is the real end. The rest is just cheating." (Coveney echoes that suggestion.) A year before Hemingway offered his comments, his friend, fellow author and literary rival, F. Scott Fitzgerald, noted that "*Huckleberry Finn* took the first journey back" and that Twain's "eyes were the first eyes that ever looked at us objectively that were not eyes from overseas." While Hemingway viewed the novel as a literary experiment with language, Fitzgerald saw it through the lens of his experience as a Minnesota born and raised writer and Princeton undergraduate who migrated to New York and to Europe.

Nearly every critic who has had something original to say about *Huckleberry Finn* has projected something of himself or herself onto the novel. In *Was Huck Black? Mark Twain and African American Voices,* Shelley Fisher Fishkin suggests that Twain's novel "may be more subversive, ultimately than we might have suspected" and that "segregation is alive and well among literary historians." Even Leslie Fiedler, the author of the landmark 1948 essay, "Come Back to the Raft Ag'in Huck Honey," which defines the relationship between Huck and Jim as homoerotic, aimed not so much to honor homosexuality but to provoke for the sake of provocation by positing a kind of outlaw sexuality that cuts across racial lines.

Huckleberry Finn lends itself to so many contrary interpretations because braided patterns are embedded in the novel itself as it wanders from river to shore, downstream to upstream, freedom to slavery, and from tainted civilization to a wild paradise for two in which the main characters talk, sing, laugh, dance, eat, tell stories, gaze at the stars, sleep, wake and wander. Mosaic, collage and montage, *Huckleberry Finn* moves in linear fashion and also in a series of circles that widen and narrow as it undermines itself, sabotages easy readings and satirizes nearly everything and everyone. No wonder that the modernist James Joyce regarded it as seminal work and paid homage to it in *Finnegan's Wake*, which redefines the English language.

Twain's novel also lends itself to a variety of interpretations because Huck isn't one person but several. An orphan who rejects his father figures, along with his mother figures, he gives birth to himself and as he points out is "born again." Hedonist, Puritan, chameleon, hypocrite, rebel, racist, egalitarian, outcast, mime, teller of tall tales, and the truth, too — which he claims is "better, and actually safer than a lie" — Huck plays the role of the all-American boy, even as he dresses up as a girl and mimics the feminine. Shaped by civilization even as he tries to reject it, he loathes property and possessions but can't escape from the world of property and possessions. Mean to Jim and kind to Jim, the only person who really loves him, he's terrified that the good citizens on the shore might think he's a radical abolitionist.

"I didn't do him no more mean tricks," Huck says of Jim in chapter fifteen, about one-third of the way through his narrative. Soon enough he's playing mean tricks again, as though Twain aims to demonstrate how deeply ingrained racism is in American society and in the American psyche, and how difficult it is to escape from it, even with the best intentions. Obsessed with the bogeyman of civilization and its stepchild, slavery, Huck is a captive of the moral code of his own society, caught on the horns of a dilemma that he thinks will send him to hell or to heaven, bring him salvation or damnation.

Much of the time, he's lonely, lonesome or afflicted by lonesomeness. There's no place for him in any society and no society he'd like to join; he's inherently antisocial and asocial. There's no one like him in Twain's world: not Tom Sawyer, though they call one another comrade; and not Jim either if only because they're divided by the color of their skins. Much of the time, Huck is eager to go into the woods. But he always comes out of the woods. He gets into trouble and avoids trouble by running away.

The literary son of Cooper's Bumppo and Melville's Ishmael, he's also uncle to Kerouac's Dean Moriarty in *On the Road.* The hot-rod, road companion of Sal Paradise, Moriarty goes on a joy ride that takes him, not on a North and South axis, but East and West from New York to California and back. Kerouac's protagonists cover a lot of ground but they don't make spiritual progress any more than Twain's protagonists. Take Huck off the raft and put him behind the wheel of a speeding vehicle and he blends in with Kerouac's hipsters, "White Negroes" — as Norman Mailer called them — and native-born existentialists.

Asexual and pansexual, the knightly defender of innocent white women against the machinations of con artists, he's a con artist himself who in turn is conned by Tom Sawyer, his best (white) friend. The author of his own autobiography, and a reader as well as a disciplined artist, he apologizes for his rudimentary writing skills. In the midst of telling a tale about the novel's bogus "King," Huck begs the indulgence of his audience. "I can't give the old gent's words, nor can I imitate him," he explains, though he's able to imitate almost everyone else he meets. In the beginning, the middle and at the end, he steps to the front of the stage to remind readers that he's telling the story. "The End. Yours Truly, Huck Finn," he signs off.

Cool, calculating and collected, he means to con the reader into thinking he's the real author of *The Adventures of Huckleberry Finn* and not somebody he refers to as "Mr. Mark Twain." Huck assures readers that he's read *The Adventures of Tom Sawyer*, the fiction in which he appears as himself. At the start of his autobiography and all the way through its pages, he takes readers into his confidence, tells them what he's thinking and the schemes he plans to execute. He also tells the audience its feelings. When readers least expect it, he lowers the boom and delivers a comment meant to snap them out of their collective delirium. In the next-to-the-last chapter and in the nightmarish world of chains, lynching, lies and hypocrisies, Huck delivers an ungrammatical comment that makes him, along with Mark Twain, an American barbarian and a critic of civilization.

"The people that's always the most anxious for to hang a nigger that hain't done just right," he says, "is always the very ones that ain't the most anxious to pay for him when they've got their satisfaction out of him." His abuse of the vulgar word "nigger," which he draws habitually from his bag of well-worn tricks, has long offended readers both white and black and after years of debate it's a challenge to clear the air. Still, it might be worth saying that the word "nigger" plays a therapeutic role in Huck's world.

By lifting the addictive racial slur out of the ordinary, Twain's manchild liberates it and redeems all the "niggers" of the world who were born free and are everywhere in chains. Like Twain's mother, Jane Clemens, Huck knows not what he says and knows everything he says, as when he blurts out, "I'm a nigger." The only home that he can aspire to inhabit is the house inhabited by black people, whether slave or free. The rules of white society aren't big enough or wide enough for the likes of Huck Finn.

The African American Harvard Law Professor Randall Kennedy argues in *Nigger: The Strange Career of a Troublesome Word* against censorship of the "n" word, though he knows that it's the most hurtful word in American history. Like Twain, Kennedy understands the power of the forbidden. Like Twain, he uses the word throughout his book. Kennedy argues that banning *Huck Finn* because of the word "nigger" has never ended the problem of racism or the issue of ethnic slurs. It hasn't stopped anyone from reading the novel if he or she wants to read it. Banning it has prompted the curious to seek it out, discover its secrets and try to make sense of the controversy it generates. Twain himself understood the self-defeating power of censorship. He explained that Adam "did not want the apple for the apple's sake, he wanted it only because it was forbidden." He added, wryly, "The mistake was in not forbidding the serpent; then he would have eaten the serpent."

Unlike his alcoholic father and unlike Jim who is running away from slavery, Huck isn't wild, though he enjoys living in the woods and on the lawless Mississippi. He's so busy looking, listening, thinking, scheming and telling his tale that he doesn't have the time to go wild. He never goes native, never becomes an "Injun," as he calls Indians, and never cuts the umbillical cord that connects him to civilization. Restless Huck never finds unending peace and serenity, not on the shore and not on the "raft of trouble" that attracts troublemakers like the King and Duke.

Twain condemns Huck to purgatory along the Mississippi where well-mannered, Bible-thumping, Southern gentlemen and pseudo-aristocrats shoot and kill the members of enemy clans. Here, too, Calvinist ministers offer sermons on "the brazen serpent in the wilderness" and invite the members of the congregation, "black with sin," to repent and redeem themselves. Twain grew up listening to Calvinist ministers; their words echoed in his head when he wrote about small Southern towns and half-crazed

Christian congregations desperate for salvation.

Huck's biological father, Pap, and his spiritual father, Jim, are the only two characters in the book that Twain brands with the word "wild." Jim is good wild, black wild; Pap is bad wild, white wild. Huck's father is mean, ornery, out of control, a sadist and a child beater who hates the government, hates African Americans and who wears a face white enough "to make a body sick." You might meet him in America today denouncing Barack Obama, food stamps and medical care for all, all the while insisting that he isn't a racist. And beats his own children.

Jim adapts to the wild, and, like fugitive slaves all through the nineteenth century, he uses the woods as a cover while he flees from the plantation. As novelist Ishmael Reed, the author of *Mumbo-Jumbo*, observes, "he finds a way to survive in the wilderness." Still, at times, he's little more than a comic black man in a white minstrel show. As Ralph Ellison, the author of *Invisible Man*, noted, *Huck Finn* presents a black man "seen through the condescending eyes — partially of a young white boy." Jim is also more than a cliché. Patient, deferential and dignified, too, he endures by almost any means necessary, and escapes lynching and humiliations until, by the end of the novel, he's legally free at last — though as a human being with the inalienable rights accorded to all humans he's always been free.

NOSTALGIA

Huck survives by his wits not because he's physically fit. He returns again and again in book after book (albeit mostly of them unfinished) because Twain felt a deep attachment to him and couldn't bear to retire him from active duty. In Twain's imagination, Huck is always the same lost boy, trapped between Jim and Tom, never able to grow older or to evolve, but rather doomed to repeat a future that's already past. In that sense, he's kin to Gatsby who, Fitzgerald wrote, "believed in the green light, the orgiastic future that year by year recedes before us." Fitzgerald added a line that's as perfect a last line as any in American literature. "So we beat on, boats against the current, borne back ceaselessly into the past," he wrote. Huck is also carried backward even as he's carried forward.

The British literary critic and short story writer, V. S. Pritchett, noted in a 1941 essay about Twain that "American nostalgia" had a "peculiar power." It harkened to "something lost in the past," and, at the same time it posited "the tragedy of a lost future." That description fits *The Great Gatsby*, *Huck Finn* and Twain's *A Connecticut Yankee in King Arthur's Court*, a parable about feudalism and capitalism in which past is future and future is past.

Twain's Medieval England, the setting for the tale, doubles as the American South, a land in which, Twain explains, the poor whites were "despised" and "insulted" by the "slave-lords," but sided with "the slave-lords in all political moves for the upholding and perpetuating of slavery." As the son of a poor white man, Huck inherits his worldview, and, while he defies the authority figures in his own world, he can never bring himself to cut himself off from them completely. No one understood the psychology of poor southern whites better than Twain. They fought in the Civil War, he explained, "to prevent the destruction of that very institution which degraded them."

Slavery came back to haunt Twain in the short novel *Pudd'nhead Wilson* in which he plays with doubles, twins, accidents of birth and breeding and civilization itself — which he describes as a monstrous fiction that engulfs slaves and masters, whites and blacks and that robs everyone of his and her humanity. Roxy, a black slave who looks white and is "to all intents and purposes...as white as anybody," switches two infants at birth. The black child, her own boy, grows up white, while the white child and son of the slave master grows up black. Roxy thinks she's doing a good deed, though both boys suffer immensely.

Ironies abound in *Pudd'nhead Wilson* — a "novel of social significance" the African American writer Langston Hughes called it. The black boy becomes the white master and the lord of his own mother, the author of the monstrous fiction of whiteness and blackness as it applies to her two boys. "Deceptions intended solely for others gradually grew practically into self-deceptions as well," Twain writes. "The little counterfeit rift of separation between imitation slave and imitation master widened and widened and became an abyss."

COLONIAL WORLD

In the summer of 1895, deep in debt and poor in health, Twain began a twelve-month lecture tour that took him to Australia, New Zealand, India and South Africa and that led to *Following the Equator*, the last major masterpiece he wrote and published in the nineteenth century. In *Following the Equator*, he adopts a global perspective and looks through a glass darkly at the history of colonialism and at the violent clashes between whites and natives in Africa and Asia. An anti-imperialist in name and in the sinews of the book itself, Twain explains that in Australia, as elsewhere around the world, whites "did not kill all the blacks, but they promptly killed enough of them to make their own persons safe." Still, they never felt entirely safe and so they went on killing.

More than ever before, the perils of communication loomed large and inescapable in his world. "Language is a treacherous thing, a most unsure vehicle," he wrote. "It can seldom arrange descriptive words in such a way that they will not inflate facts — by help of the reader's imagination." Still, in *Following the Equator,* he wrestled with most of the big social and political themes that preoccupied him all his adult life. Once again he offers his reflection about Fenimore Cooper, Ulysses S. Grant, the Civil War, the American imitation of all things English and his own boyhood in the Mississippi Valley. His memory is as sharp as ever and he's as funny as ever, too, perhaps even more so. In one chapter, he provides a garbled view of half a dozen or so crucial events in history that he attributes to a young pupil who can't keep facts straight: "The Puritans found an insane asylum in the wilds of America"; "Chaucer was succeeded by H. Wads Longfellow."

Pithy remarks by Twain's fictitious southern lawyer and mouthpiece, Pudd'nhead Wilson, appear at the start of each chapter. "When in doubt, tell the truth," Wilson insisted. "Truth is stranger than fiction." The real world that Twain encountered seemed more unreal and more wonderful than anything he might have invented or imagined. But he was wise enough to know that truth telling wasn't always a reliable way to communicate. "Often, the surest way to convey misinformation is to tell the strict truth," he says.

In *Following the Equator*, Twain pulls no punches. From beginning to end, he savages modern civilization, recognizes the achievements of ancient civilizations, and especially Indian civilization that produced the Taj Mahal which, he notes, "represents man's supremest possibility in the creation of grace and beauty." Not white but brown is, in his view, the most beautiful color. Of "Indian brown," he writes, "there is no sort of chance for the average white complexion against that rich and perfect tint." (He has in mind the brown of East Indians not West Indians or the American Indian.)

The wild and the wilderness, both literal and metaphorical, appear throughout the text. Twain calls the islands of the South Pacific an "Island Wilderness" and means that they're a jumble and not a jungle. "The wilderness stretches," he explains, "across the wastes of the Pacific." Twain ends the book with a magnificent story about a disgraced English woman who settles in South Africa, chooses "to change her name and her sex and start anew in the world." She becomes Dr. James Barry, a "wild young fellow." Dr. James Barry's "Cape wildness" fascinated Twain and he concludes the narrative with his/her death and the discovery that "he was a woman."

There were no big surprises for Twain as he approached death and died in 1910. He watched his wife, Livy, die in 1904. Nearly a decade earlier, just before he began to write *Following the Equator*, he watched his daughter Susy die. Death, both individual and collective, dogged him nearly all his life.

Near the end of *Following the Equator*, he repeats a story he once told Grant about his own two-week ordeal as a soldier in the Confederate Army. His strategy, he insisted, was not to engage Union soldiers in combat, but to tire them out. He adds, "I tired out and…yet never had a casualty myself nor lost a man." According to Twain, Grant told him that if the Civil War had been fought on his, (Twain's), principles "much bloodshed would have been spared."

Shrewd Mark Twain abandoned the Confederacy, skipped the Civil War and went West. He never stopped going into the West of myth and legend and beyond. A tireless pilgrim, he told the truth through the voices of a distinguished cast of fictional characters that includes Jim, Huck, Tom, Pudd'nhead, the Connecticut Yankee, and in his own voices, guises and disguises as Samuel Clemens and Mark Twain.

CHAPTER 11

TWENTIETH CENTURY & BEYOND

Jack London, Mary Austin, Willa Cather & F. Scott Fitzgerald

"If we kill off the wild, then we are killing a part of our souls."
— JANE GOODALL

"Our people went to America because that was the place to go. It had been a good country and we made a mess of it."
— ERNEST HEMINGWAY

CALLING THE WILD

In his most famous novel, *The Call of the Wild* (1903), Jack London (1876-1916) presents a tame California dog that turns into a fierce wolf in the Yukon. The wilderness outside rekindles the wild inside. Buck becomes a killing machine and survives everything and everyone that comes his way. Natty Bumppo would see him as a kindred spirit. He's the fittest of the fit and at the end of the tale he lives as a ghost dog in the snow and cold, haunting and terrifying the Indians he murders after they attack and kill his white master. The story illustrates London's racism, or racial thinking if racism is too strong a word. It also reflects his contradictory thinking about freedom and power. On the one hand, he believed that the environment had the power to shape everyone and everything. No one was immune from that law. On the other hand, he described the power of super humans to make and remake their environments. With London, nothing could change the world and everything could change the world; so he drifted from optimism and individualism to revolution and nihilism.

In his explosive world, human beings are "plastic." Implacable forces shape them. At the same time, they have the power of plasticity and can change their shapes and fit in most anywhere. A member of the American Socialist Party for most of his adult life, London was also an American jingoist and imperialist who swung from hope to despair. In the novel *Martin Eden*, his depressed hero goes to sea on a luxury liner, then crawls through a porthole and lowers himself beneath the waves. London describes his last conscious moments and the beautiful underwater journey he takes toward his own death that becomes a kind of aesthetic experience.

London also depicts the last moments before death and the final conscious thoughts of a man in the arctic in his best-known short story, "To Build a Fire." In the first published version, the man builds a fire and lives. In the second published version, he fails to build a fire and dies. London couldn't make up his mind if the human species was doomed to death or to a kind of life eternal.

A Darwinian, a follower of Nietzsche and a Marxist, he cobbled together a system of ideas that informed much of his fiction. He loved big ideas, the bigger the better. Still, much of his best work came to him spontaneously and by accident rather than by design. His original title for *The Call of the Wild* was *The Sleeping Wolf*. In the process of writing the story, he discovered "the wild" as a trope, and, while he wasn't sure what it meant to be "wild," he knew he had created a work of literary and commerical value. *The Call of the Wild* turned into a bestseller and made London famous. Not surprisingly, he vowed to take up the wild again, though he fashioned a decadent kind of wild in *White Fang*, the follow-up to *The Call of the Wild*. Theodore Roosevelt, who knew the real wild, accused London of "nature faking." Indeed, there was something fake about London, though his fiercest fans have never been able

to see that side of him. A magnificent faker and myth maker, he
plowed and planted the field of California literature and paved the
way for twentieth-century authors such as Sinclair Lewis and John
Steinbeck. Sincerity he embraced, but the Truth and truths were
elusive. About his own rough childhood, untamed sexuality and
exuberant experiences in Asia he never could confess the real story.

At the start of the twentieth century, Americans felt bloated
on civilization and longed to return to the wilderness in fiction
and in public parks that popped up across the landscape. London
gave readers what they thought they wanted in the realm of literature, though it wasn't until he wrote *White Fang* that he came to
the conclusion that the wild was death itself, the force that stalks
the land of cold and snow and obliterates the lives of white men
and Indians. The world isn't fair, London's stories seem to say.
Everyone is trapped and no one gets out alive.

London feared the wild and yet he pursued it in real life as
an adventurer and a radical, and in his writings, too, in which
he aimed for success and literary immortality. "It is not the way
of the Wild to like movement," he wrote in the opening pages
of *White Fang*. "The Wild aims always to destroy movement."
London couldn't stop moving; his life of constant motion and
unfettered freedom pratically ensured his early death.

Born in San Francisco in 1876, the same year that *The
Adventures of Tom Sawyer* was published, London aspired to be
the next Mark Twain. He wrote an early story about a hobo boy
in which he consciously aimed to imitate Huck Finn. London
traveled to Hannibal, Missouri and went down the Mississippi on
a raft, or so he claimed. It's difficult to know for certain what Jack
London really did and what he faked doing. Alfred Kazin noted
that the "greatest story he ever told was the story he lived." The
story and the life, however, are nearly indivisible and inseparable.
A great impostor, London played the game of socialism and the

game of capitalism, boxed and sailed, tried to look fit and concealed his own inner decay. Everything was a game, including the game of publishing that he beat again and again. A workalcoholic and an alcoholic, he worked hard, played hard and burned up from the inside out, all the while that he wore a mask of good health and posed as the quintessential outdoor Californian. When he died in 1916 he was a physical wreck with fifty books to his name — many of them, including *The People of the Abyss, The Road, Martin Eden* and *The Valley of the Moon,* modern classics.

The big historical event in his lifetime was the official closing of the frontier in 1890. London rightly knew that the end of the frontier — along with the growth of corporate America — meant the end of a long chapter in American history. He assumed that readers reared on Cooper, Melville and Twain would want to read about the frontier that had passed. He seized the moment and in his early short stories and novels he both extended and deconstructed frontier myths. He even created his own version of the frontiersman in the "Malemute Kid," a diminutive comic figure without the epic sweep of Bumppo.

In the field of American wilderness fiction, London looks like a lone wolf; he called himself "Wolf" and built a house for himself and his second wife, Charmian, that he called "Wolf House" — which burned down and left him feeling like a hollow man. When he first arrived on the literary scene at the end of the 1890s, he came out of nowhere in a blaze of fin de siècle glory and invited readers to think of him as a feral orphan. Uneasy about cities from Oakland to New York, he pointed to a past with heroic pioneers and to a future with universal death and destruction, and, somewhere far off in a distant time, his dream society of equality and justice for all — except the "lower races."

In *The Iron Heel* (1908), he describes vividly the coming of an oligarchy to the United States, and in *The Scarlet Plague* (1912), he portrays a pandemic that destroys mankind. London's literary trail led to Sinclair Lewis's *It Can't Happen Here*, a novel about fascism in the United States, and to George Orwell's *1984*, about the triumph of global totalitarianism. It also led to *Into the Wild*, a nonfiction narrative, in which Jon Krakauer chronicles the misadventures of Christopher McCandless, an alienated young man from a middle class American family who reads Jack London's *The Call of the Wild* and goes to Alaska to live alone and free. Sean Penn turned the book into a popular movie that called upon young men to give up the idea of beating the wilderness at its own game. Then again, it might have encouraged them to plunge into the wild.

Environmental author Philip Fradkin wrote the biography of Everett Ruess, another young man who died in the wild. Authors and readers alike seemed eager for stories about men who disappear in the wilderness, and just as eager for stories about women who survive. Cheryl Strayed tells her own story in *Wild: From Lost to Found on the Pacific Coast Trail* (2012), an uplifting and entertaining narrative about a solo 1,100-mile trek that enabled her to heal emotional wounds and psychological scars. Her mother died, her marriage to her first husband disintegrated, and friends were upended on heroin. Strayed went on an Odyssey and found herself; in a sense she feminized the "rucksack revolution" that Kerouac wrote about in *Dharma Bums* (1958), the novel about his backpacking experiences with Gary Snyder (who appears under the name Japhy Ryder).

The American wilderness narrative — or at least one thread of it — came to an end with Strayed's *Wild*, a memoir that Oprah Winfrey picked as a book her audience had to read because of its inspirational message. There's nothing deeply troubling about *Wild*; no alarm about environmental disaster, global warming or drought. "How wild it was, to let it be," the book ends. Stayed wasn't a lone voice in the field of popular books. The wild was also therapeutic

for other women writers, including Terry Tempest Williams and
Gretel Ehrlich. Jean Hegland offered a post-apocalyptic feminist
fiction in *Into the Forest* (1996). In *Women Who Run With the Wolves*
(1992) Clarissa Pinkola Estes showed that "myths and stories of the
wild woman archetype" had been around for thousands of years.

In an introduction to Mary Austin's desert classic, *The Land
of Little Rain* — published the same year as *The Call of the Wild*
— Williams looks back at Austin as "sister, soul mate, and literary
mentor." She notes that Austin had both a "radical spirit" and
a "Victorian diction" and that she believed in "wild America."
Near the end of her lyrical tribute to the desert and to its Indians,
Austin invites readers: "Come away, you who are obsessed with
your own importance in the scheme of things, and have got nothing you did not sweat for, come away by the brown valleys and
full-bosomed hills."

Born in 1868 in Illinois, Austin moved to California in 1888,
made friends with Jack London, traveled frequently to New York
and settled in Santa Fe, New Mexico in 1934. In *American Rhythm*
(1923), an aesthetic manifesto, she touted regional literature and
called for an "American form" and an "American rhythm" which
she defined as "a perception of movement arising from experiences
in an environment." Austin's own rhythm reached its peak in *The
Land of Little Rain* (1903) in which she explores the "Country
of Lost Borders," "lost rivers" and the "stark, treeless waste" of
the desert. No human beings dominate the landscape in Austin's
narrative and "Man" with a capital "M" is, in her words, "a great
blunderer going about in the woods." Austin felt lost and lonely in
the desert. She describes its "interminable monotony" and yet she
also felt at home there. Like Dickinson, she knew how to thrive on
morsels, how to see infinity in the finite and the temporal in the
eternal. In Austin's wild, everything is used, nothing is wasted and
the economy of nature offers a model for human beings.

London and Austin approached the wilds from opposite directions and had vastly different expectations. In her world small is beautiful and balanced. In his world big is beautiful and turbulent. Austin's female world moves slowly. London's male world moves swiftly. In his two famous dog stories, he presented archetypes of the male animal as warrior and survivor. In *The Sea-Wolf* (1904), his version of Melville's *Moby-Dick*, he created Wolf Larsen, the "savage," "beautiful" and doomed captain of the *Ghost*, and the "sissy" bookworm Humphrey Van Weyden, who cries out against the "wanton slaughter" of seals, becomes a He-man, falls in love, marries and survives.

London witnessed environmental destruction caused by commercial mining and logging in the Yukon in the 1890s and described it vividly in short stories such as "Li Wan, The Fair," published first in *The Atlantic* in 1902. "The hills had been stripped of their trees, and their raw sides gored and perforated by great timber-slides and prospect holes," London wrote. Everywhere he looks he sees "an army of men…scouring the face of nature."

In the short story, "In a Far Country," published in the *Overland Monthly* in 1899, he depicts "two effete scions of civilization" who are "swallowed" by the forest, by the "white silence" and by indifferent, implacable "Death." His men are small and his forests immense. London's heart of whiteness is as antithetical to civilization as Conrad's heart of darkness. But London's characters also get rich in the "Far Country." They come back to civilization, invest the gold they've unearthed, buy property and push other men around.

Burning Daylight, the hero in the novel of the same name, strikes it rich as a miner, becomes a millionaire and settles down in the "virgin wild" of northern California with his secretary, who teaches him to be civilized. London borrowed the plot from his own life. He lifted the characters from the outlines of himself and his wife Charmian, who he idealizes in the novel as a kind of therapist and psychic healer. As late as 1910, the year *Burning Daylight* was published, London was still enthralled with the centuries-old notion that America offered a "virgin wild," though he had long ceased to believe in Cooper's trinity: God, Providence and the march of civilization across the continent.

In *The Valley of the Moon* (1913), a novel about working class life in Oakland, California that made him look like a proletarian novelist in the 1930s, London hails the hearty nineteenth-century American pioneers who crossed the desert and triumphed over the Indians. He also put caustic comments about the very same pioneers into the mouth of the novel's bohemian poet, Mark Hall, who was inspired by the real life George Sterling, one of London's closest friends. "They moved over the face of the land like locusts," Hall says of the pioneers. "They destroyed everything — the Indians, the soil, the forests, just as they destroyed the buffalo. Their morality in business and politics was gambler morality." London agreed with Hall, even as he wanted to dress the pioneers in radiant garb as supermen and superwomen.

PRAIRIE

In *O Pioneers!* (1913), published the same year as *The Valley of Moon*, Willa Cather painted a large canvas that features pioneers who stop in Nebraska and rarely stray. Her European immigrants eke out a living on the "wild lands" of the Great Plains, build homes, create villages, get married, raise families and farm where nothing seems to want to grow, much less thrive. Cather borrowed her title, not from Cooper's *The Pioneers*, but from Walt Whitman's long, exuberant poem — "Pioneers! O Pioneers!" — that's as optimistic, patriotic and bellicose as anything Cooper ever wrote. "Get your weapons ready," Whitman cries. "All the rest on us depend." From beginning to end, Whitman incites pioneers to pierce mines, overturn soil, and march, fight and die crossing the continent. The patriotic tone of "Pioneers! O Pioneers!" sweeps over much of *Leaves of Grass*.

Throughout his poetry, Whitman situates himself in the boisterous West, depicts himself as a frontiersman and as a Natty Bumppo who hunts, kills, starts campfires and broils "fresh-kill'd game" over the hot coals. Whitman has no Indian companion, no Chingachgook, but he feels an affinity for the "Red aborigines." In the poem, "Starting from Paumanok," he notices that the Indian names for places, such as Wabash, Miami, Walla-Walla and Paumanok provide him with a sense of place and connect him to the earth.

Whitman is probably most akin to Cather in "We Two, How Long We were Fool'd," in which human beings are inseparable from the earth and attached to all sentient beings, and even inanimate objects. "We are Nature," Whitman exclaims. "We become plants, trunks, foliage, roots bark,/We are bedded in the ground…/We prowl fang'd and four-footed in the woods, we spring on/prey." In Whitman's world, the wild is us. For Cather, the "wild land" is a birthing center from which everything else emerges.

"The great fact was the land itself, which seemed to overwhelm the little beginnings of human society that struggles in its somber wastes," she writes at the beginning of *O Pioneers!*, her mini-epic of the midwest. Cather doesn't urge attack, invasion or occupation, but rather a kind of symbiotic relationship with the land that she associates with a European not an American way of thinking.

John Bergson, a Swedish immigrant on the Great Plains, has "the Old-World belief that land, in itself, is desirable." His daughter, Alexandra, inherits that belief, along with his land. She befriends old, solitary men, such as Ivar, who build sod homes, live in the land and not on the land, and who do so "without defiling the face of nature anymore than the coyote that had lived there before him had done." *O Pioneers!* is an environmentally friendly novel and a paean to wilderness.

Working with symbols, such as "wild birds" and with a poetic prose, Cather infuses her novel with a sense of romance and creates a timeless time and an eternal place in which seasons come and go and tragedy unfolds gradually and inexorably. The point is not to harness, yoke, or kill the "wild things," Cather insists, but to live with and among birds, badgers and the wild men and women of the prairie, too. Cather's men, especially Alexandra's brothers, show no flair for frontier life or farming. "A pioneer should have imagination," Cather explains; the Bergson boys have none. She adds, "it was no fault of theirs that they had been dragged into the wilderness when they were little boys."

Unlike her brothers, Alexandra has imagination, compassion and empathy. She looks at the land not with fear, anxiety or horror but with "love and yearning." To Alexandra, the land is beautiful and "rich and strong and glorious." Perhaps only an American woman raised on the prairies could have written a hymn to them and about them. Writing nearly one hundred years after Cooper began his literary career, Cather feminized the wilderness that he mapped and explored. She also ventured bravely beyond territories known to Melville, Twain and Jack London.

Far less bound by ideologies and theories than London, who chafed at earth-bound existence and longed for the stars, Cather was far more grounded in her own native soil. Her frontier women, especially Alexandra Bergson, love "wild lands," "wild creatures," "wild soil," "wild homesteads," "wild flowers" and "all the wild things." A creature of the Great Plains, Alexandra looks beneath the surface and sees the soul of the earth itself. She also peers beyond the appearance of the outcasts and sees their essential humanity. *O Pioneers!* burns with much the same intense heat that burns in Emily Bronte's masterpiece, *Wuthering Heights*.

Like Bronte, Cather turned with hope to barbarians. She felt that only barbarians could cleanse decadent empires like that of the Romans that had "grown monstrous in its pleasures." Even as she looked back at the decline and fall of the Roman Empire, she kept an eye on the emerging American Empire of the twentieth century, alarmed by the growing spectacle of conquest and decadence she saw. The raw, barbaric prairie acts as an antidote to the imperial enterprise. For Cather, the wildness of youth and the wild dreams of madmen, visionaries and misfits must be protected, even though it's the wild ones who sow the seeds of their own destruction and bring disaster to the community itself. For Cather, the wild ones are "too beautiful, too full of life and love." They perish on the prairies, while the practical, patient Alexandra's of the world survive.

Lyrical fiction by women about the wild didn't end with *O Pioneers!* Cather herself continued to write about the West and about pioneers. But perhaps the most innovative novel about pioneers that followed Cather's prairie epic was F. Scott Fitzgerald's *The Great Gatsby*, a compact work of fiction that manages to suggest the sweep of American history. Fitzgerald's fictional midwesterners flourish and perish not on the prairies and frontiers close to home, but on Long Island, where they live in comfortable homes, dance with love and death and consort with the rhythms of the Jazz Age.

Growing up on the Island in the 1940s and 1950s, I turned instinctively to Fitzgerald's *The Great Gatsby*, hoping I might meet people like Gatsby and Daisy in the big mansions along the shore where my schoolmates and their parents lived the isolated lives of the rich: survivors of Prohibition, the Depression and the Atomic Age. Fitzgerald and *The Great Gatsby* belonged to my world or perhaps it was I who belonged to theirs.

Fitzgerald's characters felt closer geographically and emotionally, too, than Faulkner's Mississippi hunters, Indians, white men and African Americans who I read about in *The Sound and the Fury*, *Absalom, Absalom!* and *Light in August*. I loved Faulkner's wild but I couldn't see myself in his world or his characters in mine. The South was another country. Gatsby and his crowd were also closer to me than Hemingway and his Michigan wilderness with its young boys and girls who reinvent Twain's adolescents, camping and fishing in the woods.

In the Nick Adams stories, Hemingway sounds goofy and sentimental. Nick and his sister seem like parodies of wilderness kids, more fictional than real, copies of something that was once authentic. In *Big Woods*, Faulkner sounds angry, outraged and almost indifferent to the sweep of human history in which one civilization becomes obsolete and its pioneers and settlers are dispossessed by newer waves of more up-to-date pioneers and settlers.

Gatsby gave me a keen sense of place, and my sense of Long Island as a place offered a way into Fitzgerald's 1923 novel that read like the news when I first discovered it in 1959, the year I graduated from Huntington High School. For Fitzgerald, the Dutch dispossessed the Island's Indians, the English dispossessed the Dutch and the Americans in turn dispossessed the English. New money threatened old money and the wasteland eroded the wilderness. But Fitzgerald rendered the transformations with less agitation than Faulkner. He allowed the reader to dream, revel in nostalgia and empathize with the beautiful, doomed wild ones. That's what I did when I read Fitzgerald's novel about fast cars, crafty bootleggers and beautiful women. It was the perfect novel to read at seventeen and going away from home for the first time.

The Great Gatsby, I learned in college, began as a boy-meets-girl story for *The Saturday Evening Post*, the same magazine I found on the coffee table in the living room of the house where I grew up. Fitzgerald's romantic short story turned into a lyrical prose poem about the American Dream and America itself. The French novelist Stendhal (1783-1842) helped Fitzgerald along the way. Just before he wrote *The Great Gatsby*, Fitzgerald discovered Stendhal's masterpiece, *Le Rouge et Le Noir* (1830) and was swept away by the story of Julien Sorel, the boy from the provinces who moves to the city, navigates his way through elite circles until he literally and figuratively loses his head. Fitzgerald called it "the most wonderful novel" of the nineteenth century. What's more, he funneled a sense of wonder into his own novel about young men and women from the provinces of America as they make their way in and around New York. When Fitzgerald finished writing *Gatsby*, he noted that, "the whole burden of the novel" was "the loss of those illusions that give such color to the world so that you don't care whether things are true or false as long as they partake of the magical glory." At seventeen, novels about lost illusions were hard to resist.

The magical glory of the 1920s didn't feel far away from my very own magical boyhood in the 1950s. Bootleggers I met told stories of the Jazz Age and aged caretakers on the old estates told tales about wild parties and wild men like Gatsby, who tried to roll back time and start all over again. Gatsby's Long Island Sound still beckoned and the natural world of frogs and flowers still existed, too, though suburbia nearly killed them. The roads Gatsby takes to get into and out of the city still took commuters to Manhattan and then home at the end of the day, though there were newer roads and faster cars when I grew up. While I wasn't from the midwest like Nick Carraway, Fitzgerald's narrator, I felt like an outsider who peered into the world of the wealthy and the powerful. I read the novel and watched as though in a theater with a movie on screen as Gatsby takes Daisy, the love of his life, away from her brutal husband, Tom Buchanan. And I felt a sense of tangible, emotional loss as Gatsby loses Daisy for the second time in his life.

The novel has never lost its charm for me, though the characters are irresponsible and unethical if not criminal, whether they cheat at golf, or on their wives or fix the 1919 World Series. *The Great Gatsby* was perhaps the first book I tried to analyze and interpret. I found it fascinating that almost all of the characters aim to fix things — to cheat — so that they're not caught for their crimes and misdemeanors. I could see that Nick, the moral center of the novel, aims to do the right thing and to be responsible in ways that Gatsby, Tom Buchanan and their friends aren't responsible. A representative of the world of the rational, the safe and the normal, Nick provided me with a lens to look at Gatsby, the Buchanans and the recklessness of the Jazz Age.

A millionaire with both a wife and a mistress, Buchanan hides behind wealth, property, marriage, and behind grand-sounding words like "civilization" — not unlike the fathers of the young women I took to the movies on Saturday nights. White Anglo Saxon Protestants, or WASPS as we called them, still dominated the North Shore of Long Island that seemed with its forests and mansions the most romantic place in the world. Tom Buchanan struck me then, and still does now, as the most unnatural and unlikeable character in the novel. He strikes me as emblematic of capitalist society that fell apart with the Stock Market crash of 1929 and the Depression of the 1930s, an era my father lived through and that he introduced to me with tales of his own adventures as a bootlegger and as a lawyer, too. Like capitalism, Buchanan bounces back.

The Long Island world of nature provides a stark contrast to the artificiality of Gatsby, with his silk shirts and fake identity, and Daisy, too, with her affluent friends living stilted lives. Only Carraway, I noticed, sees the natural world around him, and recognizes the destruction of that world, too. Indeed, he sees, hears and smells "frogs full of life," "lilac trees" and fields with "deep, pungent roses." He also enjoys "the great wet barnyard of Long Island Sound." I knew that world from my own experience as a boy who swam and sailed and wandered into the WASP yacht clubs on the shore where I didn't belong. The natural world of *Gatsby* is mostly expunged from the 2013 Hollywood film, staring Leonardo DiCaprio. In its place, the director Baz Luhrmann adds cars, mansions and commodities as though to say that Americans in the twenty-first century didn't care about frogs, trees and fields.

When I came back to *The Great Gatsby* as an adult I read it as a meditation on time. I saw that, as it moves forward it also moves back into the past and reverses the patterns of the nineteenth-century fictions that I read at school. Fitzgerald's pioneers, unlike Cooper's, don't move West, but East to Manhattan, the city with the "wild promise of all the mystery and the beauty in the world." As a college undergraduate in New York, I began to understand and appreciate the lure of Manhattan. I recognized that Fitzgerald's New York — like Raymond Chandler's Los Angeles and Nelson Algren's Chicago — was a modern wilderness; the bootleggers, gamblers and gangsters were the wild men in the brave new world of greed and glory. Fitzgerald's novel provided me with the ammunition I wanted and needed to feel that the world was an unjust place. Then, too, I could see that the wild wasn't really a geographical place, but a lifestyle. The wild was cool; as an advertising concept it sold coffee, jeans, cars, vacations and more.

Gatsby signaled the end of a certain kind of pioneer, pathfinder, scavenger and hunter. Fitzgerald explains that the young Jay Gatsby was a "clam-digger and a salmon-fisher" with a "brown, hardening body." He adds that he "knew women early" and became "contemptuous of them." His heart was "in a constant, turbulent riot" and the "most grotesque and fantastic conceits haunted him." Young Gatsby is very much like the characters in the pages of Jack London's adventure fiction and perhaps a parody of

London himself, who was an oyster pirate and a salmon fisherman, proud of his own brown hard body and his conquests of women.

The more I reread *The Great Gatsby* the more insights I had into the lives of the characters. Fitzgerald skewers the popular notion, expressed in Frederick Jackson Turner's essays, that the frontier was a fresh, new place that gave birth to American democracy. Fitzgerald offered a savage critique of the frontier and described Gatsby's benefactor and father figure, Cody, as a "pioneer debauchee who during one phase of American life brought back to the Eastern seaboard the savage violence of the frontier brothel and saloon."

Of Tom and Daisy, Fitzgerald wrote that, "They were careless people...they smashed up things and creatures and then retreated back into their money or their vast carelessness." He added that they "let other people clean up the mess they had made." I knew the Buchanans, or thought that I did. They lived in the big houses along the shore, drove big cars and walled themselves off from ordinary Long Islanders. They expected their servants, lawyers and bankers to clean up the emotional, financial and household messes they created.

Tom Buchanan, with his "cruel body...capable of enormous leverage," struck me as yet another archetypal male American and the last (or next-to-last) in a long line of empire builders. Twentieth-century white civilization, Tom argues, must beat back the "colored empires" of the world or be "utterly submerged." The fathers of my Huntington friends echoed those sentiments in the 1950s and 1960s, as African Americans broke free from segregation right on the Island.

Looking at the novel from the vantage point of the twenty-first century, I can see now that Fitzgerald kept his ear attuned to the ugly as well as the beautiful sounds of the Jazz Age, and to its political and moral sentiments, too. If he glamorized wealth and romanticized wealthy women such as Daisy, he was far more subversive than critics have usually allowed. Reading his letters opened my eyes to his radicalism. Shortly before he wrote *The Great Gatsby*, he observed, "I've let myself be dominated by 'authorities' for too long." His real heroes, he noted, were "the Rousseau's, Marx's, Tolstoy's." The real villains, he explained, are the "Roosevelts and Rockefellers that strut for 20 yrs. or so mouthing such phrases as 100% American (which means 99% village idiot)."

Those sentiments, I think, inform *The Great Gatsby*, which ends with a spectacular description of the New World at the beginning of the age of European exploration. And so we come full circle. Fitzgerald doesn't provide a date, a decade or even a century for the event he describes, but he probably meant the seventeenth century when Henry Hudson and his crew of Dutch and English sailors first saw the island of Manhattan. The closing passage of *The Great Gatsby* has always taken my breath away. I know, as every other reader surely knows, the series of environmental catastrophes that will follow the final image that Fitzgerald provides. "Man must have held his breath in the presence of this continent, compelled into an aesthetic contemplation he neither understood nor desired, face to face for the last time in history with something commensurate to his capacity for wonder," Fitzgerald wrote. He doesn't use the word "wilderness." Still, it's the "untrammeled" American wilderness that he has in mind. It's the Virgin Land recreated, albeit without a single Indian.

WASTE LAND

I know that I love *Gatsby* because, with centuries of environmental destruction staring him in the face, Fitzgerald imagined the New World as it might have looked to European sailors in the age of exploration. The ending is perfect — as perfect as the endings to *Huck Finn* and *Moby-Dick*. Like the Dutch sailors, Gatsby looks at life with a sense of awe and wonder, and an appreciation of beauty. Then, too, the ending is perfect, I think, because early in the novel Fitzgerald describes Long Island (at least a part of it) as a "waste land." (Fitzgerald wrote, "waste land" not "wasteland.") His images of America as a paradise and as an inferno stand at the opposite ends of the environmental spectrum. The wasteland and the wilderness frame Gatsby's personal drama. His failure mimics an American failure to live in harmony with the continent of North America, the American habit of denial and American attempts to fix things long after they're fixable.

The wasteland belonged to the zeitgeist of the 1920s. Before *Gatsby*, Eliot offered in *The Waste Land* (1922) — his avant-garde, apocalyptic poem made up of fragments — a mythic account of a "dead land" and "desert" with "cracked earth" and "stony rubbish." Spirituality is dying or dead, and yet Eliot held out hope for rebirth, renewal and redemption, too.

As a boy I saw the wasteland when I traveled by railroad from Huntington, Long Island to Manhattan, along much the same route that Nick travels when he goes to and from work. Nick describes in vivid detail the "desolate area" that's "bounded on one side by a small foul river." The deadly, toxic landscape is covered by "bleak dust." Moreover, "ashes grow like wheat" and "ash-gray men swarm." Here, Nick explains, the railroad meets "the motor road." Pollution chokes "a ghastly creek" and clouds of "rising smoke" emerge from chimneys. Between 1923, when *Gatsby* was published, and 1963, when I graduated from college, little had changed. If anything, the environmental destruction was worse. Americans had turned the green breast of the new world into a landscape of lifelessness even as they held on to the illusion of a pristine wilderness. In the early 1960s, the railroad and the car loomed larger then ever before; human beings seemed smaller, as though diminished by air that wasn't fresh, water that wasn't clean and land itself that was toxic. Nearly everything that was natural had been perverted.

In his review of *The Great Gatsby*, H. L. Mencken wrote that the Long Island that Fitzgerald "sets before us...is worth any social historian's study." The novel is also, I believe, well worth a natural historian's study. The poetic snap shots of trees and birds provide a portrait of a vital habitat that peaks out from the cracks and the crevices of a paved-over civilization. *Gatsby* gave me a sense of hope. Maybe nature itself would find a way to survive. Maybe it was more resilient than any destructive force made by humanity. Indeed, Fitzgerald's novel exudes the geography of hope.

"The best American writing," William Carlos Williams wrote in his classic of cultural criticism, *In the American Grain*, offers "not a serene acceptance but the fanatic alienation of wanting to break free from false identity and idolatry, even red-white-and-blue idolatry, even at the risk of madness if that's what it takes to reach the Promised Land." Williams might have been thinking of *Moby-Dick*, *Huck Finn*, and *The Great Gatsby* when he talked about the best American writing. Other choices exist, but for American writers it has often seemed as though blithe acceptance on the one hand, and intense alienation on the other hand are the only viable alternatives. It seemed that way to Melville, Thoreau, Dickinson and Twain who were proud to be Americans and who were also disloyal to the cant and hypocrisy of American civilization. The Beat Generation writers carried on that tradition. They opted for madness, nakedness and the kind of hunger that kept them on edge and creative.

In the 1920s, while living on Long Island, reading Stendhal, and writing *Gatsby*, Fitzgerald was deeply disenchanted with the America of bellicose Teddy Roosevelt and boisterous John D. Rockefeller. He was also impelled to create an enchanted moment when awed Dutch sailors held their breath and gazed at a green continent in bloom.

In the twentieth century, American environmental writers — Wendell Berry, Gretel Ehrlich, Aldo Leopold, Kenneth Rexroth, David Brower, Howard Zahniser, Rachel Carson, Wallace Stegner, Gary Snyder, Terry Tempest Williams, Annie Dillard, Marilynne Robinson and others — traced the destruction of the wild. In their books and in their own lives they also planted the seeds for the renewal of culture, agriculture and nature. They've popularized the concepts of ecology and the watershed, both of which raise awareness and link human beings to the environment.

HOUSEKEEPING IN THE GREAT OUTDOORS

Fiction, nonfiction and poetry about the wild skyrocketed at the end of the twentieth century, perhaps because readers saw the wild disappearing all around the world. There was much good work. Perhaps the word "great" truly belongs to Marilynne Robinson's *Housekeeping* (1981), which is as economical as *The Great Gatsby*. Robinson's first novel describes several generations of women in a matriarchal family who live in the fictional western town of Fingerbone that's surrounded on all sides by "the black wilderness." The narrator, a dreamy, intrepid young woman, describes the death of her grandfather in a railroad accident and the suicide of her mother, the twin events that shape her early life. Ruth explains that she and her sisters are freed from "success, recognition, advancement" — nearly everything that American civilization encourages. Plunged into a wayward existence outside the norms of the community, the girls become teenage outlaws who don't go to school, don't respect private property and don't come home at night.

For Robinson, as for Zora Neale Hurston (1891-1960), the twentieth-century African American novelist, folklorist and anthropologist, the wild belongs to a social class as well as to a geo-graphical location. In *Their Eyes Were Watching God* (1937), Hur-ston's heroine, Janie, loses much of her wildness when she marries a successful black man and moves into the black middle class. Wildness, she's told, isn't ladylike or proper. After the death of her husband, Janie reconnects with her own wildness and with the wil-derness of the world. In the Florida Everglades, she lives with Tea Cake, the love of her life. "Ground so rich that everything went wild," Hurston writes of the land where her lovers settle down and are also violently dislocated. She adds, "People wild too."

In *Housekeeping* the two fictional sisters, Ruth and Lucille, explore the woods outside Fingerbone, a hardscrabble community where citizens struggle to survive poverty and isolation. At times, the novel feels like a female version of *The Adventures of Tom Saw-yer*. Ruth and Lucille opt for a kind of housekeeping in the woods, rather than at home. "The deep woods are as dark and stiff and as full of odors as the parlor of an old house," Ruth explains. She adds, "I went into the woods for the woods' own sake, while, in-creasingly Lucille seemed to be enduring a banishment there."

Robinson can be as dark a writer as Twain, though her prose is far more poetic and compact. *Housekeeping*, with its lyrical, lush prose, offers a portrait of the artist as a poor young woman growing up on the edge of a "black wilderness," gifted with a rich imagination and a love of language. Ruth grows up, becomes a writer and tells the saga of several generations in her family.

Not surprisingly, her sister, Lucille with her fierce neatness, opts for an existence more orderly than life with her own family. Ruth and her aunt, Sylvie, leave Fingerbone and travel as vagabonds from place to place. They don't go downriver like Huck and Jim or across the country by road like Dean Moriarty and Sal Paradise in Kerouac's *On the Road*, but rather around the West by railroad.

Housekeeping shows that an author steeped in the past and

gifted with a fertile imagination can reinvent the wilderness and recreate characters with the kind of religious zeal that haunted the early New Englanders. Fingerbone, with its violence and isolation on the edge of the wilderness, feels like it could be an early pioneer settlement almost anywhere along the American frontier. An intellectual historian as well as a novelist, Robinson has written brilliantly about John Calvin and his influences on writers. "Behind the aesthetics and the metaphysics of classical American literature, again and again we find the Calvinst soul, universal in its singularity, and full of Calvinist wonder," she writes.

Her provocative essay, "Wilderness" (1998) — published seventeen years after *Housekeeping* — stirred up a generation of environmentalists, ecologists, writers, activists, teachers and artists. It has shaped much of my own thinking and feeling on the subject. "Wilderness is where things can be hidden," Robinson explains. "Wilderness and its analogues seem to invite denial in every form."

The questions that she asks are the questions that set me on fire: "What have we done for the whale, if we lose the sea?" and "How many countries in this world have bombed or poisoned their own terrain in the name of protecting it from its enemies?"

Today, her thoughts are more disquieting than ever before. Indeed, where do we turn in the twenty-first century for answers about the survival of the human species and the planet Earth? Do we turn to civilization, or do we turn to the wilderness? Should we aim for balance and meld the wild and the mild? Moreover, how can we honestly and genuinely talk about protecting, conserving, preserving and restoring the environment when the planet is overheated and countries on almost every continent are caught up in civil wars and wars of genocide?

In 1964, when the Wilderness Act and the Civil Rights Act both became law, President Johnson gave his "Great Society" speech and insisted on the need to beautify America and to create "a place where man can renew contact with nature." Six years later, at the first Earth Day, speakers around the country asked environmentally friendly crowds how the preservation of the Earth could be compatible with the bombing of Vietnam, the use of chemical weapons, and the poverty and violence in the United States itself.

Much the same questions might be asked now. How can politicians sincerely talk about wilderness protection when the arms industry provides weapons for mass slaughter of the kind that would shock James Fenimore Cooper, Herman Melville, Catharine Sedgwick, Emily Dickinson, Mark Twain, Willa Cather, William Faulker and F. Scott Fitzgerald?

At the end of her "Wilderness" essay, Robinson writes, "I think we must surrender the idea of wilderness…and accept our care and hope in civilization." I want to believe her, and yet, sharing as I do Melville's and Twain's perspectives on "snivilization," I can't help but wonder if civilization, as we know it, will only bring more bombs, more poison, more wastelands and more denial.

At his most buoyant moments, F. Scott Fitzgerald shared a sense of optimism with Williams Carlos Williams, who expressed — in the aftermath of World War I — an "infinite hope" that life might begin all over again. Today, the notion of starting all over again sounds like a fairy tale. The supply of infinite hope might have run out along with the notion of an inexhaustible supply of clean air, water and green land. Americans almost always fall prey to the false notion of plentitude. They did in the beginning and in the beginning was the end. Today, it does not seem possible to echo Thoreau's mid-nineteenth-century belief that in "Wildness is the preservation of the world." Not as emphatically as he. America, the double and the twin of itself, lives on as a dark, dirty wasteland and perhaps, just perhaps, in some way as a wilderness in a bright new day. The geography of hope won't die an easy death.

SELECTED BIBLIOGRAPHY

ANTHOLOGIES

Baym, Nina, Robert S. Levine. Eds. *The Norton Anthology of American Literature*. Eighth Edition. Vol. A, B, C, D, E. New York: W.W. Norton, 2012.

Belasco, Susan and Linck Johnson. Eds. *The Bedford Anthology of American Literature*. Second Edition. Vol. I: Beginnings to 1865. Boston: Bedford/ St. Martin's, 2014.

Cain, William E. Ed. *American Literature*. Vol. I & II. New York: Penguin, 2004.

WILDERNESS

Berry, Wendell. *The Unsettling of America: Culture & Agriculture*. San Francisco: Sierra Club, 1977.

Cronon, William. Ed. *Uncommon Ground: Rethinking the Human Place in Nature*. New York: Norton, 1996.

Glacken, Clarence J. *Traces on the Rhodian Shore: Nature and Culture in Western Thought from Ancient Times to the End of the Eighteenth Century*. Berkeley: University of California, 1967.

Nash, Roderick Frazier. *Wilderness & the American Mind*. Fourth Ed. New Haven: Yale University Press, 2001. Orig. pub. 1967.

Nelson, Michael P. & J. Baird Callicott. Eds. *The Wilderness Debate Rages On*. Athens: University of Georgia, 2008.

Oelschlaeger, Max. *The Idea of the Wilderness: From Prehistory to the Age of Ecology.* New Haven: Yale, 1991.

Peterson, Roger Tory & James Fisher. *Wild America.* Boston: Houghton, 1955.

Matthiessen, Peter. *Wildlife in America.* New York: Penguin, 1995. Orig. Pub. 1959.

Rexroth, Kenneth. *In the Sierra: Mountain Writings.* Ed. Kim Stanley Robinson. New York: New Directions, 2012.

Snyder, Gary. *The Practice of the Wild.* New York: North Point, 1990.

Stegner, Wallace. "Wilderness Letter." In *Natural Acts: Readings on Nature and the Environment.* Ed. Stephen A. Scipione. Boston: Bedford, 2009. Orig. pub. 1960.

Literary & Cultural Criticism

Achebe, Chinua. *The Education of a British-Protected Child: Essays.* New York: Knopf, 2009.

Austin, Mary. *The American Rhythm.* Santa Fe: Sunstone, 2007. Orig.Pub. 1923.

Birkerts, Sven. *An Artificial Wilderness: Essays on 20th-Century Literature.* New York. William Morrow, 1987.

Borges, Jorge Luis. *On Writing.* Ed. Suzanne Jill Levine. New York, Penguin, 2010.

Buell, Lawrence. *The Environmental Imagination.* Cambridge: Harvard, 1995.

Chase, Richard. *The American Novel and Its Tradition.* New York: Doubleday, 1957.

Cunliffe, Marcus. *The Literature of the United States.* New York: Penguin, 1986. Orig. Pub. 1954.

Doctorow, E.L. *Jack London, Hemingway, and the Constitution:*

Selected Essays, 1977-1992. New York: Random House, 1993.

Douglas, Ann. *The Feminization of American Culture*. New York: Knopf, 1977.

Eliot, T.S. *Selected Prose of T.S. Eliot*. Ed. & Intro. Frank Kermode. New York: Harcourt, 1975.

Fiedler, Leslie. *Love and Death in the American Novel*. Revised Ed. New York: Stein and Day, 1966.

Fiege, Mark. *The Republic of Nature: An Environmental History of the United States*. Seattle: University of Washington, 2012.

Ford, Boris. Ed. *The New Pelican Guide to English Literature: Vol. 9, American Literature*. New York: Penguin, 1988.

Hass, Robert. *What Light Can Do*. New York: Ecco, 2012.

Kolodny, Annette. *The Lay of the Land: Metaphor as Experience and History in American Life and Letters*. Chapel Hill: University of North Carolina, 1975.

Lawrence, D. H. *Studies in Classic American Literature*. New York: Penguin, 1971. Orig. Pub. 1923.

Marcus, Greil & Werner Sollors. Eds. *A New Literary History of America*. Cambridge: Harvard, 2009.

Marx, Leo. *The Machine in the Garden: Technology and the Pastoral Ideal in America*. New York: Oxford, 1964.

Matthiessen, F.O. *American Renaissance: Art and Expression in the Age of Emerson and Whitman*. New York: Oxford, 1968. Orig. Pub. 1941.

Mencken, H.L. *Prejudices: A Selection*. Ed. & Intro. James T. Farrell. New York: Vintage, 1958.

Mencken, H. L. *The American Language: An Inquiry into the Development of English in the United States*. New York: Knopf, 1936. Orig. Pub. 1919.

Mumford, Lewis. *The Golden Day: A Study in American Literature and Culture*. New intro. Boston: Beacon, 1957. Orig. pub. 1926.

Paglia, Camille. *Sexual Personae: Art and Decadence from Nefertiti to Emily Dickinson.* New York: Vintage, 1991.

Parrington, V.L. *Main Currents in American Thought. Vols. I, II & III.* New York: Harcourt, 1958.

Rahv, Philip. *Essays on Literature and Politics 1932-1972.* Ed. Arabel J. Porter and Andrew J. Dvosin. With a memoir by Mary McCarthy. Boston: Houghton Mifflin, 1975.

Rich, Adrienne. *On Lies, Secrets, and Silence: Selected Prose, 1966-1978.* New York: Norton, 1979.

Slotkin, Richard. *Regeneration Through Violence: The Mythology of the American Frontier, 1600-1860.* Middletown: Wesleyan University, 1973.

Smith, Henry Nash. *Virgin Land: The American West as Symbol and Myth.* Cambridge: Harvard University, 1970. Orig. Pub.1950.

Williams, William Carlos. *In the American Grain.* New York: New Directions, 1956. Orig. pub. 1925.

Woolf, Virginia. *A Room of One's Own.* Foreward Mary Gordon. New York: Harcourt, 1989. Orig. Pub. 1929.

PREFACE

Lawrence, D.H. *Lady Chatterley's Lover.* Intro. Doris Lessing. New York: Penguin, 2006. Orig. Pub. 1928.

Miller, Arthur. *The Crucible.* Intro by Christopher Bigsby. New York: Penguin, 2003. Orig. Pub. 1953.

O'Neill, Eugene. *Ah, Wilderness!* In *Complete Plays 1932-1943.* Ed. Travis Bogard. New York: Library of America, 1988.

Brower, Kenneth. Ed. *The Wilderness Within: Remembering David Brower.* Berkeley: Heyday, 2012.

CHAPTER 1

Anderson, Kat. *Tending the Wild.* Berkeley: University of California, 2006.

Barbour, Philip L., Ed. *The Complete Works of Captain John Smith. Vol. I, II, III.* Chapel Hill: University of North Carolina, 1986.

Bauer, Ralph. *The Cultural Geography of Colonial American Literatures: Empire, Travel, Modernity.* Cambridge: Cambridge University, 2003.

Calloway, Colin. Ed. *The World Turned Upside Down: Indian Voices from Early America.* Boston: Bedford, 1994.

Hudson, Henry. *Henry Hudson's Voyages from Purchas His Pilgrims.* Ed. by Samuel Purchas. Ann Arbor: University Microfilms, 1966. Orig. pub. London 1625.

Hunter, Douglas. *Half Moon: Henry Hudson and the Voyage that Redrew the Map of the New World.* New York: Bloomsbury, 2009.

McLuhan, Marshall. *Understanding Media: The Extensions of Man.* New York: McGraw-Hill, 1965.

Mitchell, Stephen. *Gilgamesh: A New English Version.* New York: Free Press, 2006.

Sale, Kirkpatrick. *The Conquest of Paradise: Christopher Columbus and the Columbian Legacy.* New York: Alfred A. Knopf, 1990.

Standing Bear, Luther. *Land of the Spotted Eagle.* Foreword Richard N. Ellis. Lincoln: University of Nebraska, 1978. Orig. Pub. 1933.

Van den Bogaert, Harmen Meyndertsz. *A Journal into Mohawk and Oneida Country, 1634-1635.* Translated and Edited by Charles Gehring and William Starna. Syracuse: Syracuse University, 1988.

Van der Donck, Adriaen. *A Description of the New Netherlands.* Ed. with an introduction by Thomas F. Donnell. Syracuse: Syracuse University, 1968. Orig. pub. 1655.

Winny, James, Ed. *Sir Gawain and the Green Knight.* Ontario (Canada): Broadway, 2007.

Chapter 2

Bercovitch, Sacvan. *The Puritan Origins of the American Self.* New Haven: Yale, 1975.

Bradford, William. *Of Plymouth Plantation.* New York: Capricorn, 1962.

Bradstreet, Anne. *The Works of Anne Bradstreet.* Ed. Jeannine Hensley. Foreword Adrienne Rich. Cambridge: Harvard University, 1967.

Bunyan, John. *The Pilgrim's Progress.* Ed. Roger Sharrock. Oxford: Clarendon, 1960.

Carroll, Peter N. *Puritanism and the Wilderness: The Intellectual Significance of the New England Frontier, 1629-1700.* New York: Columbia University, 1969.

Cave, Alfred A. *The Pequot War.* Amherst: University of Massachusetts, 1996.

Jeffers, Robinson, *The Collected Poetry of Robinson Jeffers, Vol. I. 1920-1928.* Ed. Tim Hunt. Stanford: Stanford University, 1988.

Jennings, Francis. *The Invasion of America: Indians, Colonialism, and the Cant of Conquest.* Chapel Hill: University of North Carolina, 1975.

McLuhan, T.C. *Touch the Earth: A Self Portrait of Indian Existence.* New York: Simon and Schuster, 1971.

Miller, Arthur. *The Crucible: A Play in Four Acts.* New York: Penguin, 1982. Orig. Pub. 1953.

Miller, Perry. *Roger Williams: His Contribution to the American Tradition.* New York: Atheneum, 1966.

Morgan, Ted. *Wilderness At Dawn: The Settling of the North American Continent.* New York: Simon & Schuster, 1993.

Morton, Thomas. *New English Canaan.* New York: Burt Franklin, 1967. Orig. pub. Amsterdam, 1637.

Orr, Charles. Ed. *History of the Pequot War: The Contemporary Accounts of Mason, Underhill, Vincent and Gardener.* Cleveland: Helman-Taylor, 1897.

Rowlandson, Mary. *A True History of the Captivity and Restoration of Mrs. Mary Rowlandson. American Literature.* Vol. I. Ed. William E. Cain. New York: Penguin, 2004.

Vaughan, Alden T. *New England Frontier: Puritans and Indians, 1620-1675.* Third Ed. Norman: University of Oklahoma, 1995. Orig. Pub. 1965.

Vowell, Sarah. *The Wordy Shipmates.* New York: Riverhead, 2008.

Williams, Roger. *A Key into the Language of America.* Intro. Howard M. Chapin. Bedford (MA): Applewood, nd. Orig. Pub. 1643.

_____. *The Bloudy Tenent. The Complete Writings of Roger Williams.* Ed. Perry Miller. Vol. Three. New York: Russell & Russell, 1963. Orig. pub. 1644.

_____. *The Letters of Roger Williams.* Ed. Perry Miller. *The Complete Writings of Roger Williams.* Vol. Six. New York: Russell & Russell, 1963

_____. *The Complete Writings of Roger Williams.* Ed. Perry Miller. Vol. Seven. New York: Russell & Russell, 1963.

CHAPTER 3

Austin, Mary S. *Philip Freneau: The Poet of the Revolution: A History of His life and Times.* New York: A. Wessels, 1901.

Axelrad, Jacob. *Philip Freneau: Champion of Democracy.* Austin: University of Texas, 1967.

Cain, William E. "The Age of Emerson." *American Literature.* Vol I. New York: Penguin, 2004.

Crèvecoeur, J. Hector St. John de. *Letters from an American Farmer and Sketches of 18th-Century America.* Ed. Albert E. Stone. New York: Penguin, 1981.

Emerson, Ralph Waldo. *Selected Essays.* Ed. Larzer Ziff. New York: Penguin, 1982.

Equiano, Olaudah. *The Interesting Narrative of the Life of Olaudah Equiano.* Boston: St. Martins, 1995. Orig. Pub. 1791.

Faulkner, William. *Big Woods: The Hunting Stories.* New York: Vintage, 1983. Orig. Pub. 1955.

Freneau, Philip. *Poems of Freneau.* Ed. with Intro. Harry Hayden Clark. New York: Hafner, 1960. Orig. pub. 1929.

Imlay, Gilbert. *The Emigrants, or the History of an Expatriated Family.* Intro. W. M. Verhoeven & Amanda Gilroy. New York: Penguin, 1998. Orig. Pub. 1793.

Irving, Washington. *Astoria, Or Anecdotes of an Enterprise Beyond the Rocky Mountains.* Ed. Richard Dilworth Rust. Boston: Twayne, 1976.

_____. *The Legend of Sleepy Hollow and Other Writings.* New York: Barnes & Noble, 2006.

_____. *Letters* Vol. I, II, III, IV. Ed. Ralph M. Aderman, Herbert L. Kleinfield and Jenifer S. Banks. Boston: Twayne, 1979.

_____. *A Tour of the Prairies.* Ed. John Francis McDermott Norman: University of Oklahoma, 1956. Orig. Pub. 1835.

Jefferson, Thomas. *Writings.* New York: Library of America, 1984.

Jones, Brian Jay. *Washington Irving: An American Original.* New York: Arcade, 2008.

Leary, Lewis. Ed. *The Last Poems of Philip Freneau.* Westport: Greenwood, 1970. Orig. Pub. 1945.

_____. *That Rascal Freneau: A Study in Literary Failure.* New York: Octagon, 1971.

Linklater, Andro. *Measuring America: How an Untamed Wilderness Shaped the United States and Fulfilled the Promise of Democracy*. New York: Walker, 2002.

Marx, Karl. *The Eighteenth Brumaire of Louis Bonaparte*. New York: International, 1963. Orig. Pub. 1852.

Spencer, Benjamin T. *The Quest for Nationality: An American Literary Campaign*. Syracuse: Syracuse University, 1957.

Paine, Thomas. *Common Sense, Rights of Man and Other Essential Writings*. Intro. Sidney Hook. New Foreword Jack Fruchtman Jr. New York: Signet, 2003.

Wheeler, Daniel Edwin, ed. *Life and Writings of Thomas Paine Vol. 8*. New York: Vincent Parke, 1908.

CHAPTER 4

Allen, Paul. Ed. *History of the Expedition Under the Command of Captains Lewis and Clark to the Sources of the Missouri thence Across the Rocky Mountains and Down the River Columbia to the Pacific Ocean*. Philadelphia: Bradford and Inskeep, 1814.

Ambrose, Stephen E. *Undaunted Courage: Meriwether Lewis, Thomas Jefferson and the Opening of the American West*. New York: Simon & Schuster, 1996.

Burns, Ken. *Lewis & Clark: The Journey of the Corps of Discovery*. Alexandria (Virginia): PBS, 1998.

Jackson, Donald. Ed. *Letters of the Lewis and Clark Expedition: With Related Documents, 1783-1854*. Urbana: University of Illinois, 1962.

Moulton, Gary E. *The Lewis and Clark Journals*. Abridged Ed. Lincoln: University of Nebraska, 2003.

CHAPTER 5

Audubon, John James. *Aububon's Birds of America*. George Dock, Jr. New York: Henry N. Abrams, 1979.

_____. *Aububon and His Journals*. Vol. I & II. Ed. Maria R. Audubon. New York: Dover, 1969. Orig. Pub. 1897.

_____. *The Birds of America*. Macmillan: New York, 1961.

Bakeless, John. *Daniel Boone: Master of the Wilderness*. Intro. Michael A. Lofaro. Lincoln: University of Nebraska, 1989. Orig. Pub. 1939.

Baym, Nina. "The Women of Cooper's Leatherstocking Tales." *American Quarterly*, (23) 1971.

Boone, Daniel. *The Life and Adventures of Colonel Daniel Boone: The First Settler of the State of Kentucky*. Written by Himself. C. Wilder: Brooklyn, 1823.

Brent, Linda. *Incidents in the Life of a Slave Girl*. Edit. & Intro. L. Maria Child. San Diego: Harcourt Brace Jovanovich, 1973.

Cooper, James Fenimore. *The American Democrat, or Hints on the Social and Civic Relations of the United States of America*. Intro. H. L. Mencken. New York: Vintage, 1956. Orig. Pub. 1838.

_____. *Gleanings in Europe*. Vol II. England. Ed. Robert Spiller. New York, Kraus, 1970.

_____. *The Letters and Journals*. Vol. I, II, III, IV. Ed James Franklin Beard. Cambridge: Harvard, 1964.

_____. *Notions of the Americans*. Vols. I & II. New York: Ungar, 1963.

_____. *The Pathfinder, or The Inland Sea*. Ed. & Intro. Richard Dilworth Rust. Albany: State University of New York, 1981.

_____. *Precaution*.

_____. *The Spy*. New York: Hafner, 1960.

_____. *The Deerslayer, or The First War-Path* (1841) Intro.

Bruce L. R. Smith. New York: Barnes & Noble, 2005. Orig. Pub. 1841.

_____. *The Leatherstocking Tales*. Vol. I. *The Pioneers, The Last of the Mohicans & The Prairie*. New York: Library of America, 1985.

De Tocqueville, Alexis. *A Fortnight in the Wilderness*. Delray Beach (Fla.): Levenger, 2003.

_____. *Democracy in America*. Trans. Edit. & Intro. Harvey C. Mansfield and Delba Winthrop. Chicago: University of Chicago, 2000.

Dekker, George & John P. Williams. Eds. *James Fennimore Cooper: The Critical Heritage*. London: Routledge & Kegan Paul, 1973.

_____. *James Fenimore Cooper: The Novelist*. London: Routledge & Kegan Paul, 1967.

Douglass, Frederick. *My Bondage and My Freedom* in *Autobiographies*. New York: Library of America, 1984.

_____. *Narrative of the Life of Frederick Douglass, an American Slave*. Ed. & Intro. Houston A. Baker, Jr. New York: Penguin, 1982. Orig. Pub. 1845.

Eisler, Benita. Ed. *The Lowell Offering: Writings by New England Mill Women, 1840-1845*. Philadelphia: J. B. Lippincott, 1977.

Fiedler, Leslie. "Come Back to the Raft Ag'in, Huck Honey!" *Partisan Review* June 1948.

Finseth, Ian Frederick. *Shades of Green: Visions of Nature in the Literature of American Slavery, 1770-1860*. Athens: University of Georgia, 2009.

Flint, Timothy. *Biographical Memoir of Daniel Boone: The First Settler of Kentucky Interspersed with Incidents in the Early Annals of the Country*. Ed. James K. Folsom. New Haven: College & University, 1967. Orig. Pub. 1833.

Grossman, James. *James Fenimore Cooper*. New York: Sloane, 1949.

Hobson, Archie. Ed. *Remembering America: A Sampler of the*

WPA American Guide Series. Intro. Bill Stott. New York: Columbia, 1985.

Lukacs, Georg. *The Historical Novel.* London: Merlin, 1962. Orig. Pub. 1937.

Martineau, Harriet. *Society in America.* Ed. & Intro. by Seymour Martin Lipset. Garden City: New York, 1962.

Peattie, Donald Culross. Ed. *Aububon's America: The Narratives and Experiences of John James Aubudon.* Boston: Houghton Mifflin, 1940.

Rhodes, Richard. *John James Audubon: The Making of an American.* New York: Knopf, 2004.

Sanders, Scott Russell. ed. *Audubon Reader: The Best Writings of John James Audubon.* Bloomington: Indiana, 1986.

Streshinsky, Shirley. *Audubon: Life and Art in the American Wilderness.* Athens: University of Georgia, 1998. Originally published 1993.

Trollope, Frances. *Domestic Manners of the Americans.* London: Century Publishing, 1984. Orig. pub. 1832.

Thwaites, Reuben Gold. *Daniel Boone.* New York: D. Appleton, 1911.

Turner, Frederick Jackson. *The Frontier in American History.* New York: Holt, Rinehart and Winston, 1967. Orig. pub. 1920.

Zeitlin, T.M. *Liberty, Equality, and Revolution in Alexis de Tocqueville.* Boston: Little Brown, 1971.

CHAPTER 6

Child, Lydia Maria. *Hobomok. A Tale of Early Times.* New York: Garrett, 1970. Orig. Pub. 1824.

_____. *Letters.* Boston: Houghton, Mifflin, 1883.

_____. *The American Frugal Housewife.* Bedford: Applewood, n.d. Orig. Pub. 1828.

Cooper, Susan Fenimore. *Essays on Nature and Landscape.* Ed. Rochelle Johnson & Daniel Patterson. Foreword John Elder. Athens: University of Georgia, 2002.

Cooper, William. *A Guide in the Wilderness.* Dublin (Ireland), 1810.

Heckewelder, John. *An Account of the History, Manners and Customs of the Indian Nations.* Philadelphia: Historical Society of Pennsylvania, 1881. Orig. Pub. 1819.

Kaplan, Cora. *Sea Changes: Essays on Culture and Feminism.* London: Verso, 1986.

LaBastille, Anne. *Women and Wilderness.* San Francisco: Sierra Club, 1980.

Melville, Herman. *The Confidence-Man.* New York: Grove, 1961. Orig. Pub. 1857.

Paulding, J.K. *The Backwoodsman: A Poem.* Philadelphia, M. Thomas,1818.

Sedgwick, Catharine Maria. *Hope Leslie: or, Early Times in the Massachusetts.* Ed. & Intro. Carolyn L. Karcher. New York: Penguin, 1998.

_____. *The Power of Her Sympathy: The Autobiography and Journal of Catharine Marie Sedgwick.* Ed. & Intro. Mary Kelley. Boston: Massachusetts Historical Society, 1993.

_____. *Redwood: A Tale.* New York: Garrett, 1969. Orig. Pub. 1824.

Simms, William Gilmore. *The Yemassee.* Ed. Alexander Cowie. New York: Hafner, 1962. Orig. Pub. 1835.

_____. *Views and Reviews in American Literature, History and Fiction.* First Series. Ed C. Hugh Holman. Cambridge: Harvard, 1962.

CHAPTER 7

Shepard, Odell. Ed. *The Journals of Bronson Alcott. Vol. I.* Port Washington (N.Y.): Kennikat, 1966.

Canby, Henry Seidel, Ed. *The Works of Thoreau.* Boston: Houghton Mifflin, 1937.

Parrington, V. L. *Main Currents in American Thought. Vol. II.* New York: Harcourt, 1958.

Sullivan, Robert. *The Thoreau You Don't Know: What the Prophet of Environmentalism Really Means.* New York: Collins: 2009.

Thoreau, Henry David. *In Wildness Is the Preservation of the World:* Selections & Photographs by Eliot Porter. Intro. Joseph Wood Krutch. San Francisco: Sierra Club, 1962.

_____. *The Natural History Essays.* Layton (Utah): Gibbs Smith, 1980.

_____. *Walden and Other Writings.* Ed. Joseph Wood Krutch. New York: Bantam, 1982.

Wade, Mason. Ed. *The Writings of Margaret Fuller.* New York: Viking, 1941.

CHAPTER 8

Abbey, Edward. *Desert Solitaire: A Season in the Wilderness.* New York: Simon & Schuster, 1968.

Ehrlich, Gretel. *John Muir: Nature's Visionary.* Washington, D.C.: National Geographic, 2000.

Arvin, Newton. *Herman Melville.* New York: Sloane, 1950.

Bronte, Emily. *Wuthering Heights.* New York: Penguin, 1994. Orig. Pub. 1847.

Franklin, H. Bruce, *The Wake of the Gods: Melville's Mythology.* Stanford: Stanford, 1963.

Geismar, Maxwell. "Intro." *Moby-Dick*, New York: Pocket, 1955.

Hawthorne, Nathaniel. *The Blithedale Romance.* Cambridge: Harvard, 2010. Orig. Pub. 1852.

_____. *The House of the Seven Gables.* New York: Bantam, 1985. Orig. Pub. 1851.

_____. *The Scarlet Letter.* New York: Bantam, 1981. Orig. Pub. 1850.

James, Henry. *Hawthorne.* Ithaca (New York): Cornell, 1956. Orig. Pub. 1879.

Melville, Herman. *The Letters of Herman Melville.* Ed. Merrell R. Davis & William H Gilman. New Haven: Yale University, 1960.

_____. *Moby-Dick or, The Whale.* Intro. Andrew Delbanco. New York: Penguin, 2003.

_____. *Redburn: His First Voyage.* New York: Doubleday Anchor, 1957. Orig. Pub. 1849.

_____. *Typee.* New York: New American Library, 1964, Orig. Pub. 1846.

Miller, Perry. *The Raven and the Whale: The War of Words in the Era of Poe and Melville.* New York: Harcourt, Brace & World, 1956.

Muir, John. *My First Summer in the Sierra.* Sellanraa (Georgia): Berg, 1972. Orig. Pub. 1911.

Olson, Charles. *Call me Ishmael.* New York: Reynal & Hitchcock, 1947.

Orwell, George. "Herman Melville by Lewis Mumford." *The Collected Essays, Journalism and Letters of George Orwell.* Vol I. *An Age Like This,* 1920-1940. New York: Penguin, 1979.

Poe, Edgar Allan. *The Tell-Tale Heart and Other Writings.* New York: Bantam, 1982.

Stade, Nancy. "Introduction." *The Scarlet Letter.* New York: Barnes & Noble, 2003.

Williams, David R. *Wilderness Lost: The Religious Origins of the American Mind.* Selinsgrove: Susquehanna University Press, 1989.

CHAPTER 9

Charyn, Jerome. *The Secret Life of Emily Dickinson*. New York: W. W. Norton, 2010.

Dickinson, Emily. *Emily Dickinson's Herbarium*. Facsimile Edition. Cambridge: Harvard, 2006.

_____. *The Poems of Emily Dickinson*. Ed. Thomas H. Johnson. Cambridge: Harvard, 1963

Ferlazzo, Paul J. Ed. *Critical Essays on Emily Dickinson*. Boston: G.K. Hall, 1984.

Franklin, R.W. Ed. *The Poems of Emily Dickinson*. Vols. I, II, III. (Variorum Edition). Cambridge: Harvard, 1998.

Gordon, Lyndall. *Lives Like Loaded Guns: Emily Dickinson and Her Family's Feuds*. New York: Viking, 2010.

Habegger, Alfred. *My Wars Are Laid Away in Books: The Life of Emily Dickinson*. New York: Modern Library, 2002.

Higginson, Thomas Wentworth. *Outdoor Papers*. Ann Arbor: University of Michigan, 2013. Orig. Pub. 1863.

Howe, Susan. *My Emily Dickinson*. Berkeley: North Atlantic Books, 1985.

Johnson, Thomas, H. *Complete Poems of Emily Dickinson*. Boston: Little, Brown, 1960.

_____, and Theodora Ward. *The Letters of Emily Dickinson*. Vols. 1, II, III. Cambridge: Harvard, 1958.

Lawrence, D. H. T*he Complete Poems of D.H. Lawrence*. Ed. & Intro. Vivian de Sola Pinto and Warren Roberts. New York: Penguin, 1988.

Leyda, Jay. *The Years and Hours of Emily Dickinson*. Vols. I & II. New Haven: Yale, 1960.

Longsworth, Polly. *Austin and Mabel: The Amherst Affair & Love Letters of Austin Dickinson and Mabel Loomis Todd*. New York: Farrar, Straus, Giroux, 1984.

Matthiessen, F. O. "The Problem of the Private Poet." *Kenyon Review.* Vol. VII, 1945.

McNeil, Helen. *Emily Dickinson.* London: Virago, 1986.

Rosenbaum, S.P. *A Concordance to the Poems of Emily Dickinson.* Ithaca (N.Y.): 1964.

Whitman, Walt. *The Complete Poems.* Ed. & Intro. Francis Murphy. New York: Penguin, 2004.

Wineapple, Brenda. *White Heat: The Friendship of Emily Dickinson and Thomas Wentworth Higginson.* New York: Knopf, 2008.

Wolff, Cynthia Griffin. *Emily Dickinson.* New York: Alfred Knopf, 1986.

CHAPTER 10

Black Elk. *Black Elk Speaks: Being the Life Story of a Holy Man of the Oglala Sioux.* As told through John G. Neihardt. Intro. Vine Deloria, Jr. Lincoln: University of Nebraska, 1979. Orig. Pub. 1932.

Brinkley, Douglas. T*he Wilderness Warrior. Theodore Roosevelt and the Crusade for America.* New York: HarperCollins, 2009.

Coveney, Peter. "Introduction." T*he Adventures of Huckleberry Finn.* New York: Penguin, 1985.

DeVoto, Bernard. ed. *Mark Twain in Eruption.* New York: Capricorn, 1968.

Fishkin, Shelley Fisher. Ed. *The Mark Twain Anthology: Great Writers on His Life and Work.* New York: Library of America, 2010.

_____. *Was Huck Black : Mark Twain and African-American Voices.* New York: Oxford, 1993.

Hemingway, Ernest. *Green Hills of Africa.* London: Jonathan Cape, 1936

Loving, Jerome. Mark Twain: *The Adventures of Samuel L. Clemens.* Berkeley, University of California, 2010.

Reed, Ishmael. "Mark Twain's Hairball." *A New Literary History of America.* Ed. Greil Marcus and Werner Sollors. Cambridge: Harvard, 2009.

Smith, Janet. ed. *Mark Twain on the Damned Human Race.* Preface Maxwell Geismar. New York: Hill and Wang, 1962.

Twain, Mark. *The Adventures of Huckleberry Finn.* Intro. John Seelye. New York: Penguin, 1985. Orig. Pub. 1884.

_____. *The Autobiography of Mark Twain.* Vol II. Ed. Benjamin Griffin & Harriet Elinor Smith. Berkeley: University of California, 2013.

_____. *A Connecticut Yankee in King Arthur's Court.* New York: Bantam, 2005. Orig. Pub. 1889.

_____. *Following the Equator: A Journey Around the World.* Ed. Roy Blount, Jr. New York: Library of America, 2010.

_____. *The Innocents Abroad or The New Pilgrims Progress.*New York: Harper& Brothers, 1911. Originally published 1869.

_____. *Life on the Mississippi.* New York: Penguin, 1986, Orig. Pub. 1883.

_____. *Roughing It. The Works of Mark Twain.* Vol. II. Berkeley: University of California, 1972.

CHAPTER 11

Austin, Mary. *Essential Mary Austin.* Ed. Kevin Hearle. Berkeley: Heyday, 2006.

_____. *Land of Little Rain.* Intro. Terry Tempest Williams. New York: Penguin, 1997.

Bruccoli, Matthew J. & Margaret M. Duggan. Eds. *Correspondence of F. Scott Fitzgerald.* New York: Random House, 1980.

Bryer, Jackson R. Ed. *F. Scott Fitzgerald: The Critical Reception.* New York: Burt Franklin, 1978.

Cather, Willa. *O Pioneers!*. Boston: Houghton Mifflin, 1941. Orig. Pub. 1913.

Estes, Clarissa Pinkola. *Women Who Run With the Wolves: Myths and Stories of the Wild Woman Archetype*. New York: Ballantine, 1992.

Farmer, Jared. *Trees in Paradise: A California History*. New York: W.W. Norton, 2013.

Fitzgerald, F. Scott. *The Great Gatsby*. New York: Collier, 1986. Orig. Pub. 1925.

Fradkin, Philip L. *Everett Ruess: His Short Life, Mysterious Death, and Astonishing Afterlife*. Berkeley: University of California, 2011.

Hemingway, Ernest. *Green Hills of Africa*. London: Jonathan Cape, 1936.

_____. *The Nick Adams Stories*. New York: Scribner, 2003. Orig. Pub. 1972.

Krakauer, Jon. *Into the Wild*. New York: Anchor, 1996.

Leopold, Aldo. *A Sand County Almanac*. New York: Oxford, 1966. Orig. Pub. 1949.

London, Jack. *The Call of the Wild, White Fang, and Other Stories*. Ed. Andrew Sinclair. Intro. James Dickey. New York: Penguin, 1993.

_____. *Martin Eden*. Intro. Paul Berman. New York: Modern Library, 2002.

_____. *Northland Stories*. Ed. Jonathan Auerbach. New York: Penguin, 1997.

_____. *The Sea-Wolf* in *The Sea-Wolf and Other Stories*. New York: Penguin, 1989. Orig. Pub. 1904.

_____. *The Valley of the Moon*. Foreword Kevin Starr. Berkeley: University of California, 1999.

Mizener, Arthur, ed. T*he Fitzgerald Reader*. New York: Charles Scribner's Sons: New York, 1963.

Morrison, Jim. *Wilderness: The Lost Writings of Jim Morrison*. Vol. I. New York: Vintage, 1989.

Pearce, T. M. *Mary Hunter Austin.* New York: Twayne, 1965.

Slote, Bernice, ed. *The Kingdom of Art: Willa Cather's First Principles and Critical Statements 1893-1896.* Lincoln: University of Nebraska, 1966.

Strayed, Cheryl. *Wild: From Lost to Found on the Pacific Coast Trail.* New York: Knopf, 2012.

INDEX

*(The words "wild," "wilderness," "nature," "civilization," "forest," "woods," "frontiers,"
trees," and "Indians" appear so often that to include them here
would defeat the very purpose of the index.)*

Y

Z

About The Author

JONAH RASKIN has taught American literature at Sonoma State University, the State University of New York at Stony Brook and as a Fulbright professor at the University of Antwerp and the University of Ghent in Belgium. The author of fifteen books, he earned his B.A. at Columbia College in New York, his M.A. at Columbia University and his Ph.D. at the University of Manchester, Manchester, England. He lives in northern California and has written for *The San Francisco Chronicle, The L.A. Times, The Nation, The Redwood Coast Review* and *Catamaran*.